SACRAMENTS

SACRAMENTS

REVELATION
OF THE HUMANITY OF GOD

*Engaging the Fundamental Theology
of Louis-Marie Chauvet*

Edited by Philippe Bordeyne and Bruce T. Morrill

A PUEBLO BOOK

Liturgical Press   Collegeville, Minnesota

www.litpress.org

A Pueblo Book published by Liturgical Press

Cover design by David Manahan, OSB. Illustration by Frank Kacmarcik, OblSB.

The contributions of Philippe Bordeyne, Patrick Prétot, André Birmelé, Philippe Barras, Elbatrina Clauteaux, and Jean-Louis Souletie were translated by Michael S. Driscoll.

Published simultaneously in French under the title *Les Sacrements, révélation de l'humanité de Dieu* (Paris: les Éditions de Cerf, 2008).

The English translation of the *Exsultet* (Easter Proclamation) from *The Roman Missal* © 1973, International Committee on English in the Liturgy, Inc. (ICEL). All rights reserved.

Unless otherwise noted, Scripture texts in this work are taken from the *New Revised Standard Version Bible* © 1989, Division of Christian Education of the National Council of the Churches of Christ in the United States of America. Used by permission. All rights reserved.

Library of Congress Cataloging-in-Publication Data

Sacraments. English.
　　Sacraments : revelation of the humanity of God : engaging the fundamental theology of Louis-Marie Chauvet / edited by Philippe Bordeyne and Bruce T. Morrill.
　　　　p. cm.
　　"A Pueblo book."
　　"Bibliography of Louis-Marie Chauvet"—P.
　　Includes bibliographical references and indexes.
　　ISBN 978-0-8146-6218-2 (pbk.)
　　　1. Sacraments—Catholic Church.　2. Catholic Church—Doctrines.
3. Chauvet, Louis Marie.　I. Bordeyne, Philippe.　II. Morrill, Bruce T.
III. Title.

　　BX2200.S2313　2008
　　234'.16092—dc22　　　　　　　　　　　　　　　　　　2008028272

Contents

Acknowledgments

This book was made possible, in part, due to grants from:

The Committee on Research and Publication of the University
Research Council of Boston College,
Dr. Kevin Bidell, Vice Provost for Research at Boston College,
Rev. Paul F. Harman, SJ, Rector, and the house consultors of the
Jesuit Community at Boston College.

The editors wish to express their sincere gratitude to all of these for
their generous support toward deferring translation, research, and related production costs.

Louis-Marie Chauvet: A Short Biography

Philippe Bordeyne

"All theological discourse depends upon the dominant discussion of the era that preceded it, either to argue against it or to reinforce it. It is obvious that mine has been partly constituted as a reaction against the scholastic discourse of my formation at the theological faculty of Angers." Thus Louis-Marie Chauvet begins the contextual rereading of his theological work in an article dedicated to Joseph Doré in 2002.[1] He was sixty years old then. He is greatly indebted to his upbringing, to his teachers and friends, but also to encounters that have marked his life. These have allowed him to leave his familiar surroundings without abandoning them totally, since Chauvet is a faithful person. You only need listen to him speak. During his courses, the examples drawn from everyday life do not distract from his lively, brilliant, and speculative thought. In the little anecdotes he tells, you perceive the immense respect that Chauvet has for those who passed the faith onto him because they truly lived it. In that respect, his reference to Scholastic discourse as a repelling factor that led him elsewhere can be misleading. This because Chauvet was well grounded. He draws his audacity of thought from a land that continues to nourish him.

He hails from the devoutly Catholic region of the Vendée. He was born on January 26, 1941, at Chavagnes-en-Paillers to a peasant family. His mother had left school at the age of eleven to tend sheep, but she had absorbed the literary culture that was lavished upon her in the elementary education of the time. She bequeathed to her son the taste for reading and respect for the rules of writing. In this village of three thousand inhabitants, all, without distinction among the social classes, practiced religion. Like many other boys of his village, Louis-Marie was attracted to the priesthood. After schooling at the seminary of

---

[1] "Quand la théologie rencontre les sciences humaines," in F. Bousquet, H.-J. Gagey, G. Médevielle et J.-L. Souletie, *La responsabilité des théologiens: Mélanges offerts à Joseph Doré* (Paris: Desclée, 2002), 401–15: 401.

Luçon, he was ordained a priest in 1966 for his home diocese. Soon thereafter he was sent to pursue his studies at the Catholic University of the West at Angers.

He received his formation by Thomist professors, among whom he recognized that some were "excellent." But this Scholastic theology did not sufficiently feed our curious and inventive student, who wished like many others that theology might better respond to the questions of the time.

He was anxious that church history and biblical exegesis be able to effect change, since they introduce a sense of plurality. Jean Colson's course on ministries in the Acts of the Apostles impassioned him, as it demonstrated the complexity of approaches according to the contexts and the times.[2] Chauvet received his canonical license degree in theology in 1967, after having defended a thesis on the priesthood of Christ in the Epistle to the Hebrews.[3] As a student, he benefited from the readings and the reflections of his brightest fellow students. Wine country and wine encouraged sharing in friendship. Due to numerous conversations "to the bottom of the barrel," particularly with Jean-Paul Resweber who was a fellow student at the seminary at Luçon, he was initiated into the Heideggarian critique of metaphysics.[4]

---

[2] At that time, Colson was a recognized specialist on the theology of ministries (Jean Colson, *L'épiscopat catholique: collégialité et primauté dans les trois premiers siècles de l'Église*, Preface by Yves M.-J. Congar, Unam sanctam 43 [Paris: Cerf, 1963], and he was preparing a work on Luke (*L'énigme du disciple que Jésus aimait*, Théologie historique 10 [Paris: Beauchesne, 1969]). Colson became the favorite theologian of Msgr Rodhain, founder of *Secours Catholique* in France that sought to construct a theology of charity. Cf. Jean Colson, *Le Sacerdoce du pauvre: réflexions sur le sacerdoce prophétique du Messie, roi des pauvres, dans l'Évangile selon saint Luc* (Paris: S.O.S., 1971).

[3] Three years earlier, the Sulpician Joseph Doré defended his thesis at the Angelicum in Rome on the priesthood of Christ *Secundum ordinem Melchisedech*. Doré became the dean of the theological faculty of the Institut Catholique of Paris in 1988. He left the Faculty in 1997 when he was named archbishop of Strasbourg.

[4] Jean-Paul Resweber defended his thesis in Catholic theology at the University of Strasbourg in 1973, under the title *Essai sur le discours théologique, à la lumière de la critique heideggerienne de la métaphysique* [Essay on theological discourse in the light of the Heideggarian critique of metaphysics]. Later he became professor of philosophy at the University of Metz. Notably he pub-

Chauvet left to write a dissertation in Paris, but he began by taking courses at the Superior Institute of Liturgy (hereafter ISL), where he received his diploma in 1969. During this time he acquired a solid understanding of liturgical history, all the while benefiting from the pastoral ferment after the council. Alexandre Ganoczy, who was teaching at the Institut Catholique of Paris, proposed a research topic to him on penance in the thought of Calvin, in order to study how the Reformer from Geneva conceived of the fruits of justification. Ganoczy received a scholarship for him, allowing him to spend the academic year of 1970–71 at the Institut für Europäische Geschichte at the University of Mainz. There he worked with professor Joseph Lortz, author of a new Catholic interpretation of the Reformation in Germany.[5] When he returned to Paris, Ganoczy was named to the University of Würzburg. Chauvet pursued his doctoral studies at the École Pratique des Hautes Études with Richard Stauffer.[6] But Stauffer abruptly had to suspend all professional activities for health reasons when Chauvet's dissertation was nearly finished. Pierre Burgelin, a specialist of Leibniz,[7] agreed to join his committee in extremis; he determined that the last chapter was more than sufficient for a dissertation.[8] Chauvet defended his first doctoral dissertation at the University of Paris I-Sorbonne in 1973, under the title *Jean Calvin: critique théologique et pastorale des doctrines scolastique et tridentine du sacrement de la pénitence* [John Calvin: Theological and Pastoral Critique of Scholastic and Tridentine Doctrines on the Sacrament of Penance]. It is of the end of a formation process where history plays a critical function regarding Scholastic theology.

Chauvet then returned to a parish in Vendée, where he was appointed as a vicar at Les Herbiers. The Dominican Pierre-Marie Gy,

---

lished on Heidegger, on the philosophy of language and on interdisciplinary methods, a theme very dear to Chauvet. Cf. Jean-Paul Resweber, *La Méthode interdisciplinaire* (Paris: PUF, 1981).

[5] Joseph Lortz, *Die Reformation in Deutschland* (Freiburg im Breisgau: Herder, 1939–1940).

[6] Richard Stauffer, *Dieu, la création et la Providence dans la prédication de Calvin*, Basler und Berner Studien zur historischen und systematischen Theologie 33 (Bern: Peter Lang, 1978).

[7] Pierre Burgelin, *Commentaire du "Discours de métaphysique" de Leibniz*, Études d'histoire et de philosophie religieuses (Paris: PUF, 1959).

[8] Only about a hundred of the five hundred pages drafted were included in the doctoral defense. The others continue to sit in boxes.

director of the Superior Institute of Liturgy, noticed this young diocesan priest. With the agreement of Pierre-André Liégé, the dean of the Theology Faculty, Gy wanted Chauvet to replace Alexandre Ganoczy and sought permission from the Most Reverend Charles Paty, bishop of Luçon, who readily acceded to the request. But Chauvet loved the pastoral life. He was not convinced that his place was in Paris. It was his pastor, Father Jacques David, the future bishop of La Rochelle, then at Évreux, who heartily encouraged him to accept the offer. In 1974 Chauvet began his teaching at the Institut Catholique of Paris, but he always kept a foot in pastoral ministry, at first half time at Vendée until 1981. Then he continued pastoral ministry from 1982 in the Diocese of Pontoise, near Paris, where he still is the pastor in charge at Saint-Leu-la-Forêt. His dissertation in theology, defended in 1986, was already a mature work. It quickly attracted an international audience to his research.[9] In 1989 Chauvet was elected professor by the counsel of the Theology Faculty of the Institut Catholique of Paris.

During all these years, he gave numerous workshops in dioceses around and sometimes outside France on theology and pastoral practice of the sacraments. There he collected those working in the field who sought to proclaim the Gospel and to form believers in a rapidly evolving world. Chauvet's theology is difficult to understand if you omit his constant comings and goings between liturgical life, where one receives whomever comes for sacramental preparation and university teaching. Chauvet is the heir to a tradition of reciprocal interaction between pastoral practices and theological research at a high level that gives witness to the strict relations between the National Center of Pastoral Liturgy (hereafter CNPL[10]) and the ISL.

At the Institut Catholique of Paris, Chauvet benefited from a stimulating environment, as much from the numerous disciplinary fields as from the friendly encounters with colleagues and students. In the framework of the ISL, which was his primary job, the teamwork generated some wonderful research insights. On the one hand, Chauvet

[9] Chauvet, *Symbole et sacrement: une relecture sacramentelle de l'existence chrétienne* (Paris: Cerf, 1987).

[10] Translator's remark: CNPL signifies *Centre National de Pastorale Liturgique*. *Pastorale* is the noun and *liturgique* is the adjective. In English we say "pastoral liturgy" but in French the term implies "liturgical pastoral practice." For the sake of clarity according to English usage, *"pastorale liturgique"* will be rendered "pastoral liturgy."

could be proud of the certainty with which Pierre-Marie Gy plunged him into the liturgical tradition, and on the other hand, he appreciated the audacity of Jean-Yves Hameline, well rooted in liturgical and musical practices, but who was always open to new approaches regarding ritual experience through the social sciences.[11] In the wider framework of the Theology Faculty, Chauvet often contributed to seminars or interdisciplinary colloquia. In 2001 he was assigned to teach the course in fundamental theology by the dean at that time, Henri-Jérôme Gagey, who succeeded him in the course of sacramental theology.[12] Chauvet recognized that this request was the occasion of a happy "awakening" that would force him to leave sacramental theology the better to find it in rereading Barth, de Lubac, Rahner, and particularly Balthasar.[13]

This brief return to the biography of the French theologian will be useful to the readers who followed his teaching, those who heard him in workshops, or simply those who had access to his books and articles. The paradox is that this man who has contributed so much to the radiance of the Institut Catholique of Paris to the outside world has traveled very little outside France. He reads the medieval theologians in the original text, he speaks Latin and sings it beautifully, but he doesn't have the habit of speaking in languages other than French. Nevertheless, his work is translated, read, and commented upon everywhere in the world, especially in North America. Numerous doctoral dissertations have been dedicated to his sacramental theology. From this came the idea to write this book in two voices, one American and the other European, and to publish it simultaneously in France and in the United States, thanks to a happy collaboration between Éditions du Cerf and Liturgical Press. Most of the French-speaking authors have many times joined their voices to speak about the contribution of Chauvet to contemporary theology. In the United States and in other English-speaking countries, students are well acquainted with his two major books. In this work, thought and written in common, we would like to assist readers to understand better the current

[11] Jean-Yves Hameline, *Une poétique du rituel* (Paris: Cerf, 1997).

[12] It was due to the suggestion of Gagey that Chauvet published *Les sacrements: Parole de Dieu au risque du corps* (Éd. de l'Atelier, 1993), which placed his thesis on symbol and sacrament at the disposition of the general public.

[13] Academic session marking Chauvet's retirement, Institut Catholique of Paris, June 21, 2007.

endeavor of sacramental theology and liturgy, all the while demonstrating how our teacher and friend has contributed to it directly or indirectly. You will see that the accents are sometimes different from one side of the Atlantic to the other. Chauvet, impassioned by interpretation, will not be surprised by this. The best way to honor him is publicly to lay our foundation of the varied interpretations of his work that is not found solely in the texts but also in the integrity of a life dedicated to liturgical action.

Building on Chauvet's Work: An Overview

Bruce T. Morrill

Liturgical theologians have been fond of asserting that the *lex orandi*, the law of prayer, establishes the *lex credendi*, the law of belief, even as they continuously debate just exactly what this patristic principle, as crystallized in Prosper of Aquitaine's famous sentence, means in the life of the church. Over several decades of a prodigious academic and pastoral career, Louis-Marie Chauvet has produced a systematic treatment of why and how sacramental liturgy is essential to Christian faith. Liturgical theologians largely tend to approach the topic on the basis of the history and elements of the Christian rites, whereas Chauvet, while continuously affirming and drawing from the irreducibly ritual nature of the sacraments, does so in the genre of a fundamental theology.

Fundamental theology methodologically reflects on the nature of divine revelation as conveyed through Scripture and tradition, as well as on the conditions that dispose humans to receiving that revelation. The methodological beauty of Chauvet's highly theoretical work lies in his constant consideration of actual liturgical practices such that pastoral insights abound. The beauty of its content emerges in his arguments for the corporality of our redemption in Christ, the particularity of that divine Word as the Spirit writes it on the universal body of the church through the ritual activity of the sacraments, the ethical human imperative inherent to that divine self-gift, and the grounding of this sacramental ethics in the biblical revelation of the crucified God.

The theological concept repeatedly refreshing such a demanding, thoroughgoing argument is Chauvet's elucidation of *grace*. Of utmost importance for a Christian sacramental anthropology and ethics (a life of justice, mercy, and sharing) is the thankful recognition of the utter gratuity of God's saving presence to humanity. By means of symbolic-language theory Chauvet argues that the divine gracious presence is only possible due to the nature of the God revealed in the Gospel.

God reveals God in what is most different from God. God reveals the divine self ultimately as God when God "crosses out" God in humanity. God reveals God as human in God's very divinity. This does not just mean that God is "morally" more human than humans, who so often are inhuman, but that "ontologically" it belongs to God to be the only one fully human. The relation of love alone makes one fully human . . .[1]

Salvation comes through the risks the triune God took in the death and resurrection of the Son and continues to take as the Spirit reveals the "humanness" of the God of Jesus Christ in sacramental liturgy, enabling our lives to be liturgy, a spiritual sacrifice glorifying God.

Chauvet has thus argued vigorously for grounding the theology and practice of liturgy in the paschal mystery:

To start from the Pasch . . . is first to locate the sacraments within *the dynamic of a history,* that of a Church born, in its historic visibility, from the gift of the Spirit at Pentecost and always in the process of becoming the body of Christ all through history. To start from the Pasch is consequently to be obliged to build sacramental theology not only on the *Christological* but also the *pneumatological principle.*[2]

Chauvet's insistence on history is crucial for the implications of his argument. Embracing the scandalous particularity of history opens us to the liberating content of Jesus' life, to the words, actions, and decisions through which he revealed the character of God as boundless mercy, forgiveness, and strength. To insist on history as the medium of God's redemptive work is to accept the sometimes consoling, other times unsettling revelation that, like Jesus, we meet God in the concrete circumstances of our own lives, both as participants in various social bodies and in the waxing and waning of our personal bodies. For such was Jesus' life-story unto death, empowered by the Spirit of the God who

---

[1] Chauvet, *The Sacraments: The Word of God at the Mercy of the Body* (Collegeville, MN: Liturgical Press, 2001), 163. Key sources for Chauvet's argument for the humanity of God are E. Jüngel and J. Moltmann. See Chauvet, *Symbol and Sacrament: A Sacramental Reinterpretation of Christian Existence,* trans. Patrick Madigan and Madeleine Beaumont (Collegeville, MN: Liturgical Press, 1995), 492–509.

[2] Chauvet, *Symbol and Sacrament,* 487.

raised him from the dead and thereby revealed the divine presence in a life spent in self-sacrificing love for fellow humans.

The risen Christ's gift of the Spirit sets the lives of believers in the same pattern of encountering the unseen God in the concrete circumstances of their own time and place. The "eschatological memorial of the Pasch, that is, the very specificity of the Christian liturgy"[3] places the lives of every believer in the present-tense drama of the mystery of salvation. This language of mystery should tell us that our faith is at once a profound trust in God's saving, redemptive, vindicating will for humanity but also an ongoing call to accept the incomprehensibility of that God of love, our inability to control how the human story of God will finally come to completion.[4] As St. Paul teaches, the same Spirit of the one who raised Jesus from the dead now lives as the first fruits of his resurrection in the lives of those baptized into his death, working all for the ultimate good in us, just as for Jesus. What characterizes such a life of faith is hope: "Now hope that is seen is not hope. For who hopes for what he sees? But if we hope for what we do not see, we wait for it with patience."[5]

At the heart of Chauvet's fundamental sacramental theology is his recognition and insistence that the sacraments of the church are practices of *faith*. Chauvet describes faith as "the assent to a loss,"[6] a continuous letting go of our projections of what we imagine God should be like, so that the totally other yet lovingly near God revealed in the crucified and resurrected Christ might really be present to us in our lived experience. Chauvet identifies our imaginary projections of God as part of the larger human challenge of struggling with reality in all the difficulties and surprises with which historical existence presents us. This imagining of total presence, of complete possession or perhaps fulfillment, most often does not result from a moral failure of the will but, rather, arises in individuals' unconscious as they face harrowing challenges or chronic disappointments or limited personal qualities. Yet upon reflection we realize that it is precisely the resistance of the other to our expectations that tells us we are dealing with the real and not an emotionally driven projection of our own desires onto

[3] Ibid., 485.

[4] See Edward Schillebeeckx, *Church: The Human Story of God*, trans. John Bowden (New York: Crossroad Publishing, 1991), 168–86.

[5] Rom 8:25. See also Rom 6:3-4; 8:23, 28.

[6] Chauvet, *The Sacraments*, 39.

what is around us. Heavily influenced by Heidegger's phenomenology, Chauvet describes how genuine presence always entails absence. "The concept of *'coming-into-presence'* precisely marks the absence with which every presence is constitutively crossed out: nothing is nearer to us than the other in its very otherness . . . nothing is more present to us than what, in principle, escapes us (starting with ourselves)."[7]

Here an example may help, one I would argue is germane to any human relationship: being hurt by someone or being the one who inflicts pain on another. This experience may well entail the sort of alienation within oneself to which Paul so honestly attests: "For I do not do the good I want, but the evil I do not want is what I do."[8] Precisely in such wrestling we are at our most real, spared any illusions of immediate presence to ourselves or another, called to grapple with what matters through the very bodily matter of our lives and, in so doing, to construct our own subjectivity in the world that is given us. To reflect upon the human engagement of reality in this way is to reject the Western dualistic valuing of soul over body, mind over matter, invisible over visible, unchanging essence over becoming-in-existence. Instead, with Chauvet, one comes to recognize that "the sensible mediations of language, body, history, desire" comprise "the very milieu within which human beings attain their truth and thus correspond to the Truth which calls them."[9] This lack of immediate access to reality is what constitutes the human need for language, by which is meant the entire range of symbols whereby humans submit to the otherness intrinsic to life, to the rule-bound cultural layers through which they perceive the raw data of the physical universe affecting their senses. Constantly working with the signs, words, gestures, and narratives—the "language"—of their society, people participate in a world at once given—through symbolism and language usually so conventional to the native user as to seem "natural"—yet continuously under construction.

What has too long plagued the Western Christian understanding, and therefore practice, of the sacraments, Chauvet argues, is the metaphysical notion that the (ideal) human subject exists prior to and outside the world of language (symbolism), that some level of immediate access to reality is available to humans. From this arises thought and

---

[7] Chauvet, *Symbol and Sacrament*, 404.

[8] Rom 7:19.

[9] Chauvet, *The Sacraments*, 6.

practices that value the "internal" over the "external," the invisible over the visible, thereby mistaking language (the symbolic) for a mere instrument to be overcome so as to enter into the total presence or pure essence of reality. Nothing could be further from the truth! The very "language" of the symbols that people of a religious tradition share, specifically in the manner they choose to engage them, are what comprise their particular experience of the divine and their view of the world, their commitment to its order, their ethics, their willingness to spend their lives in its realization.

> To say "there is speaking" constantly in human beings is to say that every perception of reality is mediated by their culture and the history of their desire. In the absence of these, this reality would be left to its raw factualness and would be only a chaos or meaningless jumble. In order for the subject to reach and retain its status of subject, it must build reality into a "world," that is to say, a signifying whole in which every element, whether material (tree, wind, house) or social (relatives, clothing, cooking, work, leisure) is integrated into a system of *knowledge* (of the world and of society), *gratitude* (code of good manners, mythical and ritual code ruling relationships with deities and ancestors), and *ethical behavior* (values serving as norms of conduct). The infant as well as the adult have to deal with this world, *always-already* constructed, and not with things in their crude physical state. By theses means, the universe and events form a coherent whole which is called "the symbolic order." Subjects can orient themselves by it because each thing can find in it its own signifying place.[10]

Thus, language is not the instrument but the womb of our subjectivity, society the "space" constructed of knowledge, gratitude, and ethical behavior wherein people dynamically engage the symbols already present as cultural tradition in ever-original acts of meaning, such that the subject, language, and culture are contemporaneous.

Chauvet's theological move is to interpret the practice of Christianity, the ongoing formation of Christian identity, as a particular engagement in this essential anthropological structure of knowledge, gratitude, and ethics. Christian identity is not self-administered but, rather, lies in the "assent to faith in Jesus as 'Christ,' 'Lord,' 'Son of God,'" an assent to "the confession of faith from which the church was

[10] Ibid., 13.

born."[11] The church is the milieu within which believers come to and exercise an empowering competence in the symbolic order given by the Spirit of the risen Christ in a consistent pattern: the knowledge of faith's content through the proclamation of Scripture, the inscribing of that word on the bodies of believers through the symbolic gestures, and the sacramental experience of Christ's absence as an indwelling presence compelling believers to action.

Luke's Emmaus account (24:13-35), Chauvet demonstrates, is paradigmatic of the ecclesial pattern, set in the context of the day of the resurrection, which had become the Lord's Day, the day of the Sunday assembly. In the story, Christ comes to the two disciples who have quit Jerusalem, leaving behind their expectations of immediate divine deliverance through Jesus, abandoning those hopes with the corpse of the would-be messiah. Jesus fills the empty space of their long walk home with his exposition of the Scriptures as revelatory of the meaning of his life and death. The beginning of faith, then, is the renunciation of the immediate sort of divine deliverance they expected, and their consenting to the meaning mediated through the crucified and risen Jesus' interpretation of the Scriptures. While Christ's proclamation may have burned in their hearts, however, they only come to recognize him when they are drawn into the reality of that word for them through the ritual of his taking, blessing, breaking, and sharing the bread at table. The pattern of the symbolic gesture is identical to the evangelist's description of Jesus' action at the Last Supper, a tradition we know the earliest ecclesial communities practiced as having come from the Lord (see 1 Cor 11:23). Thus, "it is in the church celebrating the Eucharist as his prayer and his action, as it is in the church welcoming the Scriptures as his word, that it is possible to recognize that Christ is alive."[12] That climax to the Emmaus story, nonetheless, results in Jesus' immediate vanishing from their sight, an absence that, far from leaving them with a hopeless feeling of abandonment (as in the story's opening), inspires them with the power to go back to Jerusalem to share the good news. This, Chauvet argues, signals the ethical dimension of ecclesial faith: The sharing in word and sacrament is verified—realizes its truth (verity)—in the *koinonia* of practical care, concern, and service among believers. Ethical praxis in daily life is as

---

[11] Ibid., 19.
[12] Ibid., 26.

much a performance of the word written on the body as is sacramental rite, the work of one and the same Spirit.

Chauvet thus arrives at an explanation for the ecclesial practice of faith as a taking up and converting of the basic three-dimensional structure of human subjectivity. Chauvet's sacramental theology is a philosophical interpretation of how God's having taken up and saved the human condition in the life, death, and resurrection of Jesus becomes real in the lives of those baptized into that same paschal mystery. The church's symbolic order of Scripture, sacrament, and ethics makes of the human pattern of knowledge, gratitude, and ethics a sacrament—an embodied revelation—of the reign of God, the salvation of human beings. What keeps this way of life explicitly Christian is ongoing balance between these three constitutive poles of the practice of faith. Only by submitting to the resistance of reality revealed in each dimension's juxtaposition to the others do believers continue to give themselves over to the otherness, the presence-in-absence of the God of Jesus. Such ongoing praxis of Scripture–sacrament–ethics keeps the faith real in its sometimes consoling, other times painful openness to the revelation of the God of Jesus.[13] By submitting together as church to the performance of Scripture, sacrament, and ethics—face to face in liturgical gathering, far and wide in daily living—Christians discover over and again that otherness, finally, is not a threat but an invitation, that the God of Jesus can be trusted.

The corporality of the practice of the sacraments, precisely as language-laden, communal acts of symbolic mediation, is what makes their celebration so essential to knowing and living the Christ proclaimed in Scripture. Participation in sacramental liturgy, as an ecclesial body given over to both the Word in Scripture and symbolic gestures that inscribe that divine word on our persons, delivers us from the human tendency to imagine that there should be no distance, no gap,

---

[13] Here I find the burden of Chauvet's argument resonant with Gordon Lathrop's liturgical theory of juxtapositions, as well as his mentor Edward Schillebeeckx's mystical-political theology of the contrast experience. See Gordon W. Lathrop, *Holy Things: A Liturgical Theology* (Minneapolis: Fortress Press, 1993), 15–83, 204–25; and *Holy Ground: A Liturgical Cosmology* (Minneapolis: Fortress Press, 2003), 53–79, 197–225; and Edward Schillebeeckx, *Christ: The Experience of Jesus as Lord*, trans. John Bowden (New York: Crossroad, 1981), 817–19; *Church*, 5–14; and *The Schillebeeckx Reader*, ed. Robert Schreiter (New York: Crossroad, 1987), 272–74, 257–59.

no otherness between ourselves and the fullness of God. The members of a liturgical assembly bring precisely their bodies to the celebration, their daily action (ethics) as persons engaged in the social and cosmic bodiliness of the human story being written in history. By participating in the traditional body of the church's sacramental worship, we submit to the mystery of God revealed in the crucified and resurrected Jesus, a God who comes to us in and through the shared bodily medium of our human knowing, suffering, and loving. Thus does the God of Jesus become really present to our lives, even as that sacramental ecclesial presence always recedes in its coming, sending us in the Spirit to discover the Word as living and active in us and our world.

The celebration of the sacraments is for revealing the transformative presence of the (scriptural) God *of Jesus* in all the ambiguity of our (ethical) living,[14] not for repairing to some sacred precinct where we get to witness God for God's own sake. Here trinitarian faith is not a puzzling theological abstraction but the heart of embodied faith. Here faith in the crucified God scandalizes theism (with its monolithic god). The Christ who comes to us in the sacraments is the one who lived a human solidarity unto death, revealing the *difference* in God that is the source of our salvation, crossing out the gods of human imagination and establishing a similitude between God and humans. In the paschal mystery the love between Father and Son becomes the love between God and humanity. The Spirit is the difference, the holiness, the otherness of love shared between Father and Son. The Spirit wrote that difference on the person-body of Jesus of Nazareth, raised him from death to glory, and now writes that difference on the bodies of believers in the rites of the church. In celebrations of the paschal mystery "God is revealed as the one who, through the Spirit, 'crosses God out' in humanity, giving to the latter the possibility of becoming the 'sacramental locus' where God continues to be embodied."[15]

If Chauvet's fundamental theology of the sacramental structure of Christian faith strikes the reader as paradoxical, then that can only attest to its success in articulating something of the tragic beauty of the paschal mystery: God's revelation of salvation as the meeting of divine and human desire (the Spirit) in the human (bodily and historical, as-

---

[14] "In other words, *every sacrament shows us how to see and live what transforms our human existence into a properly Christian existence.*" Chauvet, *The Sacraments*, 148.

[15] Ibid., 167.

sured yet struggling, defeated but triumphant) person of Jesus. Any imaginary shortcut to the immediate presence of divine fulfillment is a sliding away from the faith, a misplacing of the hope, a malnourishment of the love that comes to us in the Spirit of the crucified and risen Christ. The assent to the particular symbolic order of human living that is the tradition of the church—the constant, mutually informing movement between word, sacrament, and ethics—is what nurtures the life of Christian faith. When the divorce of symbol from reality (body from spirit) slips into Christian practice, we lose the singular grace, the divine favor, the Gospel has to offer us. Rather than gracing us with original gifts only God (in God's saving difference) can give, liturgy becomes a mere expression of what we already know, the sacraments mere instruments for one dimension or other of human experience. The pastoral consequences can prove tragic in ways anything but beautiful, the sacramental liturgy of the church trapped in a sacred no man's land practically irrelevant to the profane commerce of everyday life—personal, ecclesial, social, economic, political.[16]

Much is at stake for the church's mission, both *ad intra* and *ad extra*, at the dawn of this new millennium. We Christians, I would suggest, currently find ourselves amidst a seismic anthropological shift no less epochal than that of the Middle Ages, a profound transformation (material, intellectual, institutional, psychological) in how humanity goes about being human. Certainly, what Western Christianity looked, sounded, ordered, and argued like in the fourteenth century was significantly different from what characterized its practices and theologies at the end of the first millennium.[17] The local and global

[16] For my own attempt at wrestling with this problem, see Bruce T. Morrill, *Anamnesis as Dangerous Memory: Political and Liturgical Theology in Dialogue* (Collegeville, MN: Liturgical Press, 2000).

[17] The scholarship, of course, is vast, allowing me here to mention only one exemplary contributor to the field, Carolyn Walker Bynum. For a collection of scholarly essays demonstrating the medieval transformation in sacramental theology and practice, see Gary Macy, *Treasures from the Storeroom: Medieval Religion and the Eucharist* (Collegeville, MN: Liturgical Press, 1999). My own thinking in this regard was opened thanks to medieval church historians' contributions to an interdisciplinary conference on Catholic ritual I codirected at the College of the Holy Cross (Worcester, Massachusetts) in 2002. See *Practicing Catholic: Ritual, Body, and Contestation in Catholic Faith*, ed. Bruce T. Morrill and others (New York: Palgrave Macmillan, 2006).

consequences of Enlightenment and modernity (scientific, technological, economic, governmental) are playing out, at accelerating pace, in ways that demand of Christian theologians work that is both faithful to Scripture and tradition and adequate to the exigencies of the publics they serve—ecclesial, academic, and public.[18] The coeditors and contributors to this present book offer here their theological scholarship in the hope of not only honoring the person and monumental work of Chauvet, but also advancing constructive thought about sacramental liturgy in service to church and world along six lines of inquiry: fundamental theology, biblical theology, ecclesiology, theological ethics, the social sciences, and theological anthropology. It remains for readers, of course, to judge whether our academic efforts approximate the personal and professional gratitude and esteem with which we hold our colleague, Father Chauvet.

---

[18] For an original discussion of theology and those publics, see David Tracy, *The Analogical Imagination: Christian Theology and the Culture of Pluralism* (New York: Crossroad, 1981).

Part 1

Theology, Fundamental and Sacramental

> It is in the church that faith finds its structure because the church is in charge of keeping alive, in the midst of the world and for its good, the memory of what [the ascended Lord Jesus] lived for and why God raised him from the dead: memory through the *Scriptures*, read and interpreted as speaking about him or being his own living word; memory through the *sacraments*, . . . recognized as being his own salvific gestures; memory through the *ethical* testimony of mutual sharing, lived as an expression of his own service to humankind.[1]

> Every human subject is born from the possibility of conceiving a world, of celebrating it, of acting in it. The discursive logic of the *sign*, the identifying challenge of the *symbol*, the world-transforming power of the *praxis* (to the benefit of everyone): these three elements coalesce and form a structure. The structure of Christian identity that we proposed turns out to be the restatement, albeit a new one, of this fundamental anthropological structure.[2]

In these two opening chapters, Lieven Boeve and Patrick Prétot introduce the reader to the basic method and goal of the present book, namely, how to continue the development of sacramental theology along the lines of Chauvet's highly constructive, original thought while always attending to Christian faith's actual practice in history.

[1] Chauvet, *The Sacraments: The Word of God at the Mercy of the Body* (Collegeville, MN: Liturgical Press, 2001), 28.

[2] Chauvet, *Symbol and Sacrament: A Sacramental Reinterpretation of Christian Existence*, trans. Patrick Madigan and Madeleine Beaumont (Collegeville, MN: Liturgical Press, 1995), 180.

Chauvet has achieved a comprehensive method that, while profitably engaged with philosophy and the social sciences, is genuinely theological. Reading Chauvet so as to discern faith's potential and demands in the contemporary world requires a double movement of contextualization and deployment. Chauvet's work must be appropriated both in its own specific context, including the theology he inherited, and in the contemporary situation. It can thereby be applied and tested in the face of new challenges. Chauvet himself has in recent years taken up such a review of his own thought, a retrospective inquiry encouraging the contributors to this present book to do the same.

Boeve describes the philosophical context wherein Chauvet's theology evolved. The linguistic turn in philosophy required his rejection of instrumental conceptions of language so as to argue for it as *mediation*. Furthermore, the Heideggerian critique of metaphysics elicited in Chauvet a hermeneutical posture emboldening him to pursue the infinite quest for truth as it unfolds in the sacraments. Chauvet has thus come to conceptualize Christian faith as an interactive triangle of Scripture, sacraments, and ethics, prohibiting any imaginary immediate access to God by insisting on the human corporality of the divine revelation Christ's Spirit works now in the church. Boeve recognizes in Chauvet's decision to engage a particular philosophical theory (in his case, Heidegger's) not centered on Christianity's God, the methodological principle of simultaneously upholding the particularity of Christianity and that of any theoretical interlocutor. Therein, for Boeve, lies the pertinence of Chauvet's fundamental theology in a postmodern age: Contrary to other philosophies and theologies that secretly revert to escaping radical particularity, the faith allows itself here truly to be affected by the context and, in so doing, is able to participate in the reconstruction of the world.

Like Boeve, Prétot recognizes the merit in Chauvet's having theorized anew the particularity at the heart of sacramental theology. For Prétot, however, the novelty lies already in Chauvet's having methodologically crossed over from the sacramental (in general) to the liturgical (in particular). By concerning himself with actual rituals in their irreducible contingency at the very point when he was rethinking the efficacy of the sacraments, Chauvet broke away from a scholasticism that had lost sight of the concrete bodiliness of their celebration. In this Chauvet is heir to another particularity, that of the liturgical movement, which strove to scrutinize the diversity of rites and the people celebrating them, thereby reestablishing the singular value of the history of the liturgy. In the end it is to the particularity of the church that Chauvet refers through his attentive resituating of sacramental theology in the pastoral efforts of a church seeking to live the sacraments more authentically in a world in full evolution. By relocating the theology of the sacraments in the personal and social bodies celebrating them, Chauvet encourages our attention to the bodily experiences whereby Christian salvation comes to us in history.

Chapter 1

Theology in a Postmodern Context and the Hermeneutical Project of Louis-Marie Chauvet

Lieven Boeve

INTRODUCTION

To celebrate its 575th birthday, the faculty of theology of the K. U. Leuven on March 7, 2007, conferred an honorary doctorate on Louis-Marie Chauvet who, in response, gave the address, "Une relecture de *Symbole et sacrement.*"[1] Upon hearing this title, and having already agreed to write the present contribution, I must admit, a tremendous fear overwhelmed me. The word *relecture* can mean many things (and definitely possesses a very strong meaning in the book under consideration[2]): from merely "reading again," to "adaptation" and "correction," to "new reading" and "drastic revision" of the old text. To my great relief, however, Chauvet did not that day present a *retractatio* or anything close. On the contrary, in his address he reviewed the background and main lines of his theological approach, situating his work in the context of the philosophical and theological resources and discussion of the 1980s. Nevertheless, in the margins of his speech he added some remarks, mostly inspired by the more than twenty years

---

[1] "Une relecture de *Symbole et sacrement,*" *Questions Liturgiques/Studies in Liturgy* 88 (2007): 111–25; in Dutch, "Een terugblik op *Symbole et Sacrement,*" trans. Lambert Leijssen, *Collationes: Vlaams Tijdschrift voor Theologie en Pastoraal* 37 (2007): 237–56; English translation forthcoming in *Louvain Studies.*

[2] Chauvet indicates this by placing *relecture sacramentelle* (trans. "sacramental reinterpretation") in his major work: *Symbole et sacrement. Une relecture sacramentelle de l'existence chrétienne* (Paris: Cerf, 1987). The English translation, cited throughout this present chapter, is *Symbol and Sacrament: A Sacramental Reinterpretation of Christian Existence*, trans. Patrick Madigan and Madeleine Beaumont (Collegeville, MN: Liturgical Press, 1995).

that have passed since the publication of this *magnum opus*. Again it became clear that the fundamental sacramental theology Chauvet developed extensively in *Symbole et sacrement* is still of importance not only to contemporary sacramentology and liturgical studies, but to theology at large, both as an encompassing project and as regards its different disciplines. Dealing with the specific questions of what is classically considered to be only one among many theological disciplines, i.e., sacramental theology, Chauvet's work has resulted in an attempt to reconstruct the fundamental framework of theology itself, with important consequences for the diverse theological disciplines, particularly biblical hermeneutics, christology, ecclesiology, ethics, and pastoral theology. Characteristic of this reconstruction is the fact that it brings together the basic elements of Christian existence—faith and praxis, sacraments, church, Christ—and not from a totalizing, systematizing perspective but, rather, an existential one. Chauvet's sacramental theology is indeed framed from within a *relecture* of Christian existence, a hermeneutics of being a Christian in the contemporary, so-called postmodern context.

In this contribution I will deal especially with the fundamental theological framework and theological method Chauvet has developed, with a view to both the problem Chauvet intended to solve and contemporary fundamental theological discussions. At the time of its publication *Symbole et sacrement*, by its framework and method, breathed fresh air into theology. Today, however, and thinking further than, though still with Chauvet, he may yet offer thought-provoking reflections and suggestions for a continued reconsideration of theology in dialogue with the present context. It is fair to state, I suppose, that Chauvet has moved theology from being structured through premodern schemes onto the threshold of the postmodern context. It is from this perspective that Chauvet's endeavor is to be appreciated while at the same time deepened and strengthened.

THE HERMENEUTICAL PROJECT OF CHAUVET

In what follows I would like briefly to elaborate on some characteristics of Chauvet's project, at the risk of over-accentuating these while at the same time forgetting many others. All of them bear witness to the fact that Chauvet's theology has not only drawn lessons from modern theology but also brings us to the verge of the challenges within the present postmodern context. When one looks at it today, it is quite remarkable how in *Symbole et sacrement* an intrinsically linked double movement takes place, both on the level of theology's subject matter and its method. First of all, Chauvet attempted to reconsider the way in which theology expresses and reflects on God's communication in history with God's people. Secondly, in doing so Chauvet practiced a theological method that not only makes possible this reconsideration but also lives up to its theological outcome. We elaborate on this in the following four paragraphs.

The Criticism of Onto-theology and the Linguistic Turn in Theology

Chauvet's project involves both a critique of former ways of thinking the sacraments and the introduction of a new approach, seeking to solve the problem he diagnoses in the classical, Scholastic approach to sacrament. The first chapter of *Symbole et sacrement* opens with: "How did it come about that, when attempting to comprehend theologically the sacramental relation with God expressed most fully under the term 'grace,' the Scholastics . . . singled out for privileged consideration the category of 'cause'?"[3] Chauvet consequently shows how Thomas Aquinas, in order to explain that sacraments realize what they signify, attempted to refine the concept of causality, harmonizing the heterogeneous categories of *signum* and *causa* "in such a way that the type of sign under examination would have these unique traits: it would indicate what it is causing and it would have no other way of causing except by the mode of signification."[4] The result, however, is that God's salvific action in the sacraments is thought of through an instrumental, productionist scheme, and it is precisely this scheme that obfuscates and even prevents a contemporarily plausible account of the sacraments. More fundamentally, it is the onto-theological presumptions of such a scheme that Chauvet, inspired by Heidegger's criticism, argues against: first, the forgetting of the ontological difference in the attempt to ground the being of beings in a first being; and, second, the dichotomy of being and language, situating being outside language and turning language into an instrument, accentuating its representational character. Today such a scheme turns theology into idolatry, a speculative attempt to take hold of God and God's grace.

As an alternative Chauvet proposes to think of sacramental mediation in terms of symbolic exchange, using the dynamics of interhuman

---

[3] Ibid., 7.
[4] Ibid., 17–18.

communication and the gift as the basic paradigm. Language is not instrumental but a mediation: the medium in and by which all speaking, thinking, and acting takes place, the space in which speakers, thinkers, and agents are already situated and by which they are constituted. It is through such a shift that Chauvet intends to realize "the replacement of an onto-theological logic of the Same . . . with a symbolic representation of the Other."[5]

From Philosophy to Theology: A Homology of Attitude

Chauvet not only shares Heidegger's criticisms of onto-theology,[6] but in order to start his theological reconstruction he claims a "homology of attitude" between Heidegger's anthropological thinking and a contemporary theological anthropology. The relation between a human subject (*Dasein*) and Being is homologous to the relation of the believer to God. God's presence relative to the believer is to be thought of in a similar thinking pattern to that of Heidegger's thinking the manifestation of Being, which is also and at the same time the withdrawal of Being: in revealing, God constantly withdraws. This positing of a homology in no way intends to identify the two; on the contrary, it implies that neither is reducible to the other. "The crucified God is not crossed-out Being."[7]

As a matter of fact, for Chauvet, Heidegger's accounts of *Dasein* and the Christian faith are both distinct ways of living, anchored within two irreducibly different, coexisting, symbolic orders. For, with Heidegger, Chauvet accepts that, because of the fact that Being always has already withdrawn, we are left abandoned in a historically determined particular context. As such, we are embedded in a narrativity anterior to our identity; we belong to a symbolic order that irreducibly surrounds and determines us. By so doing Chauvet implicitly asserts the "co-originality" of both discourses, whereby the one cannot be considered an ontic particularization of the ontological other. The homology between Heidegger's philosophy and theological discourse concerns two irreducible discourses, shaping two irreducible and even irrecon-

---

[5] Ibid., 45.

[6] See also L. Boeve, "Method in Postmodern Theology: A Case Study," in L. Boeve and J. C. Ries, eds., *The Presence of Transcendence: Thinking 'Sacrament' in a Postmodern Age*, Annua Nuntia Lovaniensia 42 (Leuven: Peeters Press, 2001), 19–39.

[7] *Symbol and Sacrament*, 74. See also 82.

cilable worlds. Their homology implies "without building a foot-bridge between the Heideggerian Being and God, to reject a fundamental divorce between the philosophical and theological ways of thinking."[8]

In terms of positing the relationship between philosophy and theology, Chauvet thus appreciates the assistance philosophy can offer for a contemporary theology by its preventing theology from falling back into mere fideism. The concept of "homology" (instead of "analogy," which is still dependent on onto-theological presuppositions[9]) succeeds in this regard to underline the proper role of philosophy in theology's search for understanding, while at the same time safeguarding the integrity of theological discourse itself. Chauvet indeed refuses any reduction of one to the other, or confusion between the two. Methodologically, philosophy serves theology both in situating the Christian faith in an anthropological and epistemological perspective and in helping to express theologically what faith is.

At the same time, and probably more than Chauvet would want to admit,[10] positing the reflexive Christian discourse, although both homologously structured and "co-originary," as a distinct, particular discourse, next to and even over against the Heideggerian philosophical discourse, particularizes this philosophical discourse. It thereby qualifies itself as an expression of a contingent, historical, particular symbolic order: a symbolic order without (the Christian) God. I would add, it is only when this move is continued that the profoundly hermeneutical character of both the philosophical and theological attempts to come to understanding may be appreciated. It may also shed light on the dynamic processes of dialogue, learning, criticism, and reconstruction that the Christian discourse is involved in—a process we will describe in what follows as "recontextualization." Moreover, one may suggest that adequately grasping the particular nature of both these discourses will offer room, in a context of growing plurality, for other discourses to be engaged as well. It may enable theology to deal more fruitfully with one of the current major challenges in theological discussions: the engagement with the plurality of (religious) discourses and the (religious) other.

---

[8] Ibid., 76.

[9] See ibid., 37–43.

[10] There is, for example, no indication of this in "Une relecture de *Symbole et sacrement.*"

Chauvet finds his resistance to metaphysical theological foundations and his openness to symbolic thinking as the way to escape onto-theology confirmed in psychoanalysis. In the perspective of Lacan, every foundation of absolutely secured identity belongs to the imaginary. Living from this insight, i.e., coping with the insatiable desire for secured identity without attempting to give into it by wishing to satisfy it completely, implies entering a (particular) symbolic order, circling around what is revealed in the desire. Identity construction, therefore, is coping with the rupture in one's identification, learning to live with the desire of desire without fulfilling it completely.[11]

The Question of Reference—
Toward a More Radical Hermeneutical Theology?

Sacraments from now on, therefore, should be reflected upon in terms of symbolic exchange, following the model of human communication, in terms of linguistic mediation with its proper symbolic efficacy. It is through the symbolic work of mediation that the relation of the believer to God is realized: a relational identity never accomplished, yet a way ever to be continued. From this mediation, realized in everyday life the sacraments are the major symbolic expressions, constituted in particular, contingent, historical-cultural materiality (corporeality).[12]

For Chauvet it is crucial to affirm that the Christian symbolic order is not a double of an anthropological reality already present there anyway but, rather, generates its specific reality, efficacious in its own right. This efficacy moreover is not only of an intralinguistic nature, but urges—on theological grounds—an extralinguistic referent, even if one can only intralinguistically bear witness to it. In Chauvet's words:

> if this kind of symbolic work is to be correctly placed within the purview of *intra-linguistic* efficacy, it cannot, as far as God's grace is concerned, be reduced to this socio-linguistic process: this would be to transform theology into nothing more than a peculiar form of anthropology and to diminish the absolute otherness of God. We must say, then, that "sacramental grace" is an *extra-linguistic* reality, but with this distinction, in its Christian form it is comprehensible only on the (intra-linguistic) model of the filial and brotherly and sisterly alliance established, *outside of us (extra nos)*, in Christ.[13]

[11] See *Symbol and Sacrament*, 76 ff., 95 ff.
[12] See ibid., 109.
[13] Ibid., 140. See also 438–44.

10

At this point Chauvet would seem to share the intuitions of Paul Ricoeur when dealing with the question of reference, deepening the dynamic concept of metaphorical reference (is/is not) to the imaginative-productive notion of the "world before the text," while at the same time stressing the thoroughly theological urgency of this reference. Although the "theo-ontological" vehemence of the Christian discourse is only to be testified to from within Christian discourse itself, thus fundamentally growing from within its hermeneutical circle, it is nonetheless crucial for that discourse's integrity and plausibility.

More than ever, this insight pushes theology's hermeneutical turn further toward its full realization, pressing the challenge that Chauvet should continue along the way Ricoeur also traveled during the closing decades of the past century.[14] In his reflections on time, narrative, and narrative identity, Ricoeur increasingly relativized the borders between concept and metaphor, reflection and poetics, thinking and narrating, and as a result, between phenomenology and hermeneutics.[15] For Chauvet this implies that what he has repeatedly presented as "the triple determination of truth,"[16] as an alternative to metaphysics, ultimately is profoundly qualified by its hermeneutical nature. The "metafunction" of our thinking (which Chauvet borrows from S. Breton) and the phenomenological explorations into truth finally do not escape or, put more positively, find there appropriate place in the more fundamental third, hermeneutical determination of truth. Chauvet's approach here opens the door to a fully realized hermeneutical theology, finding its locus in actual lived Christian existence. From there forward theology can make such claims, which do not escape the dynamics of the hermeneutical circle while at the same time searching for general validity.

[14] And this also with regard to his *relecture* in "Une relecture de *Symbole et sacrement*."

[15] This point has been convincingly developed by Christophe Brabant in "*Ricoeurs hermeneutische ontologie*," *Tijdschrift voor Filosofie* 69 (2007): 509–34; here, 530.

[16] Chauvet develops this triple determination in "The Broken Bread as Theological Figure of Eucharistic Presence," in L. Boeve and L. Leijssen, eds., *Sacramental Presence in a Postmodern Context: Fundamental Theological Perspectives*, BETL 160 (Leuven: Peeters Press, 2001): 236–62. (French original in *Questions Liturgiques/Studies in Liturgy* 82 [2001]: 9–33; and more recently again in his "Une relecture de *Symbole et sacrement*.")

Theology, Christian Existence, and Corporeality—
On Mediation and the Refusal of Immediacy

Such is indeed one of the main assets of Chauvet's renewal: the irreducible intrinsic link between theology and the very particularity and materiality of Christian existence. In line with this, Chauvet concluded "Une relecture de *Symbole et sacrement*" thus: "[The] entire project can be resumed in the idea of the positive consent to corporeity as the mediation of the most spiritual relationship with God. Faith holds us to the body, and a sacrament is nothing other than the Word of God happening 'at the risk of the body.'"[17] By so doing Chauvet not only forged a more plausible and relevant alternative to the classical onto-theological schemes. At the same time, and to his credit today, he corrected the often unilateral political-ethical interpretations of Christian praxis in many Western modern (political and liberationist) theologies, themselves reacting against too traditionalist and intellectualist accounts of Christianity. Indeed, the praxis-oriented answers of these theologies to the urgent questions about the plausibility and relevance of the Christian faith in a modern context often failed to situate the sacraments and other concrete religious practices in relation to the legitimate ethical-political praxis they called for (except, e.g., in terms of "conscientization").

The shift Chauvet thus proposes is

> to think the most "spiritual" through the mediations of the most
> "corporeal," and to think this theologically, in fidelity to the
> reception of our condition as God's creature, as grace, not with
> resentment as if it would be seen as a small evil but, "with joy"
> . . . as the place where our relation to God is carried out.[18]

Sacraments then are no longer to be considered as a supplementary means to assist a communication between God and human beings, a communication that should take place primarily in the interiority and immediacy of the believing subject. Nor are they instrumental in constructing the ecclesial community or inspiring political-ethical Christian action. On the contrary, because of their corporeal and institutional constitution, the sacraments are the paradigm in which to conceive of divine-human communication.[19] It is in this way that the

---

[17] "Une relecture de *Symbole et sacrement*," 124. See also *Symbol and Sacrament*, 152 ff.

[18] "Une relecture de *Symbole et sacrement*," 121.

[19] See ibid., 121. See also *Symbol and Sacrament*, 140–41.

efficacy of the sacraments should be understood, and therefore obviously cannot be undervalued. And here Chauvet formulates the answer to his initial question about the relation between *signum* and *causa* in the sacraments: "that means that there is nothing more effective than that which however is only a sign, because language is like the matrix within which the subject happens and within which he is led as a subject."[20] Of this the Eucharist is the prime and paradigmatic example. Because of this, Christian faith is fundamentally sacramental in structure, mediated, to be distinguished and safeguarded from the temptation of the immediate—the desire to have an immediate grasp, an unmediated contact with God, Christ, grace, salvation, which is the desire for onto-theological presence.

Further elaborating on this point, Chauvet unfolds the structure of Christian identity and the role of the church as symbolic order in which this identity is constituted and lived. In this order he distinguishes the constitutive triangle of Scriptures, sacrament, and ethics. Through these three dynamically interrelated elements the church, as a proper symbolic order, performs its fundamental sacramental mediation. Moreover, when only one of the three prevails, the integrity of Christian existence is endangered: privileging the cognitive dimension of faith (Scripture) turns into dogmatism; overvaluing the sacramental element leads to magic; and the prioritization of the ethical dimension degenerates into moralism. All three are instances of the desire to master the dynamically interrelated threefold reality of Christian existence. They short-circuit the fundamental sacramental mediation, turning Christ into an object, an idol. In Chauvet's words: "These are three different methods, most often subtle, for killing the presence of the absence of the Risen One, for erasing his radical otherness. Three different ways, expressed in another way, to convert him, the 'Living' One, into a dead body or an available object."[21] And further:

> To give up the hope of finding the lost body of Jesus by consenting to meet him, alive, in the symbolic mediation of the Church thus requires a good joining of the three elements in their mutual differences. . . . Now, as risen, Christ has departed; we must agree to this loss if we want to be able to find him.[22]

[20] "Une relecture de *Symbole et sacrement*," 122.
[21] *Symbol and Sacrament*, 174.
[22] Ibid., 177.

Christ is not at our disposal. Encountering him only occurs in and through an event of the symbolic mediation of the church, itself resulting from the dynamic interrelation of Scriptures, sacrament, and ethics. Only a Christ who is not turned into an object, into a presence, but is (in onto-theological terms) absent, can be symbolically mediated. Only as such can Christ become sacramentally present (*la présence du manque de Dieu*). It is at this point that Chauvet reminds us of the homology of attitude between Heidegger's philosophy and his own theological approach. For the Christian believer, the concrete modality of authentically engaging this absence is living in the church as the symbolic Body of the risen Christ.

One might wonder whether the language of absence and of lack is ultimately the most appropriate to express "post-onto-theologically" God's salvific revelation in the risen Jesus Christ. Chauvet's language here indeed remains dependent on the onto-theological structures he intends to overcome instead of developing a more appropriate language to express Christ's sacramental presence in the church. The latter, of course, has nothing to do with an absence as such but with qualitatively other ways of being present.

RECONTEXTUALIZING THEOLOGY IN A POSTMODERN CONTEXT

It is the awareness of a theological urgency that drives Chauvet to his reconsideration of the sacramental structure of Christian existence. The gap between classical sacramental theology and contemporary culture puts the very plausibility and relevance of the sacraments, and of Christian existence as a whole, under pressure. Consequently, because of the fact that the epistemological conditions have changed (of which the linguistic turn is the prime indication), theology is in need of reconsidering the way it performs its age-old task of "faith in search of understanding." It is with this aim that Chauvet engages in an interdisciplinary dialogue with contemporary philosophy, psychoanalysis, anthropology, ritual studies, etc., in order to reconfigure the proper rationality of Christian faith, both *ad intra* (for Christians), but also *ad extra* (explaining what Christianity is about to the culture at large). Indeed, Chauvet's project is one of the better contemporary illustrations of what I have termed in other places "theological recontextualization."[23] His engagement in such an exercise allows a better situating of

[23] See L. Boeve, *Interrupting Tradition. An Essay on Christian Faith in a Postmodern Context.* Louvain Theological and Pastoral Monographs 30 (Leuven/

his theology in the contemporary field of philosophical-theological reflection on religion today.

Recontextualizing Theology: A Theological-Methodological Urgency

As a theological category, recontextualization implies that Christian faith and tradition are not only contained in a specific historico-cultural, socioeconomic, and sociopolitical context but are also co-constituted by this context. Certainly, faith cannot be reduced to context, nor can tradition's development be reduced to mere adaptation to shifting contexts. Nevertheless, there is an intrinsic bond between faith and tradition, on the one hand, and historical context, on the other. Hence, contextual novelty puts pressure on historically conditioned expressions of Christian faith and their theological understanding, driving these toward recontextualization. Contextual sensitivities and thought-patterns start shifting; older forms of tradition lose their familiarity and plausibility; and effects of alienation arise. Both through taking part in and confronting itself with this changed context the Christian faith community is urged to find new ways to express its faith in fidelity to the tradition as well as to the context in which it is situated, balancing between continuity and discontinuity. The concept of recontextualization thus functions both descriptively and normatively. As a descriptive category, it assists in analyzing the ways in which tradition has been challenged by contextual change and novelty, varying from stubborn condemnation and suppression of this novelty to its uncritical embracement and adaptation. As a normative category, recontextualization calls for a theological program. The theological insight in the intrinsic link between faith and context inspires theologians to take the contextual challenges seriously, motivating them to come to a contemporary theological discourse that at the same time can claim theological validity and contextual plausibility.[24]

Grand Rapids: Peeters / Eerdmans, 2003), chap. 1; *God Interrupts History: Theology in a Time of Upheaval* (New York: Continuum, 2007), chap. 2; and *Theology, Recontextualisation and Contemporary Critical Consciousness: Lessons from Richard Schaeffler for a Postmodern Theological Epistemology*, in E. Gaziaux, ed., *Théology et Philosophy*, BETL 206 (Leuven: Peeters Press, 2007): 455–83.

[24] As a normative theological category, recontextualization can be theological motivated from a renewed understanding of the doctrine of incarnation, as I have tried to show in "Christus Postmodernus: An Attempt at Apophatic Christology," in T. Merrigan and J. Haers, eds., *The Myriad Christ: Plurality and*

The dialogue with philosophy and other human sciences has been and is still elementary in this process. Most often philosophy offers a reflexive account of contextual worldviews and sensitivities. To a large part it constitutes the intellectual horizon in which theologians seek to express an understanding of Christian faith. On many accounts the historical involvement of theology with philosophy has clearly led to new ways of doing theology.[25] Theologians have borrowed models, patterns, ideas, and terminologies from philosophy and the human sciences in order to develop, structure, support, or flesh out their own understanding of what Christian faith is about. They use thinking patterns, categories, etc., from philosophy in order to reflexively express the truth of faith—which, by its own nature, is never absolutely grasped or completely understood—and to signify it both in a theologically and contextually plausible and relevant way. Theologians do not thereby become philosophers as such with the philosophers (or human scientists with the human scientists). On the contrary, in the best tradition of *philosophia ancilla theologiae*, they use philosophy to consider anew the specific claims of their theological tradition. Such dialogue implies not only engaging in a confrontation with contextual critical consciousness (self-criticism) but also, and more importantly, searching for a contextually anchored understanding of Christian faith, i.e., developing a theology for the present day. In both, philosophy's assistance is at once necessary and also welcome.

Chauvet's approach not only gives answer to the descriptive usage of recontextualization but also illustrates the normative impetus of the concept, doing this both on the level of the legitimization of his approach and the interdisciplinary dialogical way in which he elaborates the latter. At the same time, however, and of primary importance here, is his explicit attention to the particular theological features of the Christian faith. To whatever degree the theological *relecture* of Christian existence may be helped, and even reconfigured, by the dialogue

---

the Quest for Unity in Contemporary Christology, BETL, 152 (Leuven: Peeters Press, 2000), 577–93; and in God Interrupts History, chap. 8.

[25] The prime example is the way in which the rediscovery of Aristotelianism influenced Scholastic theology, at best illustrated by the new synthesis performed by Thomas Aquinas, between Augustinian tradition and Aristotelian thought patterns and vocabulary. See, for example, O. H. Pesch, *Thomas von Aquin. Grenze und Größe mittelalterlicher Theologie. Ein Einführung* (Mainz: Mathias-Grünewald, 1988, 1989).

with philosophy, anthropology, etc., Christian faith can never be reduced to merely philosophical or anthropological structures—as if it were a kind of narrative double or illustration of these structures. Through dialogue Chauvet succeeds, with the help of contemporary philosophy, etc., in not only reconsidering the reflexivity of being a Christian today but also testifying to the proper legitimate position of theological discourse in relation to these other discourses. Exemplary in this regard is the homology of attitude that Chauvet claims between Heideggerian and theological discourses, and thus their "co-originality." This motivates, for example, his refusal to reduce theology to merely "ontic" discourse, secondary to the "ontological" discourse of philosophy. This approach not only offers theology a structure for rethinking the dynamics of Christian faith but also posits Christian faith and theology as distinct and irreducible discourses, to be taken on their own terms.

This, I would claim, is what theological recontextualization in the contemporary, so-called postmodern context is about. This is also what enables us to situate Chauvet's theological methodology in the current broader postmodern philosophical-theological field. It would lead us too far astray to attempt to present the full picture of this field. It is, however, most enlightening to relate Chauvet's approach to two discussions that have colored the scene for at least the last two decades: first, the postconciliar theological discussion on the relation between Christian faith and the (post)modern context and, secondly, the "turn to religion" in contemporary phenomenology, hermeneutics, and deconstruction.

Theology and the Dialogue with the Context:
Between Continuity and Discontinuity

First, the post–Vatican II discussion on theological methodology and the relation between Christian faith and the contemporary context has been modified by the postmodern criticism of modernity.[26] The theological dialogue with modernity, answering the call for aggiornamento argued for and enacted in *Gaudium et Spes*, lost much of its

---

[26] For a further elaboration of this argument, including bibliographical references, see *God Interrupts History*, intro. and chap. 2. See also L. Boeve, "Beyond the Modern and Anti-modern Dilemma. *Gaudium et Spes* and Theological Method in a Postmodern European Context," *Horizons* 34:2 (2007): 292–305.

attractiveness and plausibility once the modern dialogue partner got deconstructed. So-called correlationist theologies, such as Edward Schillebeeckx's, suffered even more when the still-existing overlap between Christianity and culture progressively disappeared.[27] For a long time the latter functioned as the unquestioned, and thus facilitating, background for correlating Christian faith and modern rationalities and sensibilities. Theologians such as Joseph Ratzinger, who were hesitant to engage in the dialogue because of the ambiguities of the modern context (e.g., secularization, secularism), saw their point proven and further reinforced by their even more pessimistic evaluation of postmodernity (nihilism, relativism, amoralism, aestheticism, individualism, etc.). Other so-called postmodern theologies, such as John Milbank's Radical Orthodoxy, joined in and, as an alternative to the modern secularism and postmodern nihilism, presented a neo-Augustinian counter-narrative, reclaiming the world from a Christian participationist perspective.

More fundamentally, however, the difference between the two positions is not so much a question of whether a dialogue of theology with the modern context is productive or not as whether such a dialogue is of any theological necessity. Those rejecting that necessity perceive Christian faith as in essence not affected by it. The contrary position starts from the basic theological premise, also in the background of the normative conception of recontextualization, that Christian faith's involvement with the context very much makes a difference. Because of the incarnational dynamics of Christian faith, there is even an intrinsic link between revelation, faith, church, tradition, and the context in which they are situated. Faith and church are not unaffected by, let alone in opposition to, the world; they participate in constituting it. Furthermore, they are in part constituted by the world. Given the fact that God reveals Godself precisely in history, history is ultimately co-constitutive of faith's truth. However, because of the postmodern criticisms of modernity, modern correlation as a dialogical strategy indeed lost a lot of its plausibility due to its excessively accentuating the continuity between faith and context. Therefore, contrary to those pleading for discontinuity, it is not the necessity of the dialogue that should be put into question but the nature of such dialogue, and this because of the altered situation.

[27] This becomes very clear when one studies the evolution apparent in the results stemming from the three European Values Studies, a survey undertaken in most of the European countries during the last three decades (1981, 1990–1991, 1999).

It is here that Chauvet's interdisciplinary, hermeneutical theological approach, which, as we mentioned, could further be radicalized, renders its service. It not only seeks continuity with the present context but also accentuates the specificity of Christian existence in relation to this context. In so doing Chauvet successfully holds together both continuity and discontinuity in the relation between Christianity and context. This is due to not only contextual reasons (the particularity of different symbolic orders) but also the theological structure of Christian faith itself: answering the call of God, which can never be grasped or ever mastered, but to which it has access only in the sacramental mediation of the symbolic order of the church.[28]

Chauvet and the "Turn to Religion" in Contemporary "Continental" Philosophy: On Incarnation and Contamination

A wide range of philosophers belonging to the phenomenological, deconstructionist and/or hermeneutical traditions, including Emmanuel Levinas, Jacques Derrida, Jean-Luc Marion, and Gianni Vattimo, have placed the theme of religion on the philosophical agenda again. Such movement occurs very often in relation to their attempts to overcome onto-theology and to engage otherness and transcendence. It is noteworthy that, in their approaches, religion is often thought of primarily as a structure in and through which the decentering of the subject is grasped. Also noteworthy, in view of Chauvet, is the merely relative importance of language, particularity, and narrative in relation to this structure. Very briefly I will illustrate this point with regard to Jean-Luc Marion, Jack Caputo, and Richard Kearney, all three of whom are very close to the catholic theological tradition but, in a particular way, also distant from it.[29]

---

[28] For a proposal for holding together continuity and discontinuity in the dialogue with the context through a theology of interruption, see my *God Interrupts History*.

[29] For a more developed elaboration of my argument, and further references, see L. Boeve, "God, Particularity and Hermeneutics. A Critical-Constructive Theological Dialogue with Richard Kearney on Continental Philosophy's Turn (in)to Religion," *Ephemerides Theologicae Lovanienses* 81 (2005): 305–33; as well as (also in relation to Radical Orthodoxy): "(Post)Modern Theology on Trial? Towards a Radical Theological Hermeneutics of Christian Particularity," *Louvain Studies* 28 (2003): 240–54.

Jean-Luc Marion's phenomenology of givenness[30] takes as its point of departure the "saturated phenomenon," which turns the subject into the dative and, thus, the one who is given to, who receives oneself through receiving what is given. Therefore, the human response is always already secondary, consisting in nothing more than the acknowledgment of the reception of oneself from givenness. This structure, according to Marion, is given and therefore prior to language and hermeneutics. Accordingly, this dynamic of appeal and response, and the relationship it constitutes, also structures the nature of divine revelation and the role of religious language. According to Marion, therefore, it is not so much a hermeneutical approach to religion and religious language that teaches us how to understand (Christian) religion and religious truth, but a radicalized phenomenological approach, that is, a phenomenology serving as a heuristic reducing particularity and language to its primary structure (*autant de reduction, autant de donation*—the more reduction the more givenness).[31]

Following the lead of the later Jacques Derrida, John Caputo expresses the dynamics of deconstruction and the corresponding critical consciousness in explicitly religious vocabularies. This results in a so-called radical hermeneutics of religion that seeks to determine the "religious" in terms of "religion without religion," reducing religion to a (universal) structure of religious desire.[32] Caputo indeed strives to uncover the structure of "pure prayer," that is, a relation of the subject to a "You," while at the same time deferring the question of whether this You in effect exists.[33] He is concerned, as it were, with retrieving a form of spirituality uncontaminated by particularity and narrativity to the point of dropping the presupposition that there is a You to whom or which the prayer is directed.[34]

[30] See J. L. Marion, *Etant donné: essai d'une phénoménologie de la donation* (Paris: PUF, 1997).

[31] See Marion, "'Christian Philosophy': Hermeneutic or Heuristic?" in F. J. Ambrosio, ed., *The Question of Christian Philosophy Today* (New York: Fordham University, 1999), 247–64.

[32] As another way of expressing this structure of religious desire, Derrida and Caputo indicate the "messianic structure" recognized in, but at the same time distinguished from, the various particular messianisms.

[33] See J. D. Caputo, "Shedding Tears Beyond Being: Derrida's Experience of Prayer," in Marco Olivetti, ed., *Théologie negative*, Biblioteca dell' 'Archivio di Filosofia' 59 (Rome: CEDAM, 2002), 861–80.

[34] Caputo, however, is also aware of the fact that neither Derrida nor he himself escapes from linguistic contaminatio. See, for example, B. Keith Putt,

Finally, Richard Kearney, following Ricoeur, criticizes the "short-cut" approaches of both phenomenology and deconstruction, claiming in *The God Who May Be*[35] to perform a "phenomenological-hermeneutical retrieval" of (the Christian) religion, thereby indicating the importance of the "metaphorizing role" of hermeneutic mediation in understanding religion. Ultimately, nevertheless, Kearney, borrowing from Derrida and Caputo the concept of messianism, also tends to reduce religion to a quasi-universal ethico-religious structure, thus placing at risk his own starting point. This is well illustrated by his view on the plurality of religions: in the end, for Kearney, all religious traditions, in one way or another, share the "same" caring for justice and peace, for human wholeness and fulfillment. All convey narrative wisdom in order to realize this fulfillment. The God-who-may-be is revealed and witnessed to in many traditions, whose insights may well be analogous or complimentary. Thus, in the end, language and narrativity differentiate and divide again.[36] Religious truth is finally to be situated in what is radically beyond language, beyond narrativity. Hermeneutics becomes a tool to evoke and point at this beyond. Language again risks being considered as a contaminate of the quasi-universal purity of an ethico-eschatological religious desire.

Although all, albeit each in his own voice, display a hermeneutical sensibility for particularity, in practice they tend to situate the basic structure of the religious outside or beyond particularity, deeming language contamination. Yet is it legitimate to equate language with contamination? From a fundamental theological perspective, at least, this challenges the importance of incarnation as the theological-epistemological category par excellence to name God and to think about religious truth. Or is Christianity, with its christocentric and thus incarnational approach, from the very outset always doomed to be too

"What Do I Love When I Love My God? An Interview with John D. Caputo" (by B. Putt in J. H. Olthuis, ed., *Religion With/out Religion: The Prayers and Tears of John D. Caputo* (London/New York: Routledge, 2001), 150–79; here, 165.

[35] See R. Kearney, *The God Who May Be: A Hermeneutic of Religion* (Bloomington, IN: Indiana University Press, 2001).

[36] This is the reason Kearney opposes the very explicit "confessionally partisan" truth-claims of religions. For Kearney the uniqueness and definitiveness of the fullness of God's revelation in the incarnation in Jesus Christ qualifies to be such a claim. See his *Strangers, Gods and Monsters: Interpreting Otherness* (London: Routledge, 2003), 41.

particular, too historical, too positive? Chauvet definitely would oppose and reverse this argument, both on philosophical and theological grounds. Concerning the philosophical, he would argue for the irreducibility of the symbolic order and for the very corporeality of its operations in dealing with religions and their efficaciousness. On the theological level, he would add that it is only in the concrete materiality, particularity, and narrativity of Christian existence—thus in its arch-sacramental features—that God's word and grace are mediated. Language should not be looked at in terms of contamination or fall. The latter ultimately makes any "pure" or "authentic" concept of religion impossible, compelling hermeneutics to leave its entanglement with particularity behind and move in the direction of a pure, but nonetheless untenable, religious structure. In Chauvet's account, however, a hermeneutic of religion, and definitely a hermeneutics of Christianity, does not lead "beyond," let alone "behind," language, but to language itself: to the concrete stories, practices, texts, and traditions wherein religion is lived and experienced. For it is through concrete corporeal mediations that the spiritual is communicated and lived. Language is constitutive for religion. As a matter of fact, this may well be Christian reflection's particular contribution to Continental philosophy's recent turn to religion.

CONCLUSION

It may sound awkward, but in attempting to forge an alternative to the premodern sacramental thinking patterns, Chauvet has presented us with a theology and theological method that lead us at least onto the threshold of the postmodern context. His hermeneutical-theological project, with its strong accent on mediation, language, praxis, and corporeality, not only offers a plausible and relevant *relecture* of Christian existence today, with many consequences for theology and its disciplines, but also, because of its approach, takes sides in the theological-methodological discussion on the relation between Christian faith and context. This has important consequences for the positioning of Christian faith in relation to today's (European) culture and society. Finally, it allows theologians to take part in the philosophical discussion on religion, criticizing those forms of religious hermeneutics that claim a religious purity beyond the mediations of language and the symbolic order.

At the same time it remains true that, because of its starting point and dialogue partners, *Symbol and Sacrament* testifies to the theological struggle of a particular generation, a struggle with which many of my generation, children of the linguistic turn, are hardly still familiar. Moreover, the hermeneutical-theological drive is challenged by new questions. For example, it is confronted by accusations of, on the one hand, particularism and narrativism, while on the other, relativism and false universalism. These challenges would seem to inspire certain theologians today to halt prematurely the hermeneutical turn, returning again to more short-cut onto-(theo-)logical approaches due to fearing the consequences of a fully hermeneutical theology. The latter deliberately sets aside the will to master its subject and secure identity, pursuing instead the never-ending and in-securing way of faith seeking understanding in the concrete, material mediations of our Christian existence. For many, however, this would seem an excessively dangerous and insufficiently reassuring position in a context too easily evaluated as nihilistic and relativistic.

A second challenge for a contemporary hermeneutical theology is the confrontation with otherness in and the engagement with religious plurality. This challenge does not in the first place imply the reflection on otherness in one's own discourse (which Chauvet evidently has done), but concerns coping with the challenge of the concrete, external other, who is also the religious other. The context in and for which Chauvet has written his theology, however, is still predominantly seen as marked by secularization, challenging theology to profile itself vis-à-vis the alternative of an existence without God. In this regard the particularization of the Heideggerian philosophical discourse could be a first step to invite other religious and ideological discourses, themselves exponents of different particular symbolic orders, to enter into a critical-productive dialogue. A theological reflection on the possible productive relation between the other in one's own discourse and the other (of another) discourse, then, could be a second step. It is in such a direction that a future *relecture* of Chauvet's hermeneutical theology could go.[37]

---

[37] For an engagement of these challenges, see my *God Interrupts History*.

Chapter 2

The Sacraments as "Celebrations of the Church": Liturgy's Impact on Sacramental Theology

Patrick Prétot

INTRODUCTION

The theological work of Louis-Marie Chauvet represents a kind of Archimedean point: it takes seriously the fact that the sacraments are liturgical actions. As actions of the church, they operate not only on those who receive them but also on the assembly, the first subject of liturgical action, and through it upon the entire people of God. This attention to the sacramental order takes into consideration not only the anthropological dimension of the sacraments but also the ecclesiological dimension, including christology and pneumatology, since "the Church's mission is not an addition to that of Christ and the Holy Spirit, but is its sacrament: in her whole being and in all her members the Church is sent to announce, bear witness, make present and spread the mystery of the communion of the Holy Trinity."[1] I am of the opinion that this is what is most dynamic in Chauvet's work, *The Sacraments: The Word of God at the Mercy of the Body*, in which he relies upon the teachings of Vatican II according to which "every Eucharistic assembly truly realizes the Church of God," affirming that "the liturgical assembly, inasmuch as it is church, is for everyone the chief *concrete mediation* of her relationship with the living God revealed in Jesus."[2]

---

[1] *Catechism of the Catholic Church*, Vatican website, http://www.vatican.va, no. 738.

[2] Chauvet, *Les sacrements: Parole de Dieu au risque du corps* (Paris: Ouvrières, 1993), 55, that refers to the Constitution on the Liturgy, no. 26; Chauvet, *Symbole et sacrement*, Cogitatio fidei 144 (Paris: Cerf, 1987), 3rd part, 329 ff.; Chauvet, *Symbol and Sacrament: A Sacramental Reinterpretation of Christian Existence* (Collegeville, MN: Liturgical Press, 1995), 319 ff.; *The Sacraments: The Word of*

It is above all this that undergirds the schema of the structure of Christian identity[3] wherein the church as fundamental sacrament envelops a ternary structure in an almost "womb-like" way. This aspect is sometimes ignored by those who rely on the thought of Chauvet, separating it from its fundamental liturgical field at the risk of creating another form of Scholasticism in which the category of "symbol" would play a role that in the past was assigned to hylomorphism (substance-changing). This aspect is also ignored by some critics who think they have disclosed the risk of Chauvet's drowning the sacraments—with their irreducible ritual, bodily, and institutional abutment—in the "sacramental," claiming that he gives the symbolic so much weight as to absorb the contingency of ritual actions.[4]

All too often we forget that sacramental theology of the twentieth century is a recent heir to the liturgical movement in general, and to the history of the liturgy in particular. Because the work of liturgists in the twentieth century was often concerned with the historical perspective, it warned forcefully against any ahistorical conceptualization, the historicity that penetrates not only ritual itself (which has a history) but also the individuals and the groups who are the subjects of it. Consequently, reflection in sacramental theology is inseparable from liturgical research, to which the work of Dom Odo Casel gave fundamental shape.[5] In fact, after the course centuries during which sacramental

---

God at the Mercy of the Body (Collegeville, MN: Liturgical Press, 2001), 37–38. Hereafter the corresponding page numbers for the English language versions of *both Les sacrements* and *Symbole et sacrement* will be indicated by "ELV, p." The reader may discern which work is being referenced from the French work cited.

[3] Chauvet, *Symbole et sacrement*, 177; ELV, 172.

[4] Cf. for example P. Gisel, "Du symbole au symbolique," *RSR* 75 (1987): 357–69.

[5] O. Casel, *Le Mystère du culte dans le christianisme*, Traditions chrétiennes (Paris: Cerf, 1983); (1st French ed., Lex orandi 6, 1946; 2nd ed. expanded, Lex orandi 38, 1964); Casel, *Faites ceci en mémoire de moi*, Lex orandi 34 (Paris: Cerf, 1962); Casel, *"Art und Sinn der ältesten christlichen Osterfeies,"* JahrbLit 14 (1934): 1–78, Fr. trans.: *La Fête de Pâques dans l'église des pères*, Lex orandi 37, 1963; Casel, *Le Mystère de l'Église, Union de Dieu et des hommes*, (texts Dom Casel, ed. S. Théodora Schneider, OSB) (Paris: Mame, 1965); cf. Dom B. Neunheuser, "La théologie des mystères de Dom Casel dans la tradition catholique," *Eph. Lit.*, 94 (1980): 297–310; Dom A. Gozier, *Dom Casel*, Théologiens et spirituels contemporains (Paris: Fleurus, 1968), H.-I. Dalmais, "Le "Mystère,"" *La Maison Dieu* 14 (1948): 67–98.

theology and the liturgy maintained adjoining, particularly juridical considerations—respect for rubrics as the guarantor of validity of the sacramental celebration—the liturgical movement returned to the category of "mystery." This category, more global than that of "sacrament," allowed for rediscovering liturgy as ritual action, the church's becoming a body under the ecclesial motif of "mystery," and the work of grace implied in the sacramental order.[6]

As H. de Lubac has demonstrated, it is in the Middle Ages that the link between these three aspects had disintegrated under the influence of the medieval debates that dealt with the sole question about efficacy (and its conditions) to the detriment of the union between efficaciousness and effectiveness of the sacramental celebration in the church.[7] Rediscovering the unity of liturgy and sacramental theology, the liturgical movement thus opened a new paradigm for sacramental theology, but without relinquishing ways to think about sacramental efficaciousness. It did so by affirming the realization of the salvific work of redemption through and in the celebration of the liturgy without using a demonstration equivalent to the brilliant Scholastic synthesis. It is in returning to the category of "symbol" (a category that attempts to integrate better the dimension of relationships and therefore to greatly facilitate the consideration of the ecclesial dimension) that Chauvet tries to propose a model of sacramental theology responding to the demands of the work of liturgists.

In this chapter I would like to show how Chauvet's theology takes its place in this new situation, which axes he proposes to demonstrate that the sacraments are celebrations of the church, and by which extensions this decisive work calls us to confront current questions in a contemporary world sometimes called "post" or "hyper" modern.

A THEOLOGY OF THE "CELEBRATION" OF THE SACRAMENTS

Teaching a course on the "theology of celebration"—wherein he carefully distinguished it from a "theology of the liturgy"—Chauvet proposed the idea that "the most spiritual communion with God is brought about (here we mean *in the celebration*) through the carnal or

---

[6] Cf. Chauvet, "Sacrements," *Catholicisme*, vol. XIII, 1992, fasc. 60.

[7] H. de Lubac, *Corpus mysticum. L'Eucharistie et l'Église au Moyen Âge, étude historique* (Paris: Aubier-Montaigne, 1944).

fleshy layer of material, traditional and institutional things."[8] Let us notice the focus on two adjectives, "traditional" and "institutional," related to the fact that the sacraments are "celebrated." Chauvet insists upon considering them as actions of the church and even more the manifestation of the symbolic act of the church, a church that takes form through and in the liturgical institutions received and transmitted in a tradition.

In an article that appeared in 1982, Bishop Albert Houssiau had already traced this perspective, calling to mind the "rediscovery of the liturgy through sacramental theology,"[9] a phenomenon that he placed "between 1951 and 1980" and that necessitated overcoming three major obstacles: (1) rediscovering the profound meaning of the adage *lex orandi, lex credendi,* moving past the fear provoked by its use in the modernist crisis; (2) isolating less the sacramental moment, that is, dropping the concentration on the exact moment—that of the "conjunction" in an almost "astrological" sense, between matter, form and minister—to move to a broader perspective, taking into better consideration the temporal unfolding of the celebration; and finally (3) rediscovering history not as *confirmatur* of a predetermined theological thesis but as "original source of knowledge of the *an sit* and the *quid sit,* that is, the establishment of a truth and of the interpretation of reality."[10] In spite of these "rediscoveries," it remains that sacramental theology must continue to try to consider the dimension of communal celebration of the sacraments that cannot be taken only as ecclesial acts administered by competent ministers.

THE IMPACT OF CASEL'S THEOLOGY ON THE THEOLOGY OF CELEBRATION

Casel's theology of the liturgy deeply marked the framework of thought on the sacraments. This proposition that we normally call *Mysterienlehre* rests upon the idea of the actualization of the events of salvation and notably of the Passover (*Pascha*) of Christ in the liturgy. To speak thus is to think about the sacraments as places of encounter of humans with the living God who throughout history pursues his work of creation and salvation. In his groundbreaking work E. H.

---

[8] Institut Supérieur de Liturgie, *Programme 2007–2008,* 16.

[9] A. Houssiau, "La redécouverte de la liturgie par la théologie sacramentaire (1950–1980)," *La Maison Dieu* 149 (1982): 27–55.

[10] Ibid., 34.

Schillebeeckx proposed the idea of the encounter of Christ in "the sacraments" of the church, Christ who is the "sacrament" of the encounter with God.[11] The biblical notion of "memorial," for structuring a conception of liturgical celebration in its relationship with Scripture, is consequently homogeneous to the theology of the mysteries. It is definitely the encounter between humans and the work of God in which contemporary sacramental theology is especially sensitive. It finds for example a compelling resonance in John Paul II's letter on the occasion of the twenty-fifth anniversary of the Constitution on the Divine Liturgy from Vatican II: "Because the liturgy is the exercise of the priesthood of Christ, it is necessary to maintain always present the affirmation of the disciple before the mysterious presence of Christ: 'It is the Lord!' (Jn 21, 7). Nothing that we can do in the liturgy can seem as more important than that which Christ does, invisibly but really through his Spirit."[12]

The "doctrine on the mysteries" has often been badly understood,[13] in part because it was more intuitive than demonstrative and, for this reason, much different than the theological customs fashioned through scholastic theology and the manuals inspired by it. We often summarize a phrase borrowed from St. Leo the Great that inspired Casel: "What is visible in our redeemer has now passed into the Mysteries."[14] But this shorthand version has possibly not served the thought of Casel to the degree that Leo's phrase focuses attention on the actualization of the *events* of salvation to the detriment of the consideration on the efficacy of the celebration of the mysteries, while raising the question: how can a past event be made present in a liturgical celebration?

[11] Cf. E. H. Schillebeeckx, *Le Christ, Sacrement de la rencontre de Dieu, Etude théologique du salut par les sacrements*, Lex orandi 31 (Paris: Cerf, 1960; 1st ed., 1957; 3rd, 1959).

[12] John Paul II, Lettre apostolique pour le 25e anniversaire de *Sacrosanctum Concilium*, sur la sainte liturgie du 14 mai 1989, DC 1985, June 4, 1989, 518–24, n. 10, p. 520.

[13] Cf. T. Filthaut, *La théologie des mystères, exposé et controverses*, trans. J. C. Didier and A. Liefooghe (Tournai: Desclée, 1954); I. H. Dalmais, "La 'doctrine des mystères' (*Mysterienlehre*) de Dom Casel," A. G. Martimort, ed., *L'Église en Prière*, new ed. (Paris: Desclée, 1984), vol. I, 275–81.

[14] Leo the Great, *Sermon 74,2*, PL 54:398: "*Quod redemptoris nostri conspicuum fuit, in sacramenta transivit*"; "The appearances of the Lord and Redeemer have passed into the Mysteries" (*Le mystère du culte dans le christianisme*, 1983, 18).

The crux of the problem is found in the relationship between several realities: Christ as a personal mystery, that is, as he shows in the flesh the invisible divinity; his salvific works that are the saving acts, especially his death and resurrection; and finally the communication of this salvation to humanity through the worship of the church and especially in the sacraments.

The content of the mystery of worship, as Dom Casel perceived it, is none other than Christ himself and his work of salvation. If there is a difference between the mystery of worship and the mystery of Christ, it "consists in that the first is the worship representation, a way of being sacramental of the first mystery. The difference therefore only reports on the way of being, not about its essence."[15]

It is possible that this collection of views on the liturgical actualization of the mysteries may have led to an excessive concentration on the relationship between Christ on the one hand, and the liturgy and the sacraments on the other. This christocentrism is the hallmark of a text such as Pius XII's encyclical *Mediator Dei* (1947),[16] but it continued at Vatican II especially through the doctrine about the presence of Christ in the liturgy and the sacraments: "In order to accomplish such a great work, Christ is always present in his Church, especially in the liturgical actions. . . . He is present in the sacrifice of the Mass, in the person of the minister . . . and to the highest extent under the Eucharistic elements. He is there present through his power, in the sacraments, so that if someone baptizes, it is Christ himself who baptizes."[17]

Since it is rooted in the patristic period, Casel's theology lends itself to an approach on the covenant between God and humans, a perspective where he advances the image of the church as a "spouse and collaborator in the work of salvation."[18] But at the same time, in a correlative way, since the church is also the "body of Christ," we should never lose sight of the "mystery of the unity of the head and the body."[19] That is what the conciliar constitution expressed in its own way noting that to accom-

---

[15] Th. Filthaut, *La théologie des mystères*, 8.

[16] Pius XII, Encyclical *Mediator Dei* on the Sacred Liturgy, November 20, 1947, *La Documentation Catholique*, no. 1010, February 15, 1948, 193–225.

[17] Vatican II, Constitution on the Sacred Liturgy no. 7 (http://www.vatican.va).

[18] Dom Casel, *Le Mystère de l'Église, Union de Dieu et des hommes*: 1st and 3rd parts.

[19] Ibid., 2nd part: "Le mystère de l'unité de la tête et du corps," notably chap. 1, "Le Christ unique," 125–30.

plish the salvific work "through which God is perfectly glorified and humans sanctified," "Christ associates himself always with the Church, His beloved Bride who calls to her Lord, and through Him offers worship to the Eternal Father."[20] The conciliar text underlines the double image of Christ, who is both mediator, as head of the body (whence the fundamental shape of liturgical prayer: *per Christum ad Patrem*) but also partner in the covenant in a spousal relationship with the Church (whence the legitimacy of the prayer *ad Christum*).

THE SACRAMENTS: ECCLESIAL CELEBRATIONS OF THE TRINITARIAN MYSTERY

But in fact that which is more suggested than truly articulated in Casel's work is better developed in Chauvet, who in replacing the sacraments in the network of ecclesial mediations allows for a true articulation of these several dimensions. Instead of isolating the sacraments in a concept centered only on the mystery of Christ, he introduces them to a trinitarian framework that has as its points of departure the paschal mystery in which the church can take her place of fundamental mediation:

> [T]he claim that encounter of and communication with the living God are done through traditional and fully human materials— gestures, postures, words—which the church assumes in the name of Christ and calls "sacraments," does not hold good unless, *the very being of God* can in some way be conceived of as "human" in its very divinity. This means that the discourse affirming "sacramental grace" can be held with assurance only if it is in harmony with a properly "theo-logical" discourse giving food for thought concerning the "humanity" of divine God. In Christianity, such a discourse is necessarily rooted in christology, which no less necessarily opens onto a Trinitarian discourse.[21]

It is by adopting the Passover of Christ as a point of departure that this articulation is offered. When classical sacramental theology departs from the Incarnation and the hypostatic union, it concludes by presenting the sacraments as instruments that prolong the holy humanity of Christ.[22] The christological concentration already raised and

[20] Vatican II, Constitution on the Liturgy no. 7.

[21] Chauvet, *Les sacrements: Parole de Dieu au risque du corps*, 171; ELV, 155.

[22] Ibid., 171–72; ELV, 155–56. Cf. *Symbole et sacrement*, 474 ff.; ELV, 453 ff.

which badly frames with the *lex orandi* of the church (we can cite here the trinitarian structure of the eucharistic prayer or the trinitarian formula in baptism and even the rite itself) hinders us to think about the sacraments outside the schema of the production of grace in which the church and notably the minister appear as place holders (literally lieutenants) substituting for Christ. Inversely the trinitarian schema allows us to think about ecclesial mediation within the trinitarian mystery itself because "Such, therefore, is the Spirit's function: *to write the very difference of God in the body of humanity*, and first of all in the body of the church, which was its first visible work after the resurrection . . . and also in the body of every believer (1 Cor 6:19)."[23]

Definitively it is thanks to a subsequent pneumatology, supported by the consideration of the place of the epiclesis in sacramental actions,[24] that the ecclesial mediation appears in full light: through the sacramental actions, the church through the power of the Spirit, who is the gift of the "Crucified-Risen One," gives body to the Word. Whereas classical sacramental theology emphasized the sacraments in regard to Christ, presenting them as ecclesial operations, contemporary research takes into consideration that the sacraments are "celebrated" in order to think about their efficacy in the order of grace. In this way it recovers the patristic insight about sacramental economy through which it is in and through the liturgical celebration that the sacraments appear as the Word that brings about salvation, a vision favored by the ritual link that structures the Easter Vigil: the celebration of the sacraments of Christian initiation is the ritual fulfillment of the proclamation of the great stories of the paschal event.[25]

But this implies a kind of reversal that depends upon the mystery of the Cross: "It is precisely when Jesus has the radical experience of the human condition that erupts through the centurion the Church's confession of faith: 'Truly this is the Son of God.' Here is the mystery: God has never allowed Himself to be so recognized as in that of the disfigured man of the cross."[26] In other words, because God reveals himself "in what is most different from God,"[27] it is a trinitarian christology—

[23] Ibid., 182; ELV, 166.

[24] Cf. P. De Clerck, "Les épiclèses des nouvelles prières eucharistiques du rite romain. Leur importance théologique," *Ecclesia Orans* XVI (1999): 189–208.

[25] Cf. *Symbole et sacrement*, Chap. VI, 195–232; ELV, 190–227.

[26] *Les sacrements*, 179; ELV, 162–63.

[27] Ibid.; ELV, 163.

we recognize here the influence of theologians such as J. Moltmann, E. Jüngel or W. Kasper—who constitute the key to the question: to what God are we witnesses but also partners when the church "celebrates" the sacraments? To say that the sacraments are "celebrated" has heavy consequences for theology in the first instance. To add that they are "a celebration of the paschal mystery" is even greater, since it is a matter of shedding light on the scandal of the Cross, this "scandalous revelation" that "requires a theology" "immanently paradoxical," that "subverts the representations which humans more or less spontaneously have of God."[28] Undoubtedly this fundamental contribution of Chauvet deserves not only to be heard but to stimulate the thinking of theologians proceeding from the sacramental rites themselves.[29]

SACRAMENTS AND ECCLESIAL EXPERIENCE: A FIELD OF RESEARCH FOR TODAY

Here let us open a research axis that can be formulated in the following way: if the liturgy is indeed the actualization of the mysteries of salvation, if the church is the first subject of the celebration, then it is right to extend the reflection on the relation between the church and the celebration as it actualizes the work of salvation.

This is pastorally decisive in a time when multiple and varied processes acting at multiple levels operate profoundly, and that tend to isolate people in search of identity who often find no place to express and fulfill themselves. The sociologist of religions Danièle Hervieu-Léger has painted the landscape designated by "ultra modernity," shedding light on several "tendencies" that characterize the new data in a state of emergency.[30]

The first tendency holds for the "affirmation of the psychological component of modernity" thanks to that of contemporary individualism that goes hand and glove with "the rise in power of the claim of each person's right to his or her own fulfillment." The relationship to the sacraments is affected today by a kind of obligation to recognize

---

[28] Ibid., 180; ELV, 164.

[29] Cf. my contribution "La liturgie chrétienne et son potentiel de formation éthique" in Philippe Bordeyne & Alain Thomasset, eds., *Les communautés chrétiennes et la formation morale des sujets, Revue d'Ethique et de Théologie Morale*, Hors série (Paris: Cerf, 2008).

[30] D. Hervieu-Léger, *Catholicisme, La fin d'un monde* (Paris: Bayard, 2003), 85–88.

individuality especially on the occasion of the rites of passage. Requests to "personalize" the liturgy (through the choice of texts and songs) favor the expression of individuals and groups at the risk of clouding the affirmation that the sacraments are celebrations of the faith of the church. How can we articulate this individualistic approach, colored sometimes by a "consumerizing" posture, with the conviction that the "liturgical actions" are "celebrations of the Church"?[31]

A second tendency faces the question of the "creational" dimension of the sacraments affirmed in the Middle Ages through a theologian like Hugh of St. Victor:[32] it consists in the "qualitative transformation of the relationship to nature that introduces the stunning advances of science and technology," which tend to separate the sacramental symbols drawn from nature like water, bread, wine, oil, fire, from the foundational events of the history of salvation. How can we resist then certain tendencies that under the cover of "symbolism" tend to "re-enchant" the world and creation, giving to them meanings of an esoteric or even magical character?

Finally, "the generalized contractualization of social relations" that "is true in every area from the bonds of marriage to teaching relations, from the relations between parents and children to the connections at the heart of business," tends to call into question "the idea that these bonds are able to find some kind of legitimacy outside the will of the individuals who established them between themselves." This third tendency weakens the meaning of the liturgical assembly as the primary actor of the celebration of the sacraments. The liturgical assembly is not the product of a pact between the members, and its composition is not the result of co-opting. But the etymology of *ecclesia* returns to a precedence, contained in the idea of a call and a gathering.[33]

In fact, it is the enrollment of the Christian life in the communal framework, and not the liturgy alone, that creates a problem in the contemporary world. If it is a "sensitive" place, it is because it shows

[31] Vatican II, Constitution on the Liturgy, no. 26.

[32] Hugh of Saint Victor, *De sacramentis christianae fidei* I, 9, 2: PL 176:317–18; cf. P. De Clerck, "Pour un dépassement de la notion d'institution des sacrements. Un essai théologique," *Revue de l'Institut Catholique de Paris* 53 (1995): 53–69, especially 61–62.

[33] Cf. Vatican II, Constitution on the Liturgy, no. 106, concerning Sunday.

the more general difficulty of the connection between individuals and the community. The sacraments reveal the difficulty of living together. We willingly claim respect for individuals seeking their own way, forgetting that the liturgy and the sacraments confront a normative and structured experience. This is why the celebration of the sacraments—more than the sacraments as such—often appears as a stumbling block, since the celebration beckons people to sacrifice their personal wishes and their unique "sensitivities" to enter into the dynamic of covenant but also into the great game of symbolic exchange, where the order of grace demands the renunciation of all mastery in order to open oneself to receive what we cannot give ourselves. This invites us to pursue a dialogue between sacramental theology and contemporary cultures or "subcultures." Beginning with the idea of celebration, and considered subsequently in its essential relationship with the liturgy, sacramental theology thus may constitute a major contribution of Christianity to a new relational order.

SACRAMENTAL THEOLOGY GROUNDED IN LITURGICAL HISTORY

But since sacramental theology is deeply rooted not only in the unforgettable contributions of ritual anthropology, but also in the slow process of canonization of rituals affected through the Christian tradition, itself an heir of discernment influenced by Jewish and pagan inheritances, the confrontation with the history of liturgical practices occupies a decisive place. In an article on the celebration of the sacrament of reconciliation,[34] Chauvet proposed the relationship between the research of sacramental theologians on the celebration of the sacraments and fundamental theology. We would like to suggest here a "rereading" of this article not on the basis of the question—that of the theology of the sacrament of reconciliation—but on the applied theological method.

Beginning with a historical overview, Chauvet maintained that "baptism is the first sacrament of reconciliation" and that this sacrament has known "several upheavals": from the institutionalization of unrepeatable penance, thanks to Hermas toward the middle of the second century, to the arrival of the so-called modern penance toward

---

[34] Chauvet, "*Nova et vetera*, Quelques leçons tirées de la tradition relative au sacrement de la réconciliation," P. De Clerck and E. Palazzo, eds., *Rituels, Mélanges offerts au Père Gy op* (Paris: Cerf, 1990), 99–124.

the end of the eleventh century or the beginning of the twelfth century (and which causes a veritable about-face of the penitential sequence)—passing through both the development and then failure of canonical penance and the system of "tariffed penance."[35] He emphasized above all that the "event of each penitential system is partly connected to the socio-cultural situation of the Church."[36] Here appears the work of a theologian who constrains himself to consider the cultural context of the celebration in order to ascertain from this field of "Christian practices" the dialogue between faith and reason. In this way he shows how "each penitential system accentuates a different aspect." From this point of view, from the Middle Ages onward the essential fact is that reconciliation is no longer a communal liturgical celebration marking the reintegration of the sinner or several sinners (having committed serious sins) back into the communion of the church, in terms of an ascetical process comparable to that of the catechumenate and bringing with it a lengthy and costly penitential course. It became progressively an individual practice in which the admission (of even minor faults) played the role of the "principal element" of the satisfaction according to Peter the Chanter: "*confessio oris habet maximam partem satisfactionis.*"[37] The system of "tariffed penance" established by the Irish monks during the early Middle Ages did not constitute an essential change except through the abandonment of an ancient principle, so strongly affirmed that it seemed intangible, concerning the non-repeatability of the sacrament.[38]

When the 1979 French-language ritual adopted the title "To Celebrate Penance and Reconciliation" to translate the Latin *Ordo penitentiae* (the naming of the ritual therefore was already a theological wager),[39] it is thus the sign of *ressourcement* in the tradition: one meant to rediscover the ancient insight of a "celebration of the reconciliation of penitents" through the ages where one entered the sacrament begin-

---

[35] Cf. M.-F. Berrouard, "La pénitence publique durant les six premiers siècles. Histoire et sociologie," *La Maison Dieu* 118 (1974): 92–130; C. Vogel, *Le pécheur et la pénitence au Moyen Age*, Traditions chrétiennes 5 (Paris: Cerf, 1969).

[36] Berrouard, "La pénitence publique durant les six premiers siècles. Histoire et sociologie," 107.

[37] Ibid., 106.

[38] Ibid., 102–5.

[39] *Célébrer la pénitence et la réconciliation* (Paris: AELF, Chalet-Tardy, 1978, 1991); French trans. of *Ordo Paenitentiae* published at Rome, December 2, 1973.

ning with a notion of "administration of penance," with its quasi-judicial connotation.

The title of the article published in a festschrift offered to P. Gy, "*Nova et vetera*, Quelques leçons tirées de la tradition relative au sacrement de la reconciliation" [Some Lessons Drawn from the Tradition Relative to the Sacrament of Reconciliation], referred to the work of K. Rahner[40] but also to a dialogue between sacramental theology and the history of the liturgy. It is in particular an echo of the concept *ressourcement en tradition* through which Père Gy explained the work of the liturgical reform operating after Vatican II.[41] He described the purpose in the history of sacramental theology of distinguishing in the Catholic world "an immutable part, that which is of divine institution," and "the parts subject to change that can vary from age to age and even must change if any elements are introduced that badly correspond to the intimate nature of liturgy itself, or if these parts have become inadequate."[42] This distinction, essential for the actors of the liturgical movement as it created the possibility of a reform taking into consideration cultural evolution,[43] relied upon the teachings of the Council of Trent that had established the principle on the occasion of the debate on Communion under two species, all the while insisting that the power of the church over the sacraments cannot extend to touch their substance: *salva illorum substantia.*[44]

Therefore the liturgy was renewed by beginning with a process of *ressourcement en tradition* borrowing often from the first millennium of the practices whose use had disappeared over time. The revised ritual of penance contains also several "forms" of celebration: next to the "individual" form, a communal form was rediscovered with a view to demonstrating "more clearly the ecclesial nature of penance."[45] This

[40] Cf. K. Rahner: "Vérités oubliées concernant le sacrement de pénitence," *Ecrits théologiques* II (Paris: DDB, 1960), 149–94.

[41] Cf. P.-M. Gy, "La liturgie de l'Eglise. La tradition vivante et Vatican II," *Revue de l'Institut Catholique de Paris* 50 (1994): 29–37, particularly 34–37.

[42] Vatican II, Constitution on the Liturgy, no. 21.

[43] Cf. L. Bouyer, "Ce qui change, ce qui demeure dans la liturgie," *La Maison Dieu* 40 (1954): 86–107.

[44] Trent, Session XXI, July 16, 1562, "Doctrine et canons sur la communion sous les deux espèces et la communion des enfants," chap. 2, Denzinger, *Symboles et définitions de la foi catholique*, under the direction of P. Hünermann and J. Hoffmann (Paris: Cerf, 1997), no. 1728, p. 463.

[45] *Célébrer la pénitence et la réconciliation*, no. 34 (= RR 22), 22.

process surpassed greatly the sacrament of penance and was concerned with the whole of the sacramental edifice, with the Constitution on the Liturgy granting a privileged place to the "communal celebration with assistance and active participation of the faithful."[46]

But the work of returning to the liturgical sources, a principle already adopted by the reforms of the Council of Trent, aimed at reestablishing the liturgy "in conformity to the ancient rule and to the rites of the Holy Fathers,"[47] had not been accompanied by a new expression of the doctrine on the sacraments. The dogmatic references marked by the debates of the sixteenth century that oftentimes rested upon the "abuses" of medieval practices persisted. Sacramental theology must consider the renewed practices through rediscovery of liturgical and patristic sources, whereas the dogmatic framework inherited from the Council of Trent referred to medieval usages. Certainly, we should not exaggerate the differences and discontinuity between the patristic and medieval periods. But the theologian who agrees to face the complexity of the historical studies is sensitive to the displacements of representations between two moments in history. This being done, he is constrained to situate the relationship between liturgy and sacraments in a problematic on the Tradition that maintains the distinction between history and tradition.[48]

"Recourse to Tradition is not the same thing as recourse to history. The term 'tradition' has in fact an immediate theological value, since it implies a placing into perspective of multiple practices and theories that take the long view of the history the Church and seek some major points of equilibrium that seem to disengage themselves from the fashioning of theological doctrines, ecclesiastical institutions or liturgical practices."[49]

The question therefore is to think of the continuities—in particular those that translate the theological concepts of "substance" and "institution" of the sacraments—and at the same time, the sometimes very important evolutions of sacramental practices, with an eye to discern-

[46] Vatican II, Constitution on the Liturgy, no. 27.

[47] Cf. St. Pius V, Bull *Quo Primum* of July 14, 1570, in the *Missale Romanum ex decreto sacrosancti Concilii Tridentini restitutum S. Pii V*.

[48] Cf. also Chauvet: "La notion de 'Tradition,'" *La Maison Dieu* 178 (1989): 7–46.

[49] Chauvet, "*Nova et vetera*, Quelques leçons tirées de la tradition relative au sacrement de la réconciliation," 99.

38

ing what the Tradition as a process invites us to decide for today. In other words, the idea itself of Tradition confronted with a history of practices obliges the theologian to venture, in a responsible way, a word that takes into account the sociocultural realities of a given period. This is what Chauvet does when he creates a diagnostic, placing it in the furrow of his rereading of the invincible diversity of the historical data.

"Without wanting to proffer some hasty conclusions concerning the crisis of the sacrament of reconciliation today, we are in a position to ask, in the heart of a cultural evolution of such depth that we can speak about it as a "mutation" (correctly, if it is true that it is the matrix itself where the schemes of symbolic representations are engendered concerning values, norms, legitimacies, the roles that are touched), if we are not in one of these periods where the system of penance, which the Middle Ages has bequeathed to us, is in the process, whatever we might say, of decline."[50]

The conclusion of the article reports precisely on the relationship between history and Tradition, emphasizing that the recourse to Tradition "inevitably happens due to current problems."[51] The history of the liturgy cannot offer an indisputable discourse: the idea itself of Tradition requires a work of construction of meaning, realized from the diversity of practices, where historical research is confronted with dogmatic affirmations and the questions of a given period. If one is to be faithful to the Tradition, then the sacramental theologian must become a historian. Contrary to certain modernist presuppositions, history does not serve to "relativize" dogma, granting it a referential range but, on the contrary, it provides a double glimpse at the present and the past, without which there is no hermeneutical act.

CONCLUSION: TO THINK OF THE "CELEBRATION"
OF THE SACRAMENTS, STARTING FROM THE
CELEBRATION OF THE EASTER TRIDUUM

The Second Vatican Council called for a "general restoration of the liturgy"[52] without proposing a new presentation of sacramental theology as the Council of Trent had done in the face of the protestations

[50] Ibid., 108–9.
[51] Ibid., 124.
[52] Vatican II, Constitution on the Liturgy, no. 21: "*ipsius liturgiae generalem instaurationem sedulo curare cupit.*"

of the Reformation. For historical but also theological reasons, the work of Trent, which remained referential, was not without limits:[53] the concern to defend a contested tradition dredged a divide with the representations of modernity. The accent on the "objectivity of the sacraments" has long ignored their role in the mediation of the spiritual experience of faith, the advancement of the power of the church, and the importance given to questions of validity and liceity that has opposed sacraments and Christian freedom, while the disjunction between sacrament and sacrifice cloud the ecclesial and eucharistic dimension of the Mass. On the other hand, finding its major key in the notion of "active participation," borrowed from Pius X, the reform of Vatican II has obliged sacramental theology to consider the role of the assembly because "in the celebration of the sacraments, it is the entire assembly who is 'liturgy,' each person according to his or her function, but in the unity of the Spirit who acts in everyone."[54]

Chauvet has attempted to escape this stranglehold by reflecting upon the symbolic order that considers the heritage of the tradition other than in the medieval categories that Trent used. Placing the sacraments in the network of ecclesial mediations, he introduced a certainly demanding but fruitful way that aims to honor the cultural displacements from "ultra-modernity," keeping track of the gains of a theological tradition that values the initiative of God in the order of grace—according to the adage *ex opere operato*—whereas, since the Renaissance, the patristic Theocentrism has ceded its place to an anthropocentrism in which the sacraments are perceived with difficulty as theandric actions, "both human and divine, visible and rich in invisible realities."[55]

It is in this framework that we would like to suggest here, without the ability to develop this point fully, an axis of research that seriously extends the relationship between sacramental theology and liturgy. Because the sacramental economy that characterizes the time of the church "consists in the communication (or 'dispensation') of the fruits of the paschal mystery of Christ in the celebration of the 'sacramental'

[53] H. Bourgeois, "Evaluation de la sacramentaire tridentine," under the direction of B. Sesboüé, *Histoire des dogmes*, vol. III, *Les signes du salut* (Paris: Desclée, 1995), 200–206.

[54] *Catechism of the Catholic Church*, no. 1144; cf. no. 1188.

[55] Cf. Vatican II, Constitution on the Liturgy, no. 2.

liturgy of the Church,"[56] it is in considering the celebration of the Easter Triduum that sacramental theology finds its natural site, the place of its full flourishing as the celebration in the church and as actualization of the Mystery. In fact the three major celebrations of the liturgical year—the Mass in *Cena Domini* of Holy Thursday, the celebration of the Cross on Good Friday, and especially the summit of the paschal night—constitute the matrix of the sacramental life of the church. It is there that the anthropological, theological (trinitarian), ecclesiological, and eschatological dimensions of Christian sacramentality join together and, with the church, find their source in the open side of Christ on the cross.

[56] *Catechism of the Catholic Church*, no. 1076.

Part 2

Scripture and Sacrament

> It is absolutely traditional to affirm that the Scriptures are sacramental.[1]

> In the sacraments, as in all other ecclesial mediations, it is always as *Word*, bitter and sweet at the same time, that Christ gives himself to be assimilated . . . a Word that communicates itself only because it is carried to us and in us by the Spirit.[2]

David Power builds appreciatively, and at times critically, on Chauvet's sacramental understanding of the Bible as the book of the church, the liturgical assembly as the place where the Spirit brings the Word to life through the communion of the Body of Christ. The Spirit, for Chauvet, is the principle of God's otherness, both in the love shared by Father and Son and in the self-emptying of the Word on the cross, wherein God crosses out divine majesty for the sake of humanity. The paradox at the heart of Christian faith lies in the singular historic event of that death, of that absence and crossing out of God, becoming the source of Christ's sacramental presence through the word being spoken among a plethora of peoples. In all cases, the Spirit is the agent of this unifying love in difference.

Power notes how Chauvet has constructed his theology in the context of a Europe seized in a moment of collective anxiety, citing this as the cause for Chauvet's strong emphasis on the paschal mystery. Power argues that different social, cultural, and traditional contexts may well lend themselves to grounding their theologies of Word and

---

[1] Chauvet, *The Sacraments: The Word of God at the Mercy of the Body* (Collegeville, MN: Liturgical Press, 2001), 43.

[2] Chauvet, *Symbol and Sacrament: A Sacramental Reinterpretation of Christian Existence*, trans. Patrick Madigan and Madeleine Beaumont (Collegeville, MN: Liturgical Press, 1995), 226.

sacrament in other biblical paradigms. Indeed, Power suggests that, although insisting on his theological interpretation of the paschal mystery as grounded in ancient ecclesial tradition, Chauvet is nonetheless hard pressed to reference any particular prayer encapsulating that vision. Scripture itself provides a number of interpretations of the salvation affected in Christ and celebrated in faith. Power discusses two among these, Philippians 2:6-11 and Colossians 1:15-20, developing a highly informative and insightful analysis of how hymns break open the Word in ways allowing for the ongoing creative influence and action of the Spirit in particular communities.

André Birmelé's chapter nicely complements Power's by considering the theology of Word and sacrament within one particular tradition, Lutheranism, so as to demonstrate how an informed appreciation of its own primary sources, proper language, and particular piety reveals much in common with the renewed sacramental-liturgical theology of Roman Catholicism. Articulating the theology inherent in the Lutheran tradition's sacramental appropriation of the Gospel, Birmelé unfolds a four-step systematic argument profoundly resonant with key tenets of the contemporary Catholic theology being advanced by such important figures as Chauvet. His Lutheran exposition thus lays out a path toward a unified fundamental theology of Word and sacrament for Catholics and Lutherans that nonetheless respectfully retains each tradition's specific ways of faithfully witnessing to the Gospel.

Birmelé's first step, drawing directly upon Luther, is to situate both Word and sacrament foundationally in the person and mission of Christ. Scripture is God's word only insofar as Christ, the eternal Logos, is its source. Moreover, if sacrament refers to historical, tangible revelation of the mystery of God's redemption of humanity, then Christ is none other than the singular sacrament of the eternal, unseen God. This theology of Christ the Sacrament of God, Birmelé notes, is none other than what such twentieth-century theologians as E. Jüngel and K. Rahner (and one must add here E. Schillebeeckx) came to argue, situating particular ecclesial rituals in the fundamental sacrament of Christ himself.

Such a foundation, secondly, requires that sacraments be understood as existing for no other reason than the salvation of people, capable of redemption only because of the divine source of the grace they impart. Luther's insistence on the sacraments' purpose as *pro nobis*, we would note, finds contemporary articulation in Chauvet's theology of sacrament (both Christ and ecclesial rituals) as the revela-

44

tion of the humanity of God. Thus, Birmelé's repeated indication of the ecumenical implications in Luther's theology rings happily amidst the pages of this present volume, all the more so due to his providing several examples of how such a convergent fundamental sacramental theology helps resolve old inter-ecclesial disagreements about efficacy, Real Presence, and so forth.

Word and sacrament then, third, are not opposed but analogous means of grace, similar in structure and function in the life of the church. Birmelé's concluding step is an articulation of an ecclesiology of communion realized through participation in the event of celebrating Word and sacrament, with an insistence, however, on not only the legitimacy but the necessity of diverse practices within the one church of Christ. Power's consideration of specific contemporary ecclesial contexts fleshes out Birmelé's principle, with both authors bringing further insight into Chauvet's insistence on the utterly ecclesial nature of sacramental practice.

Chapter 3

The Word in the Liturgy:
Incarnating the Gospel in Cultures

David N. Power

Toward the end of *Symbole et sacrement*[1] Louis-Marie Chauvet asks what presentation of sacrament may allow it to speak to our contemporary existence, marked by tragedy and by a particular way of thinking that is struck by the Otherness of God and the kenosis of divine revelation in Christ. This highlights the hermeneutical issue of sacramental celebration, something that has to be related back to that part of Chauvet's theology devoted to the relation between church and Bible.

Chauvet shows that, in liturgy, the Word of God is appropriated into the life of the community of the faithful within the horizon of worship, and that this is vital to the church's interpretation of the Scriptures. It is a faith nurtured through worship that guides interpretation. This is what makes the difference between treating the Scriptures as historical texts that are a patrimony of church and of culture and listening to them as God's Word, which is a Word addressed to people whom God has called and continues to call to be the living presence of the divine in the world. Writing on the European scene, Chauvet gives the reader the challenge of a contemporary and cultural hearing and reading of the Scriptures. Facing the loss of habitual and comforting paradigms of divine revelation, he has forged an alternate foundational narrative of Christian existence in the world, one that may be conceived in relation to the distress of the time and yet, remaining within a vision of eschatological memorial, nurtures hope. It is the particularity of the

---

[1] Summarized also in Part IV of his smaller work, *Les Sacrements: Parole de Dieu au Risque du Corps* (Paris: Éditions de l'Atelier, 1997).

narrative offered that constitutes paradoxically more universal and varied possibilities in a globally conscious communion of churches.

INCARNATION OF THE WORD IN LIVING CULTURES

It is to this total hermeneutical process and the appropriation into peoples' lives of the Word of God that the present essay attends. It does so keeping in mind the plurality of peoples and cultures within which the sacraments are celebrated in a Christian communion. Chauvet gives some attention to communities of other cultural heritage, especially African, but his theology and his paschal narrative are indubitably European. The background is the recent history of chaos on the continent, the breakdown of language exchange, and the breakdown of philosophies, whether those of Christian heritage or those of the Enlightenment and modernity. This is the social sedimentation of Christian celebration, even if people are not always conscious of it. To underline the word "appropriation" is to open up the question of cultural diversity, where culture does not mean static and unchanging structures, ideas, images, and stories, but a continually creative heritage.

As the sacrament of Christ, the church is culturally diverse. It proclaims and celebrates the integration of the Gospel and of the memorial of Christ into the lives of peoples of diverse histories and different cultural heritages. The principle spelled out is that the Gospel takes root in cultures, and that, in transforming them from within, it is itself enriched. It is not to an abstractly conceived cultural heritage that the Gospel is addressed as God's living Word, but to peoples faced with their own anguish and looking to their own heritage and history for some vision of present and future in a time of decay. When the hearing of the Word is related to particular histories and cultures, there must be diversity in sacramental celebration.

The need to read the Scriptures so as to find strength and inspiration in them is very concrete. Recently, the pain and the challenge of the times in which people live and in which they need hope has been spelled out for the African continent and for the peoples of Latin and Caribbean countries. The published *lineamenta* for a second Synod of the Churches of Africa and Madagascar[2] outline quite graphically the

[2] "Synod of Bishops: Second Special Assembly for Africa. The Church in Africa in Service to Reconciliation, Justice and Peace," *L'Osservatore Romano*, Weekly Edition in English, 19 July 2006, 3–14.

issues facing churches as they seek to share the lot of peoples and be a beacon of light in their midst. For Latin America, there is a comparable location of the presence and mission of Christ's disciples whereby it is related both to a distressing past and to a largely disastrous present in which poverty increases and hope often seems lost.[3] On both continents it is asked why the Gospel has often not taken deep roots among the people but left them frequently looking to the practices of ancient or oral traditions for some consolation and hope. The preaching of the Gospel today has to be postcolonial, freed from alien dominance, but it has to address the multiple sufferings of the people in their present situation. Relating the Gospel to cultures and histories goes hand in hand with relating it to the problems outlined in documents such as those cited.

The particularity of Chauvet's narrative paradigm thus becomes a challenge to the particularity of the ways in which God's Word is heard, the divine Spirit invoked, and Christ remembered. In being received and interpreted, or indeed one may say with the Pontifical Biblical Commission, "actualized," the Gospel of Jesus Christ has to be related to who and what peoples are.[4] As described by the Pontifical Biblical Commission, actualization means applying "the message" of the Scriptures, written in one set of historical circumstances, to "contemporary circumstances." As for liturgy, the commission states that it is the "most perfect actualization of the biblical texts" since it places their proclamation "in the midst of the community of believers, gathered around Christ."[5] Granted, then, the diversity in the proclamation and actualization of the Scriptures, proclaiming them in the liturgy means attending to the way in which a people envisages life through what it receives from its cultural heritage and from a past history in which believers may seek a presence of Word and Spirit. It is this that gives the vision of a future in which, despite current calamity, it may hope.

---

[3] CELAM, V Conferencia, Aparecida, 2007, *Documento Conclusivo*, www.celam.info/download/Documento_Conclusivo_Aparecida.pdf.

[4] The Pontifical Biblical Commission, *The Interpretation of the Bible in the Church* (Washington, DC: USCC, 1993), Part IV.

[5] Placing this in an ecumenical context, the commission also notes how attending to the diverse proclamation in different Christian confessions is mutually enriching.

One has to revisit in Chauvet's sacramental outlook the way in which the Bible is the book of the church. This has a past on which communities continue to draw, but it also must have a creative present. Following the work of biblical scholars, Chauvet makes the connection between the theology of inspiration, the formation of the canon, and the hearing of the Word in liturgy. There is a close connection between the formation of the canon and sacramental memorial and vision. Related to this as a process of reception and interpretation is the history of lectionaries. Lectionaries show what communities retain as most significant in the Scriptures, bringing to the fore certain selected scriptural texts and scripturally configured meanings of tradition. That puts the question of how much of each liturgical heritage is to be retained and how much it can or needs to be changed.

Some questions have been asked about the canon itself, but here I draw attention to issues about lectionary selections that cannot go unheeded.[6] Since this is an example of how Scriptures are received and interpreted, let us start with problems in some examples of lectionary selections, never forgetting that these are put within a horizon of memorial that serves to orient their reading.

Feminist and postcolonial scholars have raised questions about proclaiming certain kinds of text in the liturgy. The household codes, for example, in Pauline books and 1 Peter, in their countenancing both the lower social condition of women and the institution of slavery, can hardly be proclaimed as good news. Some texts also, such as what Paul says in Romans 1:18-22 of the heathen world, have been used to repudiate what were deemed the pagan ways of the colonized.[7] Their place in proclamation is therefore also problematic. Behind these issues lurk questions about the canon itself, what constitutes the canon, and the significance for particular Scriptures, that they belong within the church's canon. Feminist and postcolonial interpretations question the authenticity or the authority of the canon itself on account of texts such as those mentioned. To decipher their "essential message" is not an easy thing. They cannot be read or heard without attending to what is the ongoing story of the church and its relation to social situations.

---

[6] Christoph Theobald, "La réception des écritures inspirées," *Recherches de Science Religieuse* 93/4 (2005): 545–70.

[7] R. S. Sugirtharajah, *Postcolonial Criticism and Biblical Interpretation* (Oxford: Oxford University Press, 2002), 49–50.

A more fundamental problem is the proclamation of readings whose selection depended on typological interpretations of the Hebrew Scriptures. While the readings at the Paschal Vigil vary somewhat from liturgical family to liturgical family, as well as vary within each family over time, some continuity is apparent. Three important readings connected to the memory of Christ's Pasch and to Christian baptism are Exodus 12, Genesis 22, and Exodus 14. While always read in the light of Christ and church, taking them in a typological sense today sits poorly with the respect called for in hearing the Hebrew Scriptures as the living texts of the Jewish faith community since it defies what is known of their original meaning.

We cannot return to the patristic exegesis of the Old Testament, even if we learn much about being church from it. In fact, the Scriptures cannot be presented in the liturgy as they were in past ages, given the changes in culture.[8] The reading of Scripture in the patristic age depended on a spiritual reading of texts where all passages were placed within the mystery of Christ. The liturgical import of the Scriptures in the Middle Ages was to a great extent visual and theatrical. With the invention of printing, people gradually began to read the texts and read them with the tools of historical and literary criticism. That is the form in which God's Word is given to us today. Attending to this enriches the ways in which we center our existence on God's revelation and what this asks of us. With the background of a more developed critical understanding of the formation of the Scriptures, we must treat such texts both in light of their historical composition and as literature.[9] Attention to literary form does not have to be erudite. Indeed, it will be received in different ways in different churches: those of Europe relate them in their de-Christianized milieu; those of the South hear them as Churches of the Poor who find in this literature a voice that speaks to them.[10]

[8] Jean-Paul Michaud, "Exégèse et culture à travers l'histoire," *Theoforum* 37/2 (2006): 133–69.

[9] Charles Kannengiesser, "The Bible as Read in the Early Church: Patristic Exegesis and Its Presuppositions," *Concilium* 1 (1991): 29–36.

[10] Carlos Meesters, "Listening to What the Spirit Is Saying to the Churches. Popular Interpretation of the Bible in Brazil," *Concilium* 1 (1991): 100–111. Indeed, churches that have suffered poverty and colonization have found, for example, in the Genesis and Exodus narratives a promise of liberation and of hope for their own people.

In another document, this one on the place of Jewish Scriptures in the Christian Bible (and one might add Lectionary), the Pontifical Biblical Commission suggests a reading more attentive to the literal sense of texts and to their place in history. This is what therefore would have to guide the hearing of the Scriptures in liturgical assembly. On how one may respect the intent of the patristic reading and yet go beyond it the commission says:

> The basic theological presupposition [of typological reading] is that God's salvific plan which culminates in Christ (cf. Ep 1:3-14) is a unity, but that it is realised progressively over the course of time. . . . From the outset, the action of God regarding human beings has tended towards final fulfilment and, consequently, certain aspects that remain constant began to appear. . . . The first realisations, though provisional and imperfect, already give a glimpse of the final plenitude. This is particularly evident in certain important themes which are developed throughout the entire Bible, from Genesis to Revelation: the way, the banquet, God's dwelling among men [sic]. Beginning from a continuous re-reading of events and texts, the Old Testament itself progressively opens up a perspective of fulfilment that is final and definitive. The Exodus, the primordial experience of Israel's faith (cf. Dt 6:20-25; 26:5-9) becomes the symbol of final salvation. Liberation from the Babylonian Exile and the prospect of an eschatological salvation are described as a new Exodus. Christian interpretation is situated along these lines with this difference, that the fulfilment is already substantially realised in the mystery of Christ.[11]

One needs to add that, while the mystery is "substantially realised" in Christ, Christian peoples know this means living their own history in eschatological perspective. In appropriating the Scriptures read in the light of Christ, they relate them to their own particular histories and to their own way of attending to the written word. In the course of such appropriation there may well be changes in the selection of texts for liturgical proclamation.[12]

[11] Pontifical Biblical Commission, *The Jewish People and Their Sacred Scriptures in the Christian Bible* (Boston: Pauline Books and Media, 2003), no. 21.

[12] Given the shortcomings of the revised Lectionary for the Roman liturgy, even it has to be seen as a work in progress rather than a completed project. The use made of the Hebrew Scriptures in this Lectionary is particularly unfortunate, granted that this was meant to be a remedy for a previous neglect.

LITURGICAL REFLECTION OUTSIDE LITURGY

Too much in fact may be expected from the moment of liturgical proclamation. There has to be a connection between liturgical proclamation and how communities reflect on the Scriptures in nonliturgical settings where they read and study the texts and do not simply hear them proclaimed. While communities of faith are communities of worship, much reading and rumination of the Scriptures is done before selected texts get into the liturgy. One strategy often adopted is to invite small groups or local gatherings to reflect on the authorized Sunday Scriptures in advance and thus to bring an informed faith to the Sunday celebration. This is helpful but does not seem adequate unless a more thorough approach to interpretation is found.

To guide a process of biblical reflection and actualization, it is possible to draw light from the kind of reading done for the Sundays of Ordinary Time. The purpose of the chosen texts on these Sundays is to introduce people to a continuous reading of the books of the New Testament and so to a continuous and coherent interpretation of them. In the work of appropriation, people could be invited to mark those stories and passages that resonate most strongly for them in their given cultural and historical situation. From this procedure, communities find out how the Word of God addresses them and what hope it gives them. For example, in many an African context, both because of rampant disease and because of traditional healing practices, the healing stories of the narrative of Jesus have a large place in forming their faith in him. In Asia, where Christian communities find themselves among peoples of other living faiths, they are attentive to those stories that speak of relations to the stranger. A faith so contextually formed enlivens the Sunday liturgy. On the other hand, it continues to be guided by the horizon of worship even though much of the effort to appropriate the understanding of texts to ecclesial, political, and social contexts is done outside the liturgical setting.

LITURGICAL HORIZON OF PROCLAIMING
AND PONDERING THE WORD

Taking what is proclaimed as the Word of God, it is within the liturgical setting and horizon that scriptural readings are fully appropriated as the living breath of the community.[13] When texts are put within

---

[13] See Raymond Kuntzmann, "L'herméneutique biblique. D'une lecture de la Bible à sa celebration," *Revue des Sciences Religieuses* 80/3 (2006): 371–85.

the liturgical horizon of memorial of Christ's death and resurrection, there is a decided nuance given to their actualization. The document of the Biblical Commission, *The Interpretation of the Bible in the Church*, talks about drawing out the "essential message" of a text though a hermeneutical process and then applying this to a particular place and time, for a particular people. Still, the more historically oriented document of the same commission on Christian and Jewish Scriptures offers other possibilities, more connected with the current trends in hermeneutics recalled even in the first document. Rather than speak of an "essential message" we could follow the orientation of Hans-Georg Gadamer and Paul Ricoeur in their hermeneutical approaches. This is to note the "question" that a text puts to readers and hearers in dialogical settings and to attend with Ricoeur to the polyphony of texts in the naming of God and so to the multiplicity and particular orientation of different literary genres.[14]

Taking such approaches into account would get us beyond the quest for an "essential message" and give more attention to modes of discourse and to the historical referents within which texts are heard and received. While the more immediate thought of people is of their own location in time and place (particular and global), there is a more fundamental eschatological vision of history awakened by the memorial referent to the Christ Event, to that moment to which all moments and the hope of the future are referred.

The gospel proclamation of Luke 12:13-21 may serve as an example to illustrate how, from an exegesis of a text, hearers may move to a response that is within the setting of true worship. In its historical and literary setting[15] the parable is about the uses of private property, but at a time when only a few had such holdings. The man in the story has worked hard and systematically and has harvested his fields well. Thus he has provided for his declining years and doubtless also for his posterity. His unexpected and untimely death, however, teaches that

[14] Paul Ricoeur, "Naming God," in *Figuring the Sacred. Religion, Narrative, and Imagination*, trans. David Pellauer (Minneapolis: Fortress Press, 1995), 217–35. Allied with this are warnings by other scholars to attend to ideologies that have influenced the history of interpretation but that cannot be discussed here.

[15] Rachael Oliphant and Paul Babie, "Can the Gospel of Luke Speak to a Contemporary Understanding of Private Property? The Parable of the Rich Fool," *Colloquium. The Australian and New Zealand Theological Review* 38/1 (2006): 3–26.

he has focused on self-interest and has not made the service of God's kingdom the priority in his life. What the parable says for the early disciples is that, for those who live by God's kingdom, private possession is to be put at the service of the community with social needs in mind. There is no position taken in the text against having private property, but an invitation to use it for others. Indeed, we know from the history of the early church that "having all things in common" did not mean that the rich gave up their property but that they put what they possessed at the service of the church and of its needy members. Today, especially in countries burdened by history with economic, social, and political problems, the parable still asks its questions, but in ways hearers and readers will be more conscious of advocating larger social change in the world around them. More prosperous hearers could well be awakened to global stakes.

When by liturgical proclamation the parable is related to the mystery of Christ's Pasch, it speaks to faith in Christ himself, in that moment in history when the full meaning of the kingdom is manifested. It speaks also of an eschatological horizon to history that invites people to live in expectation of God's visitation and by their faith in what they have been given to know in Christ. The response to the parable is located within the memorial of Jesus Christ and the eschatological hope of "a new heaven and a new earth," already in our time, as indicated by John Paul II in his encyclical on the Eucharist.[16] This would augur an order of justice in which the prevailing motivation is love exemplified in the justice brought about by the self-emptying of him "who was in the form of God." It is an invitation to live the testimony to the new order that Christian churches are called upon to give, within the household of the faith and by their activities in the world around them.

THE PRAYER TEXTS OF SACRAMENTAL WORSHIP

Within worship, the hearing of the Word passes to prayer in the name of Christ. It is prayer texts that ultimately allow congregations to express their commemoration of Christ in faith. A problem in Chauvet's work is that, while he relates his own theological interpretation of the paschal mystery to the "ancient tradition," he cannot point

---

[16] John Paul II, *Ecclesia de Eucharistia* (Boston: Pauline Books and Media, 2003), no. 20.

to any particular prayer that encapsulates such a vision.[17] To incorporate his paradigm of the Pasch into celebration may need some form of prayer not provided by ancient texts.

The vision of the mystery is fleshed out for a community in passing from hearing the Word to praying the Word. One would expect African, Asian, and Latin American churches to have hymns and memorial thanksgiving prayers different from traditional Western and Eastern Rite liturgies. Scholars and canonical directives now point to elements that must be incorporated into every anaphora. Knowing the framework is only the beginning of a larger consideration. It remains to be asked how prayers in their formulation of the mystery relate to the interpretation and actualization of the Word of God within specific communities.[18]

Of a blessing prayer in its expression of faith one would expect three things. First, it fits with what is most basic to an act of faith. Second, it needs to give an overarching vision of faith that responds to the appropriation of the Word of God in a given community. Third, it allows for particular application within a much larger vision.

In the basic act of faith, the kind of faith of which Paul writes in Romans and Galatians, Christians look to Jesus, to the story of his life and teaching and to his death and resurrection as the determining moment in God's revelation and self-disclosure. This is proclaimed as a defining moment in revelation and in a history broken open and made possible by God. Already in the New Testament, however, there are many configurations of the story as it is received into the life of different communities and as it is proclaimed in song and worship. That is to pass to the second factor in hymn-singing or in offering memorial prayer.

HYMNS OF PRAISE

Rather than treat directly of eucharistic prayers themselves, some insight into how prayers express an overarching vision of faith is of-

---

[17] The present writer has suggested a possible reference to the image of Christ's voluntary suffering in the prayer of the *Apostolic Tradition* and of kenosis in the prayer of Basil. See David N. Power, *"The Word of the Lord." Liturgy's Use of Scripture* (Maryknoll, NY: Orbis, 2001), 143–60.

[18] The author has examined this in more detail in David N. Power, "The Sacramental Language of the Eucharistic Prayer," *Ecclesia Orans* XVI/2 (1999): 209–32.

fered here through the example of ecclesial prayer constructs found in the New Testament.[19] While blessing prayers are a genre on their own, for the sake of reflection on texts of ecclesial composition it is possible to look for a model in New Testament hymns. These are, as a genre, configurations of faith expression within which an eschatological memorial is kept of the once-and-for-all event of Jesus.

In the New Testament, hymns[20] are cited in given circumstances and often to a specific purpose, but they escape the boundaries of the immediate context, offering more than is actually said. They are shorter than narratives, not so full of detail, yet they are larger than narratives since they offer a praise and creedal framework to which changing narratives and more varied forms of language may be related. They are sometimes said to be generative texts. This means that they are always in the process of becoming, offering constant possibilities of language exchange, signification, and expansion, yet fulfilled in particular ways in real time and never divorced from the original voice that is embodied into the text. Unlike poems as such, which of their nature float more freely, the memorial and praise purpose of the hymn puts it into the life of a body that lives by the memory of event and offers its life as a spiritual sacrifice to the God who has made the particular history of Jesus of Nazareth the divine's own mode of self-communication.

What Ricoeur says of hymns for worship is apposite. They take all forms of discourse into the hymnodic mode: "It is the privilege of worship to reactualize salvation, to reiterate the creation, to remember the exodus and the entry into the promised land, to renew the proclamation of the law, and to repeat the promises." The concentrated inclusion of the narrative in the hymn transforms it into a remembrance that is actual, for a salvation that belongs to "today."[21] As an act of mimesis, the hymn (and this may also be said of the blessing prayer) is a

---

[19] This is for two reasons. First, the way in which the faith is formulated in hymn is a model for the blessing prayer (also sung). Second, hymn composition serves the beginnings on which blessings may draw.

[20] On New Testament hymns, see E. Haulotte, "Formation du Corpus du Nouveau Testament. Recherche d'un "module" génératif intratextuel," in *Le Canon des Ecritures. Etudes historiques, exégétiques et systématiques*, sous la direction de C. Theobald (Paris: Cerf, 1990), 255–340, especially 314–47.

[21] Ricoeur, "Biblical Time," in *Figuring the Sacred. Religion, Narrative, and Imagination*, 178–79.

reconfiguration of the narrative that fits it into the world of the hearer, while suggesting a potential far beyond any immediate actualization of what the story's promise holds forth. To sing the hymn does not mean entering a world beyond the present, but finding in the Word a form that may be appropriated into varied times because it comes from God and looks ahead in hope. One could say that they are sung within an eschatological horizon. They turn the mind and heart to Christ and his mystery as key to history but by inviting those who sing them to look forward in hope and to look for the presence of Christ and his Spirit in their own stories.

Notable New Testament hymns include Philippians 2:6-11; Colossians 1:15-20; Hebrews 1:3; John 1:1-14; and 1 Peter 1:20; 3:18, 22.[22] These appear to be hymns belonging within the worship life of communities, but these books cited them for a given context and to some particular local purpose. While the immediate purpose narrows the meaning given to each hymn in itself, it nonetheless has a larger orientation. Each hymn gives succinct formulation to the mystery of salvation. It begins by evoking an eternally intended salvation of God's loving design, proclaims how this comes about within historical time, and then looks to the fulfillment in the future that is guaranteed by present gifts.[23] Two texts, Philippians 2:6-11 and Colossians 1:3-8, exemplify how a hymn may be cited to serve a particular purpose, but not confined in meaning to this purpose, while at the same time showing how hymns express the vision engendered by faith in different ways.

Each author invokes the given hymn with a very practical purpose in mind insofar as the moral behavior of the readers/hearers is concerned. The appeal to the hymn is better understood when it is seen in relation to the cross-cultural questions that the Christians face in their living situation. In citing a hymn on Christ's kenosis in Philippians 2:6-11, Paul's purpose is to exhort the members of the community of Philippi to obedience and to the practice of humility in relation to each other. It would seem that the disciples in Philippi had to resolve the meeting together of Jews and Gentiles, especially in relation to ritual

[22] I follow Haulotte's work here (see above, n. 20). Similar consideration could be given to New Testament prayers of thanksgiving (Rom 1:8-15; 1 Cor 1:4-9; Phil 13:3-11; Col 1:3-8; 1 Thess 1:3-10) or blessings of God for the works of salvation (2 Cor 1:3-7; Eph 1:3-14; 1 Pet 1:3-9).

[23] This is also true, for example, of the blessing prayer in Ephesians 1:3-14.

observances, among which the practice of circumcision looms large. Paul believes that in the midst of such a culturally determined ritual dispute, the recollection of Christ's kenosis should put them in the right frame of mind, remembering what is essential to true faith. The song is more theologically abundant and sophisticated than allowed for by Paul's hortatory use made of it. It places the community within a horizon of remembrance, adoration, and expectation that is indeed rich, but it can also be appropriated within a relatively narrow set of circumstances and needs that do not exhaust the full meaning of the hymn. Within its horizon, the people will continue to see and judge their lives as disciples of the Christ whom they follow.

Colossians 1:15-20 is a contrasting paradigm of remembrance and vision. It too is related to Christ's death and resurrection and likewise fits into a specific cultural milieu. Since the people seem to hanker after the ancient wisdom of their Greek background, Paul looks to the hymn to appeal to the idioms of Wisdom literature and to proclaim the lordship of Christ as holding sway over creation and the church, submitting everything in the heavens and on earth to the glory of the Father. Paul wishes to fetter the disciples to Christ and to keep them obedient to his teaching. While referring to the hymn here meets a certain purpose, as in Philippians the hymn has a much greater potential for fixing a vision and for drawing many things into its vision.

Though they may not explain it totally, the social and cultural differences between the people of the two churches has something to do with the use of images and metaphors incorporated into these hymns. They are similar in the eschatological perspective they give, but they illustrate how peoples may remember the same mystery in different forms and idioms. They have a common historical referent and a sense of ongoing history that is open to the future, but their poetic language and theologies are quite diverse.

This has application for examining the "great thanksgiving prayer." It is not enough to show that they have some common structure (see, for example, *General Instruction on the Roman Missal*, no. 79), but their diversity of image and even prayer forms needs to be appreciated.[24] The great thanksgiving prayers and indeed blessings belong within

---

[24] Historically the schema is not all that uniform. For an overview of scholarship, see David N. Power, "A Prayer of Intersecting Parts: Elements of the Eucharistic Prayer, " *Liturgical Ministry* 14 (Summer 2005): 120–31.

particular liturgical traditions and are influenced by doctrinal and cultural issues affecting the communities in which they originated. Historically, there is a difference in structure, poetry, and theological significance between the *Apostolic Tradition*, Addai and Mari, John Chrysostom, and the Roman Canon, to mention just the best known. Though they cannot be examined here in detail, both their diversity and their generative potential are important to the life of faith and are comparable to what has been found in New Testament hymns. Being generative texts, they are open to ongoing appropriation and textual change, as witness the uses made of the text from the *Apostolic Tradition* in present ecumenically sensitive assimilation into eucharistic celebrations. These prayers and others present a tradition to young churches from which they may draw, but in a process of weaving new songs that relate more to their own historical and cultural experience.[25] Between this and their reading of the Scriptures, there is a link for which in a sense no rules exist but which the crisscross of reality illustrates. In practice, appropriation in worship often does begin with hymns, and it may be from hymns that communities can draw the rudiments of the expression of their faith that are then brought to the great thanksgiving prayer.

THE SPIRIT AND THE OTHER

A theological grasp of this process could be drawn from what Chauvet says of the Spirit. It is to the Spirit that he attributes the living sense of God's Otherness and the capacity for the Word to take body in the church. He sees the church, and indeed the living assembly of worship, as the proper place in which the Word is interpreted and brought alive in sacramental communion of the Body through the power of the Spirit.[26] In the narrative paradigm of the latter parts of both his *magnum opus* and shorter book, the role of the Spirit is again called into play in speaking to a postmodern sensitivity to the failures of language and to the otherness of God, which is not trespassed in the Incarnation. Indeed, in the power of the Spirit, sacrament gives some expression to the mystery of divine kenosis, an emptying out of the

---

[25] For some eucharistic texts from African Churches, see Francois Kabasele Lumbala, *Celebrating Jesus Christ in Africa: Liturgy and Inculturation* (Maryknoll, NY: Orbis, 1998).

[26] The role of the Spirit in sacramental celebration explained in *Symbole et Sacrement* is summarized in Part IV of the shorter work, *Les Sacrements*.

Son of divine fullness so that God may find flesh among us without betraying the mystery of being God in its otherness to the world.

This role of the Spirit may explain how diversity in expression is not only possible but essential. Through the power of the Spirit, the self-emptying of the Word is carried over into the words of sacrament, embodied in a diversity of cultures. Greater attention to the polyphony of embodiment and interpretation, within a diversity of assemblies, in a diversity of cultures, alerts us to the role the Spirit has to play in the ongoing interpretation and embodiment of the Word by which Christ is proclaimed as Lord and the key moment of history. It is indeed the otherness kept alive through the Spirit that allows within one communion of churches a diversity of appropriations and embodiments of the Word of God, of the kerygma of salvation through the death and resurrection of Christ. If the creative role of the Spirit in bringing the Word to life, or the memory of Christ to life, is passed over, there is a risk of glossing over the diversity in the hymnic texts of blessing, beginning with the eucharistic prayer tradition(s). As the Word was emptied out on the cross, crossing out the glory that was his, so the Word is constantly crossed out in the otherness evoked by the active Spirit as it brings it to form anew among diverse peoples. It is in the nature of God's self-emptying love to take visible forms, within the circumscriptions of historic event and cultural form. But the Word is the Word of the Cross, and the Spirit enables churches to live by it, even crossing out given human and visible forms in order to allow space for new ones. Paradoxically, the once-and-for-all historic event of the Cross of Christ can be given sacrament and spoken among many peoples. It is in the Spirit that the Word continues to be present and active in the church, not only in making faith possible but also giving it the gifts of creative speech.

CONCLUSION

Taking inspiration from what Chauvet has written on the relation between Word and sacrament, this essay has pursued the question of the hermeneutical process of the appropriation of God's Word in its relation to worship. It has done so principally by asking what it means to the intersection of Word, sacrament, and the cultures embodied in a multitude of diverse histories and what it means to be able to look to Christ in the hope that is empowered by the Spirit.

Chapter 4

The Relationship between Scripture and Sacrament in Lutheran Theology

André Birmelé

Ecumenical dialogue in these past decades permits us to reopen many files that had been the object of contentious splits between the Catholic Church and the churches marked by the Reformation. Baptism, Eucharist, and Scripture have been the topics of many dialogues. The question of the sacraments as such, however, has hardly been engaged. We would like in these pages to open the debate. It seems to us that a dialogue on this theme would make sense today. In Catholic reflection, sacramental theology has experienced significant development in these last years. Louis-Marie Chauvet, to whom many of these reflections have been dedicated, has been and is by his theological, philosophical, historical, liturgical, and anthropological research on sacramentality one of the major working contributors to this evolution.

I propose four approaches to reflection where I think there is a consensus between our families and where complementary dialogues may lead to mutual recognitions. The Lutheran approach is not the same as that of the Roman Catholic tradition. But the differences that exist are not necessarily divisive. They seem to me, rather, to reveal more legitimate differences of language, religious practices, and particular theological accents in their efforts to express the same fundamental conviction and faithfulness to the Gospel.

JESUS CHRIST, SACRAMENT OF GOD

One seeks in vain in the theology of the churches marked by the Reformation a "theology of the sacrament" in the Roman Catholic or Orthodox sense of this expression. Even if they use the notion of sacrament to mean certain ecclesial acts, in particular baptism and Eucharist, the churches marked by the Reformation do not really know any "theology of the sacrament," not even a "sacramental theology." Generally there does not exist a chapter *De Sacramentis* in Protestant dogmatic theology.[1] But it obviously does contain chapters on baptism, Eucharist, absolution, or even marriage, anointing of the sick, confirmation or ordination, but it will avoid putting them all together in order to understand them under the general notion of sacrament. The heirs of the Reformation mistrust this notion that appeared in the history of the Latin Church in the first centuries to the extent that it becomes all generalizing and sought to develop some particular theological options that characterize and regroup some ecclesial acts that are very different. The stakes are not the sevenfold sacramental system fixed in the twelfth century, or some quarrel regarding the number of sacraments or of their institution, some questions that, as contemporary interconfessional dialogue shows, can easily be resolved. The stakes in the first place refer to the definition itself and to the use of the notion of sacrament.

Until 1517–18 Luther was hardly interested in the sacraments. His references were those taught to him in the theological schools at the end of the Middle Ages. His first original reflection regarding the sacraments appears in the foundational reformation writing *De captivitate Babylonica ecclesiae* in 1520.[2] One of the major theses of that text is to show that sacrament is the coming about of the Gospel. It is Gospel in itself and should not be understood as a work of the church. As a vector of the saving Word, sacrament is not only a promise of salvation but brings salvation about. It is the incarnate promise, because without a visible sign enabling this promise the Word would be only *nuda*

[1] For a more detailed description, cf. volume 3 of *Lehrverurteilungen Kirchentrennend?: Ökumenischer Arbeitskreis Evangelischer und Katholischer Theologen*; eds. K. Lehmann and W. Pannenberg (Freiburg im Breisgau: Herder; Göttingen: Vandenhoeck & Ruprecht, 1986), particularly the articles by D. Sattler and Th. Schneider, "Hermeneutische Erwägungen zur 'Allgemeinen Sakramentenlehre'" (15–32), and G. Wenz, "Die Sakramente nach lutherischer Sicht" (72–98). These volumes describe the theological steps that were taken that produced the initial document, *Lehrverurteilungen kirchentrennend?*

[2] English translation: *The Babylonian Captivity of the Church* in Martin Luther's basic theological writings. Ed. Timothy F. Lull, 2nd ed. / CD-ROM editor William R. Russell (Minneapolis, MN: Fortress, 2005).

promisio.[3] The sacrament does not supplant the Word, because it only gives what the Word has to give.

It is necessary to carefully note here that this concerns the Word, which must be distinguished from Scripture and from preaching, a distinction to which we will return. Returning to the linguistic and theological categories common to the sixteenth century, Luther noted that the very signs, which are the visible elements, could not be a sacrament in and for themselves. They are however indispensable for a sacrament, because the Word needs some visible signs in order to occur. The Word only happens thanks to the sealing of a sacramental sign. These theological convictions are obviously linked to some polemical points, especially against the understanding of the Mass as a "work of the church" or any approach that leads to some sacramental automaticism; the sacrament only effects salvation when it is received in faith—which obviously does not mean that faith makes the sacrament work.

This brief historical note directs us to the notion of the Word so fundamental in the theology of Luther. History often speaks of ecclesial traditions marked by the Reformation as being the "Churches of the Word." This discovery is true, but it often rests upon a misunderstanding because the Word is, in many cases, understood as synonymous with Scripture. This shortcut betrays the fundamental option of Luther, for which the Word is nothing other than the Logos, which is Christ himself. It is only from this point and from it alone that Scripture obtains its meaning, and it is only from here that the notion of sacrament makes any sense.

As a well-informed exegete Luther had obviously noted how the Latin idea of *sacramentum* was used by the Vulgate in the letter to the Ephesians to translate the Greek term *musterion*. Whereas the apostles are the "stewards of God's mysteries" (1 Cor 4:1), the mission of the church is to live and to proclaim the mysteries of God. What is this "mystery of God"? The letter to the Ephesians in the opening hymn celebrates the election and the incarnation of Jesus Christ, his death and his resurrection for us. "[H]e [God] has made known to us the mystery of his will, according to his good pleasure that he set forth in Christ, as a plan for the fullness of time, to gather up all things in him, things in

---

[3] *Opera omnia domini Martini Lutheri* (Wittenberg, 1562) 2, 258; hereafter, MLO. The expression *nuda promissio* (naked promise) might be translated "simple promise."

heaven and things on earth" (Eph 1:9-10). The later chapters do not say anything different: "to make everyone see what is the plan of the mystery hidden for ages in God who created all things" (Eph 3:9); "This is a great mystery, and I am applying it to Christ and the church" (Eph 5:32); "a message may be given to me to make known with boldness the mystery of the gospel" (Eph 6:19). We can add to this the wish of the letter to the Colossians: "I want their hearts to be encouraged and united in love, so that they may have all the riches of assured understanding and have the knowledge of God's mystery, that is, Christ himself in whom are hidden all the treasures of wisdom and knowledge" (Col 2:2-3). These biblical references are fundamental for Luther. Through the Incarnation, the cross, and the resurrection of Christ, this mystery is not hidden but is known and becomes the object of a public declaration, which is hereafter made visible even to the pagans.

These biblical data lead Luther, pursuing them through a tradition already present in the fathers, to consider that there exists in fact only one *sacramentum*, Christ himself: "Unum solum habent sacrae literae sacramentum . . . quod est ipse Christus Dominus."[4] From the Reformation and beyond the different traditions have certainly continued to use this term to mean diverse ecclesial acts,[5] but they will only do so in

---

[4] M. Luther, *Disputation de fide infusa et acquisita* Thesis 18, in *D. Martin Luthers Werke: Kritische Gesamtausgabe*, ed. J. F. K. Knaake et al. (Weimar: Bohlau, 1883 ff.), 6, 86; hereafter WA (= Weimar Ausgabe).

[5] We note nevertheless, that article 13 of the *Augsburg Confessions* and its explanation in the *Apology* propose at the heart of the symbolic books of Lutheranism—and elsewhere in opposition to the Zwinglian tradition—a little more general definition: "the sacraments were not instituted only to be the signs of the profession of faith among people, but rather to be the signs and witnesses to the divine will in our regard, proposed in view to arouse and affirm faith in those who need it." *La foi des Eglises Luthériennes* (cited *FEL*) (Eds. A. Birmelé and M. Lienhard) (Paris: Cerf; Genève: Labor et Fides, 1991), par. 19. The notion of sacrament seems to link baptism, Eucharist, confession, and absolution. The notion is no more precise in the collection of confessional writings. We will discover also that the different uses of the notion of sign will lead in different ways how to count the sacraments. While Luther includes absolution (cf. his Small Catechism), Melanchthon will count ordination in the number of sacraments even in his understanding of the sign of marriage or also of prayer, charity, the cross and the martyrdom of Christians. (*Apology of the Augsburg Confession d'Augsbourg*: FEL par. 238f.). In the reformed tradition Calvin can consider ordination as a sacrament but this act is not situated at the same level as baptism or the Lord's Supper (*Institution for the Religious Life* IV, 19.28).

a derivative sense, such that the Scriptures never qualify the *sacramenta* of any particular liturgical celebrations.

Numerous contemporary theologies along these lines abound on all sides today, understanding Christ himself, the mystery of God, as being the sacrament par excellence. Thus the German theologian E. Jüngel speaks of a unique sacrament: Jesus Christ, the sacrament of God. Jüngel uses the word sacrament as a "theological notion expressing mediation" between God and humans, mediation that comes in Jesus Christ.[6] Celebrating the sacraments, the community of believers confesses its faith and expresses the incarnation of Christ the unique sacrament, God who gives himself, using the givens of this world. The Catholic theologian Karl Rahner says the same thing.[7] Christ is the original sacrament (*Ur-sakrament*) who is celebrated in the community of believers, the church (*Grund-sakrament*). The point of departure for Rahner is radically christocentric, Christ being the *sacramentum* and the *res sacramenti*. Certainly one can cite other Catholic authors more critical of the option of Karl Rahner, such as Cardinal W. Kasper, who questions Rahner's approach and his notion of sacramental incarnation in the church. But he also insists in his definition of the sacraments on their finality: to celebrate Christ, the Lord over whom we have no disposal and who remains always a "mystery," Christ himself as the primordial sacrament.[8]

Insisting on Christ, the unique sacrament of God, the understanding of the particular sacramental celebrations becomes more open, not excluding other strong moments of ecclesial life as sacraments in a derivative since without their being Sacrament in the sense of Christ himself. This statement relativizes old debates on the meaning of sacrament and even the number of sacraments and their institution.

SCRIPTURE AND SACRAMENTS, IN SERVICE OF THE GOSPEL OF SALVATION

We must emphasize a second option characteristic and decisive for the Lutheran Reform of the sixteenth century. The incarnation of

---

[6] E. Jüngel, and K. Rahner, *Was ist ein Sakrament?* (Freiburg: Herder, 1971), 41 and 50.

[7] Cf. the different contributions of Rahner in the same work cited in the preceding footnote.

[8] W. Kasper, "Wort und Sakrament," in *Glaube und Geschichte* (Mainz: Matthias-Grünewald, 1970), 285–310.

Christ, his death and resurrection for us (*pro nobis*) are the central and decisive givens of the Gospel, and for this reason the criteria, or rather the hermeneutical key, for all theology, for the entire life of the church and all Christians.

The cross is our reconciliation with God; Easter is the irruption of life. We are invited to live in a new relationship with God, a new relationship with others, and a new relationship with ourselves. We are invited to live faith. The cross and the resurrection place a term on the known situation where death, limiting life, destroys all hope. Currently all death is limited through life, all life is carried through faith in this Lord, the guarantor of the future who comes to meet us. We no longer live for ourselves but for him who died and rose for us (2 Cor 5:15). This new reality is not only that of a future beyond. Whoever is in Christ today is a new creature. The old world has passed away. A new reality is here (2 Cor 5:16).

God calls us by our name, gives us our identity, and makes us witnesses of this other logic, the logic of grace that calls us to exist before we could ever merit it. We are not what we could make of ourselves; we are called to be what we are, children of God. We are signs of a new reality that precedes us, establishes us, and fulfills us.

We can choose another vocabulary and make an appeal to the many citations expressing what the Reformation called "justification by faith." The theological choice of the Reformation consisted in considering soteriology and christology as being two sides of one and the same reality. To speak of Christ means to speak of *Christus pro nobis*. This dimension *pro nobis* is evident for the Reformation, whence comes the strict connection between the work of Christ accomplished through the cross and the resurrection, and the justification of the sinner before God, the justification *sola gratia* and *sola fide*.

For the Reformation this message of salvation is not only an essential conviction alongside others, but is the *articulus stantis et cadentis ecclesiae* (the article with which the church stands or falls): "On this article (Jesus Christ) no gap or concession is possible; the heavens and the earth or all that is perishable were to collapse."[9] "The article on justification" is "guide and judge for all other domains of Christian doctrine" because "it establishes our consciousness before God. Without

---

[9] Article de Smalcalde II, 1 (1537): *La foi des Eglises Luthériennes (FEL)* (Paris: Cerf, 1991), par. 372.

this article the world is only death and shadows."[10] This central article shines on all the church says and does. It is not an article that would command the others according to a hierarchical order but the principle that radiates over all the others, giving them their meaning. This article does not only have its importance for soteriology, but it appears also as the fundamental structure of faith for the doctrines of the church as a whole and for each one among them. It is not a matter of placing a particular doctrinal formulation at the fore that would command all the others. What is at stake is the message itself of the Gospel, a message that confounds all theological approaches and denounces error from the moment these approaches do not subject themselves to God's only work, to the divine will expressed in Christ, to the message of salvation that makes the believer exist *coram deo*.

This brief evocation of the message of justification, of the Gospel of Christ *pro nobis*, key for all Christian life and of all ecclesial activity, does not make us lose sight of our initial problematic, the sacraments. Quite to the contrary, it indelibly inscribes the sacraments in the Gospel of justification, in the work of Christ *pro nobis*. The mission of the church is to propose God to the world. The incarnate Christ, dead and risen, offers himself to us and bids us accept the reconciliation that he gives us, making us his ambassadors (2 Cor 5:16-21). How can this message happen today in the world, and how can this salvation be given to the believer? To this traditional question the Lutheran Reformation responds with traditional terms: God gives himself to us through the means of grace, which are the proclamation of the Word and the sacramental celebrations.

Certainly God gives himself through numerous signs that are also proofs of his incarnation. Some world and life events are bearers of this presence of God. The greater parts of these world events, however, are difficult to interpret and for the most part remain ambivalent. But it is different with the celebrations of the Word and the sacraments. God has decided to join himself to these celebrations. We have

[10] M. Luther in 1537 in his *Disputatio* for the promotion of Palladius and Tilleman, WA 39, I, 205: Articulus justificationis "qui conservat et gubernat omnem doctrinam ecclesiasticam et erigit conscientiam nostram coram Deo. Sine hoc articulo mundus es plane mors et tenebrae. Quia nullus est error tam parvus, tam ineptus et insulsus, qui non summe placeat rationi humanae et nos seducat, si cognitione et meditatione huius articulus sumus."

the certitude that in these celebrations, God incarnates himself today and gives himself to us.

Through these means of grace, the gift of the Gospel "enfleshes itself" in the church's worship. In the hearing of the Word and the celebration of the sacraments, which are baptism and Eucharist, God proposes himself and gives himself to humans. In them Christ is truly present. For us we receive him in faith. It is not our faith that creates these means of grace, but these means only work for our salvation if we receive them in faith. Thus understood, the sacraments are the indispensable vector of salvation, the moment when we participate in faith in this new reality opened by the life, death, and resurrection of our Lord.

We have often blamed the traditions of the Reformation for being too focused in a unilateral way on the question of salvation and justification. Other dimensions of faith like creation, even certain aspects of pneumatology as a result of this, risk being shunted into second place, resulting in a narrowing or shrinkage that contemporary Lutheran theology is forced to correct. However, this problem recedes if the understanding of the Christian mystery is centered on *Christus pro nobis*. Today this is largely shared in ecumenical circles. I would like to refer to the *Joint Declaration on the Doctrine of Justification* (JDDJ) signed in 1999 by the World Lutheran Federation and the Roman Catholic Church.[11] The JDDJ exposes the common understanding on salvation in Christ, then opens the question about the place of this message in the development of theology and of the life of the church. "We also share the conviction that the message of justification directs us in a special way towards the heart of the New Testament witness to God's saving action in Christ" (JDDJ 17). This message directs unceasingly the whole of doctrine and the practice of the churches to Christ (JDDJ 18). We therefore do not make it a doctrinal point among others. More important for our subject is the fact that the JDDJ is in agreement in saying that this salvific action of God in Christ is communicated to us through the Holy Spirit, who offers this salvation "through word and sacrament in the community of believers" (JDDJ 16).

This common insistence on the salvific action of God in Jesus Christ through the Holy Spirit, the center of biblical testimony that is today

[11] Eglise catholique—Fédération Luthérienne Mondiale: *La doctrine de la justification. Déclaration commune.* (Paris: Cerf, Bayard, Fleurus-Mame; Genève: Labor et Fides, 1999).

given to the believing community "through word and sacrament," should allow us to progress toward a common understanding of sacrament. The sacraments are the means of grace. This means both that the message of salvation should be at the center of all sacramental theology and that the sacraments are indispensable for the event of grace in our time. The accent does not need to be placed so much on the definition of particular ecclesial acts instituted by Christ as on Christ himself as source, origin, and content of the reality of the sacrament.[12]

SCRIPTURE AND SACRAMENTS: AN ANALOGY

The churches marked by the Reformation of the sixteenth century have always insisted upon the authority of Scripture, the source and norm of all teaching and all Christian life. This insistence is explained through history and through the distrust of the elements of ecclesial life, lest they obtain a comparable authority. It is also theologically fundamental for Scripture to be its own interpreter and give access to the entire Gospel. Nevertheless this has resulted all too often in placing one writing ahead of another without taking into real consideration the way in which Scripture gives access to the Gospel.

Luther, we have emphasized, placed the accent on faith and the gratuitous salvation offered to humanity, the new relationship that God offers to the believer through the death and resurrection of Jesus Christ. The advancement of this conviction was the consequence of a turn to testimony and to biblical theology. But this approach also leads to distinguish carefully (without separating them) between the biblical text (the word with a small *w*) and the Word (capital *W*), which is Christ himself. It is through the Holy Spirit that the text becomes Word (*viva vox Evangelii*). It is necessary "in the Sacred Scriptures to distinguish the Spirit from the letter, that which makes a true theologian."[13] "We will never be satisfied with the letter of the external word; we want to capture the very Spirit . . . The word presented outwardly is not what teaches us inwardly. It is only the pencil and the instrument that inscribes the living word on our hearts. What the voice announces *vocaliter* should be grasped as *vitaliter* in the heart through the action

---

[12] Vatican II speaks of the church *quasi sacramentum*. Without opening the debate here on the sacramentality of the church, it is necessary to note that the council went in this direction specifying that such an approach has its meaning in Christ (LG 1, 9, 48).

[13] WA 3,12 (first course on the Psalms in 1513).

of the Holy Spirit. The Spirit is hidden in the letter."[14] Certainly only the Scriptures give access to the Gospel, but this Gospel should be distinguished to the degree that it is always the living Word, "good news, that should be spread not by pen, but by mouth."[15] Therefore, the authority of Scripture does not reside in the letter itself, even if this letter is essential, but rather in the fact that it opens up the Gospel.[16] Through the power of the Holy Spirit the text of Scripture becomes Gospel, a dynamic Word that produces what it affirms and promises. It makes us participate in Christ. When the Gospel comes to pass, when God comes to humanity, when God comes to the world, God is incarnate. There is nothing to add to it, and in this sense we emphasize the *sola scriptura* or the *solo verbo,* through the Word alone.

Departing from here, it is possible to speak of the "sacramentality of the Scriptures." Just as he chose water for baptism or bread and wine for Eucharist, things found in creation to give himself to his own, God chose to reveal himself through these writings, these witnesses of the first Christians gathered in Sacred Scripture.[17] The reading of Scripture, its preaching, is a "sacrament," the moment when through the word of the privileged testimony of the first Christians, the Logos, Christ himself, takes the Word and comes into being.

---

[14] WA 39, I, 47 (commentary on Ps 45).

[15] WA 10, I, 1, 17.—MLO X, 22.

[16] This distinction between Scripture and Word of God will lead the Reformers—Luther more than Calvin—not to put all biblical testimony on the same level. Some biblical testimony will be more appropriate to make the faith be born and the new relationship with God. Other seems more secondary but is not to be eliminated as such. Thus Luther doubted the apostolic character in the strict sense of the term of the epistles of James and Jude, of the letter to the Hebrews and of the Apocalypse of John. Calvin will be reserved regarding the epistle of the Hebrews, Second Peter, and the Apocalypse.

[17] We can complete this treatment by some references to the fathers of the church. It is first to the Scriptures that the fathers apply the sacramental vocabulary. They contain effectively a multitude of *sacramenta* relative to Christ, as St. Augustine was able to say, "*Sacramentum,* that is to say not just any word of the sacred letters." (Augustine, *Ep.* 55, 38) and Jerome adds: "Each term contains a *sacramentum,* as much the words as the *mysterium.*" Jerome, *Tract. In Ps.*, ed. Morin, *Anal. Mar.* 3 p. 33). St. Augustine will also say inversely that the *logos* does not happen only in the proclamation but also in other ecclesial celebrations, in particular baptism and Eucharist. He speaks about this as "visible forms" of the Word qualifying the proclamation of the Word as an "audible sacrament."

There exists a fundamental analogy between the proclamation of the Word, baptism, and Eucharist in that all three can be understood as forms of the Word and as sacramental celebrations or sacraments in service to the Sacrament—the Logos who is Christ himself. In order to avoid misunderstanding we must clarify that the three types of celebration should not be confused. It is a matter of three different means of grace, of three celebrations, each one having its particularity and calling for different liturgical frameworks. The proclamation of the Word has a dimension addressed more to reason, appealing to the understanding of the human person. Baptism is insertion into the body of Christ, the moment when God declares, regarding a child or an adult: "You are my child." The Eucharist is the meal of the community where communion with God and communion among believers are offered simultaneously. The three celebrations are not identical. Baptism, Eucharist, and proclamation of the Word are not synonymous but, rather, three very different forms of God's singular grace.

Four important points can help to understand better this analogy in Lutheran theology.

First, it is essential to affirm that God does not give himself to us in a spiritual way and that afterwards, in a second moment, we give witness in celebrating word and sacrament as mere signs and confirmations of the spiritual gift of God previously received. To take the Incarnation seriously means to affirm the strong link between the spiritual gift of God and these celebrations. It is at this time and in these celebrations that God offers himself and lets us participate in his salvation; it is in these celebrations that he is really present. It is on this point that Luther separates himself from the other Reformers, particularly Zwingli.

Baptism is a celebration for which recourse to water as indicative of purification is constitutive, the Eucharist an act for which eating and drinking is constitutive. But the meaning of the sacramental event goes beyond the first meaning of these actions, the fact of being washed or being satiated. The natural meaning is transcended. These actions become bearers of a new meaning that is not without relationship to the first meaning but that should not be reduced to the latter, even as simply deduced from it. The new meaning is not the work of my faith or of the church but is born from an interaction between the celebrating community and the work of Christ acting in it. Through *anamnesis* (to make a memorial) the thanksgiving (*eucharistia*) and the calling down of the Holy Spirit (*epiclesis*), the community celebrates her Lord and offers itself to him, Christ, who is offering himself to his church and offering grace, faith, love, and hope.

The same reasoning applies for the word. It is not simple information regarding God but a word, a human word and a human testimony, that in the fact of being proclaimed becomes through the Holy Spirit a performative Word, Gospel, a force that places the hearer in the whirlpool of God's grace.

Second, a believing community celebrates the word and the sacraments, but the reality of grace that happens is not a work of this faith. It is necessary here to insist upon the *extra nos* of the Logos: the gift of Christ in the sacrament. His real presence does not depend upon faith, but its reception creates and deepens faith. Only the reception of grace in faith causes faith to work salvation in me. The absence of faith on the side of the recipient, however, does not by any means lead to the absence of the reality of the presence of Christ in these celebrations. The fact that baptism or Eucharist has occurred is the work of the Holy Spirit. The participants, however, must receive the gift of God in faith so that it works for their salvation. The same applies to the word, namely, the fact that the proclaimed word becomes Gospel. The Word of God is not the work of the believer or of the believing church but, rather, is independent of this faith. God himself and not the believer makes the scriptural witness the Word that bears grace. This Word however requires reception in faith. Then only does its reality happen in the life of the hearer, nourished by faith where the promise of the Gospel is conferred upon him or her.

Third, this approach also allows for a better understanding of the Lutheran insistence upon the "real presence," a polemical question in the traditional quarrels among Christian families and also within the traditions marked by the Reformation. It is helpful to begin from Scripture. Christ is really present there, but this presence is not localized in a letter or even a verse. It is in the "celebration" of Scripture, its reading and proclamation, that the Gospel becomes real; therefore, Christ is really present. He chose to tie himself to the Scriptures in order to become really present in, with, and through this letter, all the while without being localized in the letter. When the Reformation speaks of Christ's presence in the water of baptism or in the eucharistic elements, the process is the same. We should not disassociate the presence of Christ from the water, the bread and wine, and the celebration of these sacraments, but we must do so without claiming to be able physically to localize that presence. It is in this sense that the

Reformation speaks about the real presence of Christ *in, cum et sub* the elements of the celebration.

Finally, this analogy between word, baptism, and Eucharist allows us to relativize the famous question about the number of sacraments. The Reformation only understands the proclamation of the word, baptism, and Eucharist as "means of grace." Absolution, however, was not ignored. It is simply the most radical form of the word: "your sins are forgiven." The same thing applies for confirmation, marriage, and the blessing of the dying, which are obviously retained but equally understood as forms of the proclamation of the Word. The difficulty that remains in the current ecumenical dialogue concerns the understanding of ordination. For the Reformation, ordination is a form of the word, the commitment of the ordained to God and his church and of these latter toward the ordained. Lutheran theology does not consider that a special grace, a capacity that the other baptized do not possess but is given to the ordained—more specifically, a grace conferring upon him or her the power to celebrate the Eucharist.

SCRIPTURE AND SACRAMENTS
AT THE CENTER OF THE CHURCH'S LIFE

In its confession of faith, the *Augsburg Confessions* of 1530, Lutheranism defined the church as being "the community of all believers to whom the Gospel is preached purely and the holy sacraments are administered in accordance with the Gospel."[18] This definition of the church certainly would have a polemical side in opposition to any definition of the church beginning with its structures and ministers. But this definition joins itself above all to the theological logic described above. The church is defined beginning with a means of grace that occurs in it. It can only be understood beginning with the preaching of the word and the celebration of the sacraments.

God proposes salvation to the believer. He provides it, we have insisted, through means of grace—the word and the sacraments. It is through these that the believer is declared justified before God. God certainly speaks to the individual but this address is in no way individualistic. Communion with God is simultaneously communion with other believers because the Word comes to me in and through the community of believers, enrolling me in it. Far from ignoring the

---

[18] Thus article 7 of the *Augsburg Confessions*, the confession of the faith of 1530, which is the reference to the Lutheran Churches.

church, Lutheran theology makes it a major element decisive for justification by faith. It is in the church that believers are justified. Conversely the church—the body of Christ and object of faith—is nothing other than the communion of believers who celebrate the word and sacraments in truth. The celebration of the word and sacraments is always a celebration of the church. It is celebrated by the *koinonia*, the community. The church of Jesus Christ is the communion of those who are called by the Holy Spirit to faith, affirmed by the Word, incorporated by baptism into the body of Christ, and nourished by the Eucharist, awaiting the eschatological realization of the kingdom.

Historically this has been the understanding of the church, and it remains controversial in the current ecumenical dialogues. Indeed, in Lutheran theology the church should not be defined by anything other than those things necessary for the means of salvation, the means of grace through which God gives himself. The fundamental interdependence between the church on the one hand, and word and sacraments on the other, is certainly affirmed by all the Christian traditions, but the Lutheran approach would be considered as restrictive. Indeed, it allows little or no mention of ministry, which is, in Catholic theology, constitutive of the church in a way different than is the case for Lutheranism. Here as well it is necessary to avoid misunderstandings. Lutheran theology has developed a theology of ministry, but the articulation between ministry and the means of grace is not that of the Roman tradition. One could not rightly have an ecclesial celebration, a celebration of the means of grace, without having a minister ordained for this task, but the reality and the authenticity of these celebrations does not depend upon a certain understanding of ministry. This articulation certainly remains a major ecumenical difficulty.

This point evidently enters into the very conception of the unity of the church. The preaching of the Word and the celebration of baptism and the sacraments are the means by which God justifies the believer and, through these things being given, establishes the church. Lutheran theology goes a step further and in fact logically makes it the necessary and sufficient condition for the unity of the church. Authentic celebrations of the word and sacraments become the signs of the true church. They do not replace unity, holiness, catholicity, and apostolicity, the traditional marks put forward through the creeds of the early centuries. They are at the service of these marks. Where does one find *una, sancta, catholica et apostolica ecclesia*? The Lutheran response would be that we find these where believers celebrate in truth the word and sacraments. The result is that authentic celebration of the word and sacraments becomes the necessary and sufficient condition for the unity of the church. The different ecclesial bodies will be able mutually to recognize each other as legitimate and truthful expressions of the one church of Christ, which transcends time and space, when they are able to recognize in another community the true celebration of the word and sacraments. Mutual recognition of ministries would be a consequence of this and not a prerequisite. This conviction is the basis of any contemporary ecumenical process of churches who lay claim to the Reformation.

The community is the church on the basis of the action being accomplished in it. It is not merely an assembly of the converted, who only secondarily find themselves in church. The church is the place of the advent of grace. Through it the community goes beyond the simple sum of believers; it is *koinonia* in the image of the communion that is in God himself. The church is not inactive; it is the celebrating community. But this activity must not be understood on the same order as that of God, who instituted the sacraments and who gave them to the church, offering himself through them. It is a matter of celebrations of the church and in the church, all the while being celebrations the church could never come up with on its own. These celebrations of word and sacrament are proleptic of the kingdom to come, to borrow an expression from the contemporary theologian W. Pannenberg. In Christ we do not only have a foretaste of the kingdom, but this kingdom is already realized. In it Christ has already anticipated the final realization. While we await the definitive establishment of the kingdom, the saving will of God and the fulfillment in Christ are announced and lived in earthly data still marked by a provisional quality. For this reason they are called mysteries. The celebration of the word and the sacraments each Sunday, the Day of the Lord, is the celebration of this mystery awaiting the final Day of the Lord. In these celebrations this fulfillment is revealed to us not only in the form of information but as a lived reality. We receive from them a deposit in advance of the Day of the Lord (Eph 1:14). We discover and receive from them the future and already present glory of the kingdom.[19]

---

[19] W. Pannenberg, *Systematische Theologie*, 3 vols. (Göttingen: Vandenhoeck, 1988ff.) Vol. 3, 379 ff.

Part 3

Ecclesiology, Pastoral and Ecumenical

> The other scandals concerning the faith—one thinks, for example, of the Eucharistic presence—can easily become "false scandals" masking the real one or excuses for secretly turning ourselves away from the real one. For this true scandal is that God, by the gift of the Spirit, continues to raise up for himself a body in the world—the body of the Risen One in its humiliated condition, marked by the wounds of his death. The true scandal is ultimately this, the path to our relation with God passes through our relation with human beings and most especially through our relation with those whom the judgment of the mighty has reduced to "less than nothing."[1]

The two contributors to this ecclesiological section are both acutely aware of real, historical, paradoxical aspects of a liturgically practiced and sacramentally known faith. Philippe Barras explores this humbling reality in the pastoral field of contemporary French Catholicism, while Gordon Lathrop fearlessly names and confronts the challenge in an inter-ecclesial period "when many people have lost interest in both ecumenical and liturgical questions." Whereas one might read Chauvet's articulation of faith's fundamental scandal as pointing to the ethical work of Christians *ad extra*—the church verifying its celebration of word and sacrament through openness and service to the poor and suffering in the world—these two authors turn to paradoxical dimensions of pastoral-liturgical practice within the church itself. In so doing, they highlight Chauvet's own insistence on the inevitably difficult and at times painful acceptance of the "humanity of God" revealed in the Spirit's kenotic empowerment of Christ and, now, the

---

[1] Louis-Marie Chauvet, *Symbol and Sacrament: A Sacramental Reinterpretation of Christian Existence*, trans. Patrick Madigan and Madeleine Beaumont (Collegeville, MN: Liturgical Press, 1995), 187.

church. We must accept the scandal of institutional structures and personages, of sociocultural ambiguities in genuine pastoral availability to people, of simple signs and not always elegant words bearing the divine revelation of human redemption.

Philippe Barras evaluates the ongoing pastoral challenge in the French Catholic Church requiring constant judgment on the part of local pastoral ministers and deliberation by the Conference of Bishops, namely, how to respond to the request for sacramental rites made by people who otherwise rarely participate in the liturgical and communal life of the church. The exercise of power surely is at issue, a matter of whether and how pastoral ministers and authorities can recognize and accept God's working in and through human beings who would seem by theological and perhaps even canonical standards "nonpersons" in the society (social body) of the church. Barras argues for how the paschal mystery is at work in pastoral ministers' openness to what is human and good in people's desire for rites of passage, how replacing negative judgment with pastoral creativity reveals the divine work hidden in human scenarios. Shifting the criteria for the fruitful celebration of the sacraments away from theological ideals to honest awareness of personal situations and contextual realities thereby promises pastoral practices true to the evangelical heart of the church's sacramental tradition.

Lutheran theologian Gordon Lathrop gives an unblinking assessment of and passionate proposal for the current state of ecumenical, and therefore liturgical, relations in the church. The liturgical movement from its inception has been necessarily, intrinsically ecumenical in nature. The current ecclesial climate, however, characterized by churches struggling to assert their identities in themselves or on the basis of autonomous authority, betrays a rejection of the Gospel's call to accept the scandalous way God truly becomes present to the church, namely, through our relation with those whom the ones in power judge as deficient, unacceptable, or lacking in some way. What promises ongoing liturgical revitalization is not the imposition of uniform protocols but, rather, a generous appreciation of the varied ways particular local churches practice the fundamental elements essential to the tradition of Word and sacrament: the practical integration of Scripture, sacrament, and ethics; the fostering of the participatory contribution of all in the liturgical assembly through accessible language and mutual service; liturgical ministries practiced competently, proportionately, and humbly; and an open, albeit critical, approach to local acculturation in the liturgy. These criteria, Lathrop nonetheless asserts, can only bear pastoral and apostolic fruit if practiced in a genuinely ecumenical manner, that is, through mutual transparency and respectful evaluation among churches. All forms of triumphalism must be revealed for the worldly scandals that they are. The trusting, humble honoring of differences within the Body of Christ, the pursuit of renewal and growth "under the sign of 'not without the other,'" thereby promises a genuine contemporary embrace of the scandalous faith revealed in Word and sacrament for the life of the world.

Chapter 5

Sacramental Theology
at the Mercy of Pastoral Service

Philippe Barras

Can sacramental theology be relevant for our times without taking into consideration ecclesial practices? Taking our cue from Professor Louis-Marie Chauvet, we can respond without hesitation, no. Sacramental theology must be concerned about liturgical practices and pastoral strategies. "As important as it might be, the turn to *tradition* cannot be the only determinant of theological discourse, even in sacramental theology: *ecclesial praxis, mission, spiritual welfare* of the faithful are the major parameters. Not to give enough attention to these would damage the nature of theology itself, which necessarily requires a *hermeneutical* moment."[1]

Doing theology is intimately linked to the sort of ecclesial discernment that gives a proper place and full dimension to liturgical acts in the experience of the faithful today. Such a theological posture joins Karl Rahner's legacy of associating theological reflection, with its proper technical side, and practical reflection, with its concrete questions concerning the situation of the church today in the world. This leads to true "pastoral theology"[2] or, to paraphrase the title of a well-known work by Chauvet, to a theology at the mercy of pastoral service, provided one properly understands the notion "pastoral" as applied to sacraments.

---

[1] Chauvet, "Notes sur la confirmation des adultes," *La Maison-Dieu* 211 (1997): 63.

[2] Cf. Karl Rahner, *Mission et grâce–I, Vingtième siècle, siècle de grâce? Fondements d'une théologie pastorale pour notre temps* (Paris: Mame, 1962).

The notion of pastoral theology[3] is relatively recent in the life of the church. It is also confused to the degree that it is applied as much to persons (e.g., youth pastoral ministry, family pastoral ministry, etc.) as to human realities that people live (e.g., pastoral healthcare, pastoral care to tourists), as to places (e.g., prison pastoral care, school pastoral ministry, etc.), as to ecclesial projects or to certain dimensions of Christian life (e.g., pastoral care for vocations, missionary pastoral ministry, catechetical pastoral ministry, etc.). In the spirit of liturgists coming out of the liturgical movement, pastoral liturgy and sacramental care recover both the implementation of worship celebrations and the accompaniment of persons before, during, and after the celebrations (sacramental or not). For many years pastoral liturgy was often distinguished from pastoral sacramental theology: the former meaning everything that concerns the celebration itself, drawing upon the rubrics of the liturgical books, and the latter, everything that deals with the instruction of the faithful for sacramental reception. Such a tension that marks the frequent separation if not opposition between liturgy and sacramental theology is no longer pertinent, especially since Vatican II.

It is necessary to determine what one means by "pastoral care" of the sacraments, even "pastoral liturgy." I will attempt to establish the hermeneutical milestones in the first part, then I will verify factually how Chauvet takes the risk of entering into the tension between sacramental theology and sacramental practice (second part), before searching for some of the potential benefits in the third part.

THE NOTION OF PASTORAL PRACTICE
AS APPLIED TO THE SACRAMENTS

The notion of pastoral service applied to the liturgy and the sacraments came into usage especially in France in the middle of the twentieth century. The notion that emerged first was that of *"pastorale liturgique—pastoral liturgy,"*[4] in 1941, in the wake of the liturgical

---

[3] Translator's remark: *Pastorale* is used in French as a noun but in English it is advisable to use it as an adjective modifying a noun such as service, care, practice, theology, ministry, or liturgy. For example, in English one says "pastoral liturgy," but in French the term *pastorale liturgique* is used, which implies "liturgical pastoral practice."

[4] Translator's remark: As mentioned above, *pastorale* is the noun and *liturgique* is the adjective. In English we say "pastoral liturgy," but in French the term implies "liturgical pastoral practice." For the sake of clarity according to English usage, *"pastorale liturgique"* will be rendered "pastoral liturgy."

movement,[5] and it especially concerned the celebration of the Mass. In 1951 the plenary assembly of the French bishops adopted a "directory for the pastoral administration of the sacraments." Presented by the Most Reverend Guerry, coadjutor bishop of Cambrai, who built upon the missionary momentum after the war,[6] it is noteworthy for the fact that it was adopted by all the bishops of France for the first time, but also for its subsequently offering "a great movement of sacramental evangelization" through the instruction of the faithful when receiving the sacraments, spiritual direction, and granting responsibility to Christian communities. However, it was after Vatican II that a true pastoral sacramental practice unfolded.[7] It was not simply a matter of concern about their sacramental validity, but moreover to insure their fruitful reception. Several theologians, Chauvet in particular, offered to determine the contours of such a sacramental pastoral praxis in the framework of pastoral liturgy itself.[8]

EMERGENCE OF THE NOTION OF *PASTORALE LITURGIQUE*[9] IN FRANCE

Although the notion remains relatively flexible, it conceals diverse fields and takes on a variety of meanings. It was born out of the liturgical movement initiated by Dom Guéranger who from the end of the nineteenth century tried to restore to the liturgy its proper vocation in the church and in the life of the faithful. We speak first of all about education through the liturgy,[10] then of the liturgical apostolate,[11] and we have to wait until the middle of the twentieth century, under the

---

[5] According to A.-M. Roguet, *Mens concordet voci—pour Mgr A.-G. Martimort* (Paris: Desclée, 1983), the expression "pastoral liturgy" was born in Germany between the first and second world wars. *Die Pastoralliturgik* essentially means the active place of the liturgy in spiritual direction: cf. Romano Guardini (*Vom Geist der Liturgie*, 1918), Odo Casel, Pius Parsch, etc. However, it was in France that the notion would develop.

[6] Cf. Abbés Godin et Daniel, *France, pays de mission* (Lyons: l'Abeille, 1943).

[7] Cf. Mgr Maziers, "La liturgie dans une Église en état de mission," *La Maison-Dieu* 79 (*Implications pastorales de la réforme liturgique*) (Summer 1964): 21.

[8] Cf. P. Prétot in this work.

[9] See footnote 4 above.

[10] For example, M. Flad, *L'éducation par la liturgie* (Paris: l'art catholique, 1921).

[11] For example, P. Bayart, *Un programme d'apostolat liturgique* (Tournai: Casterman, 1936).

influence of the Belgian Dom Lambert Beauduin, then exiled in a religious community near Paris, to witness the emergence of the notion of a "pastoral liturgy" whose goal was essentially promotion of the liturgy in the spiritual life of the faithful and improvement of the celebration in its form, enlightening its proper values. The Vanves Days[12] in January 1944 witnessed the birth of the Centre de Pastorale Liturgique under the direction of the Dominicans.[13] From the beginning, different concepts of pastoral liturgy collided. There was the concept of Father Doncœur and Abbot Michonneau, who both dreamed of a liturgy capable of evangelizing those who were far from the church. For them, pastoral liturgy sought to make of the liturgy a means of evangelization and even the first announcement of the Good News.[14] For this there was need for deep reform of the liturgical rites so that they might be accessible to everyone. Then the concept of Fr. Morin,[15] in the wake of Dom L. Beauduin, who, in order to develop the conscious and active participation in the liturgy, proposed an education of the faithful in Sacred Scripture as well as a better adaptation of the rites to contemporary culture and mentalities, all the while remaining with the Tradition of the church. Some years later, a third concept came into being: that of the magisterium, with the encyclical *Mediator Dei*[16] of Pope Pius XII largely recognizing the contributions of the liturgical movement, all the while limiting its daring pastoral consequences. Here, pastoral liturgy appeared as the means used by ecclesiastical hierarchy to encourage the faithful to worship practice, essentially understanding the Christian life as educating the faithful about their duties, and to insure the strict adherence to liturgical rules (through education and control of the

[12] The proceedings were published in *Étude de pastorale liturgique*, Lex orandi 1 (Paris: Cerf, 1944).

[13] This refers to Fathers Aimon-Marie Roguet and Pie Duployé. But they were not alone and depended upon the support of D. Lambert Beauduin, P. Louis Bouyer, P. Gaston Morin, P. Paul Doncœur, Ch. Aimé-Georges Martimort, Dom Basset, etc.

[14] This was opposed forcefully by Dom Basset and especially by Father Louis Bouyer, *Étude de pastorale liturgique*, 78–79 and 380–84.

[15] His interventions at the Vanves Days were determinative for the creation of the Center for Pastoral Liturgy (CPL): *Pour un mouvement liturgique pastoral*, La Clarté-Dieu, no. XIII (Lyons: Abeille, 1944); reprinted in *Études de pastorale liturgique*, Lex orandi I (Paris: Cerf, 1944).

[16] November 1947.

clergy). These three concepts, which I will call respectively "mission-ary," "popular," and "clerical," all have a commonality: they consider the liturgy essentially as an object of pastoral service. This is evident when it concerns adaptation or reform of the rites in order that they might be more meaningful and accessible, but also when it concerns the education of the faithful or clergy, because the goal consists in form-ing their perspective and understanding.

Sacramental pastoral theology is distinguished from pastoral liturgy because it does not seek to adapt the rites nor even to introduce the faithful to the rites. It can however be qualified as *missionary, popular,* and *clerical*: It seeks a place for evangelization, in the sense of explicitly announcing the Good News, particularly for those who do not fre-quently come to Sunday Mass; it also seeks religious education in of-fering a real catechesis when people ask for the sacraments; it likewise seeks education in different aspects of the Christian life, and especially those dealing with moral behavior. But unlike pastoral liturgy, sacra-mental pastoral praxis does not truly take the sacrament as an object of pastoral attention but, rather, as a pretext to put into place a cate-chetical moment as a kind of sacramental preparation.

LITURGICAL AND SACRAMENTAL PASTORAL PRAXIS SINCE VATICAN II

The Second Vatican Council marked an important turning point for liturgical and sacramental pastoral practice, a turning point that was already begun at the first international congress for pastoral liturgy in Assisi in 1956.[17] The theology of the liturgy put into place in *Sacrosanc-tum Concilium*[18] in fact invites recognizing in the celebration "of the sacraments around which revolve the entire liturgical life" not only an *office* into which the baptized are invested to accomplish the work of God, not only a *revelation* that instructs the faithful and brings them to a better understanding of God, but also an *experience*[19] both spiritual

---

[17] To note especially the intervention authorized by J. Jungmann who defined the liturgy itself in pastoral terms, and the important encounter with Pope Pius XII who reminds him that the liturgy only comes under the jurisdiction of ecclesiastical hierarchy. Cf. the proceedings *dans La Maison-Dieu* 47–48 (Spring–Summer 1956).

[18] Particularly chap. I, SC nos. 5–12.

[19] According to the category put into place Jean Mourroux, *L'expérience chré-tienne—Introduction à une théologie*, Théologie, no. 26 (Paris: Aubier, 1952). Note

and bodily of the encounter with the present Risen One[20] who acts in the midst of the gathered assembly.[21] This experiential approach leads us to envisage the liturgy itself as a pastoral experience. If it is necessary to use pastoral zeal in the church regarding liturgy and the sacraments, it is first of all to appreciate the liturgy as a pastoral force.[22] In this perspective the liturgy is considered as subject and no longer object of pastoral praxis. This has for its first objective to make the faithful appreciate the potential power of the liturgy to help them live in the sacrament, the encounter of Christ in the church. If the liturgy is the place and the moment where Christ continues his work of salvation accomplished in the paschal mystery, at the heart of the life of the world, pastoral liturgy devotes itself to the mission of seeking to make perceptible the work of divine grace through the paschal mystery into which the liturgy immerses and incorporates us.

To the degree that Vatican II again places the sacraments at the heart of liturgical life, pastoral liturgy concerns itself first and foremost with the celebration of the sacraments. Thus sacramental pastoral care is called to use the capacity of the sacraments to establish a relationship between God and humans and "to restore them to the paschal way opened by Christ."[23] It is not only a matter of catechizing on the occasion of sacramental preparation, even if this conception has had a long life and was perpetrated widely after the council until today. Indeed, we can easily understate this reason in a secularized, post-Christian society where the proclamation of Jesus Christ no longer goes without saying. Nevertheless, the reason is perhaps deeper: it is not so easy to envisage sacramental pastoral care that entrusts its entire fortune to

---

that the author never cites the liturgy itself as an eminent place of Christian experience that is "the ensemble of actions by which we grasp ourselves in relationship with God." (25)

[20] Cf. E. Schillebeeckx, *Christus sacrament van de Godsontmoeting* (Bilhoven: H. Nelissen, 1959); *Le Christ, sacrement de la rencontre de Dieu*, Lex orandi 31 (Paris: Cerf, 1967).

[21] SC no. 7.

[22] Note that the expression "Pastorale liturgique" only occurs in *Sacrosanctum Concilium* in no. 43 and means the "desire for the development and restoration of the sacred liturgy." The council fathers did not yet have the full means to take the "pastoral" turn that was operative.

[23] John Paul II, *Vicesimus quintus annus*, no. 6. *Lettre apostolique pour le 25ᵉ anniversaire de la Constitution conciliaire Sacrosanctum concilium sur la sainte liturgie* (Paris: Cerf, 1989).

the event of salvation manifested and actualized in the celebration. Already in 1970, Henri Denis wrote: "the difficulties perhaps do not arise from the liturgy—since it is always able to adapt itself—but rather from the sacrament itself. The current crisis therefore would be a crisis of sacramentalism. . . . What is the meaning of the sacraments and sacrament in general in the life of people today?"[24] If the difficulties are found more on the side of sacraments than liturgy, it is because they reveal the profound nature of all liturgy as a salvific act of Christ in the church.[25] H. Denis was correct: it is the ontological reality of the sacraments that is in question. If, as stated in *Sacrosanctum Concilium* no. 6, the sacraments around which all liturgical life gravitates are the actions through which the work of salvation accomplished by Christ dead and risen for all people is effected, then the decisive question remains: How can sacrament be perceived as a salvific act? And finally, from what do we need to be saved? Here the role of sacramental pastoral praxis is called to be soteriological. The sacramental theology of Chauvet turns out to be a precious help.[26]

In summary, I have distinguished between pastoral liturgy developed before Vatican II that considered the liturgy as an object and tried to adapt it to contemporary situations, and a pastoral liturgy emerging from Vatican II that aimed to consider the liturgy as subject of pastoral praxis and sought to develop all its capabilities. Furthermore, I can distinguish a "nonliturgical" sacramental praxis, understood as a deployment of a catechetical arsenal on the occasion of sacramental administration, and a sacramental pastoral praxis that as a part of the pastoral liturgy has for its objective to open and inscribe the way of Christian existence in its relationship to God, initiated or marked by the event that constitutes the liturgical celebration of the sacrament.

Inevitably, as in every transitional period, these two types of pastoral praxis can be found today. The two concepts confront each other quite often in the parish context. Some people privilege the education of the faithful and liturgical adaptation, while others privilege the

---

[24] H. Denis, "Liturgie et sacrement," *La Maison-Dieu* 104 (Spring 1970), *Recherches nouvelles de pastorale sacramentelle.*

[25] Whereas a liturgy separated from the sacrament can adapt itself more to the life of human beings, but at the risk of losing its theophanic dimension.

[26] The theologian himself says that that which caused this thesis to click for him was the question about the efficacy of the sacraments following St. Thomas Aquinas.

search for meaning from the liturgical act itself and work for its implementation. Like many, Chauvet finds himself at the crossroads of these two tendencies. His history and his generation bring him to the first tendency, and his theological reflection about the sacraments leads him to the second.[27] And so the pastoral concern of the theologian finds itself in permanent tension. It is a beneficial tension since it allows him to open the tenets of the first tendency to the perspectives of the second.

CHAUVET IN TENSION BETWEEN SACRAMENTAL AND PASTORAL THEOLOGY

There are numerous examples of contemporary pastoral questions that Chauvet has confronted, leading him to some original propositions in trying to reconcile theological tradition and ecclesial practices. Here we will look at one concerning the sacraments of Christian initiation, namely, the unity and sequence of the three sacraments of baptism, confirmation, and Eucharist.[28] The traditional sequence of the three (baptism, confirmation, Eucharist)[29] finds itself in critical opposition to the current method most widely practiced in France, which consists of confirming well after the celebrations of baptism and First Communion. In fact, the majority of those who are baptized as infants or in grade school and given First Communion in their childhood, are confirmed in their adolescence. Likewise, in several dioceses, adults who receive baptism and Eucharist at the Easter Vigil, in conformity to the Rite of Christian Initiation of Adults, are confirmed a year later—contrary to what is indicated in the Rite.[30] Chauvet's suggestion is

[27] His numerous interventions in the sessions on sacramental pastoral practice organized by CNPL, particularly in regards to infant baptism, funerals, or confirmation, give witness to this fact.

[28] Chauvet subscribes fully to the patristic theology that undergirds the Rituals of Vatican II. Cf. among the numerous references: "Les sacrements de l'initiation chrétienne," J. Gelineau, *Dans vos assemblée* (Paris: Desclée, 1998).

[29] Chauvet qualifies himself as not convinced by Bourgeois' position in *Théologie catéchuménale* (Paris: Cerf, 1991) who relies upon the current practice of confirmation after First Communion to develop a theology of sacramental sequence: baptism, then Eucharist, and then confirmation. "Note sur la confirmation des adultes," *La Maison-Dieu* 211 (1997): 58.

[30] *Rituel de l'Initiation chrétienne des adultes* (Paris: Desclée, 1997), no. 211 (*Ordo initiationis chritianae adultorum*, Rome, 1972, no. 3).

90

pragmatic, distinguishing the case of adults from that of adolescents and children. For the latter he prefers not to change the current practice in the church "as long as we don't have anything else to propose to young people at the moment of their adolescence,"[31] feeling that a change to establish confirmation to its original position "would end up destroying rather than building up the Church of God"[32] because "some good spiritual and missionary fruits in the life of young people" lead them to the sacrament at the time of their adolescence. In the case of adults, he proposes a fulsome application of the traditional order reestablished by the last council as an exemplary model for the entire church, that is, to celebrate confirmation at the same time as baptism and Eucharist at the Easter Vigil in every parish. Elsewhere he proposes to allow for a progressive integration into the ecclesial community (one of the reasons cited to vary the sacrament of confirmation) and to accompany this measure putting into place a true "postbaptismal year" that would conclude with a diocesan celebration (establishing the particular connection with the bishop) focused on the sacrament of reconciliation as a "dry plunge,"[33] followed by the sacrament of Eucharist.

The proposed solution shows the tension in which the theologian finds himself in seeking to clarify and challenge pastoral care. This is even more perceptible in another proposition he put forward a few years later. To make clear the particular connection with the bishop in the sacrament, what often justifies the postponement of adult confirmation, Chauvet proposes[34] to differentiate, in this case, both confirmation and First Communion to "safeguard" the order of the three sacraments according to the tradition that places Eucharist as the summit of initiation and to celebrate them all together on Pentecost

[31] Chauvet, "Notes sur la confirmation des adultes," *La Maison-Dieu* 211 (Spring 1997): 61.

[32] Ibid.

[33] Ibid., 60.

[34] Intervention at the Conference on confirmation in the Diocese of Évry-Corbeil-Essonnes in 2003: Chauvet, "Sacrements de l'Église, sacrements de l'initiation chrétienne,"*Jeunes et vocations*, no. 118 (Paris: Éd. du Service national des vocations, August 2005): 77 (article available on the internet, http://snv.free.fr/jv118chauvet.htm). The author says that he prefers this solution to that consisting of celebrating baptism and First Communion at the Easter Vigil and the sacrament of confirmation at Pentecost.

Sunday,[35] which is a major liturgical day constituting the close of the Easter season. This proposal was put into action by the bishop of Pontoise and other such dioceses, but it provoked the negative reaction of some catechumens when told they would receive Eucharist for the first time at Pentecost and not Easter: "How can you deprive me of Eucharist once I have been baptized . . . especially during the Easter season?" This reaction, which is reasonable, could not stand without a response: the current practice in the Pontoise Diocese consists, in fact, in celebrating baptisms at the Easter Vigil, each catechumen in his or her own parish, then gathering all the newly baptized a week later, on the second Sunday of Easter around the bishop, for the celebration of the sacraments of confirmation and First Communion.

This concrete example takes into account the current difficulties in holding together in a coherent way the theological position and pastoral practice to the degree that each one has its own unique heritage—the patristic concept of the sacraments of Christian initiation for the former and the magisterial decisions for the second, notably the decree *Quam Singularis* of Pope Pius X,[36] in 1910, and the position of the Conference of Catholic Bishops of France in 1985[37] that considered as "normal" celebrating confirmation well after the First Communion. Here, Chauvet's theological posture consists in recovering the theological positions of the great tradition and trying to tease from it the pastoral consequences, but also interrogating himself about these theological positions concerning the conditions for the possibility of their reception by our contemporaries.[38]

[35] French-speaking Ritual no. 59 (*Ordo christianae adultorum*, no. 56).

[36] In reaction to the very rare practice of eucharistic Communion and to the postponement of First Communion, this moves it up to the age of puberty, that is, to seven years old, without moving at the same time the age of confirmation, which results in the modification of the sequence of the three sacraments in some countries like France. (Cf. P. De Clerck, *Confirmation et communauté de foi*, Dossiers libres [Paris: Cerf, 1980]).

[37] In November 1985, the Conference of Bishops in France clarified: "As for the decision of each bishop for his diocese, the age of confirmation can be set within the period of adolescence, that is between 12 and 18 years of age" (*Bulletin officiel de la Conférence des évêques de France*, no. 30, p. 450).

[38] As already cited, Chauvet positions himself in the wake of Rahner (cf. B. Sesboüé, *Karl Rahner*) (Paris: Cerf, 2001), 75.

OPEN PERSPECTIVES
IN SACRAMENTAL-PASTORAL PRAXIS

It is not insignificant that one of the major works of Chauvet[39] concludes with a fifth part, "pastoral care," using some concrete consequences of the consideration of the body and the symbolic approach insofar as it concerns the sacraments that constitute the rites of passage (infant baptism, First Communion, marriage, and burial). Here we would like to explore this reflection, particularly the framework of infant baptism.

The penetrating pastoral question for a number of years concerns the motivation of people demanding a sacrament, especially infant baptism, as perceived by pastoral agents, and its inadequacy for the expected faith content. Some see this gap as unacceptable to the point that they refuse or, more precisely, defer the celebration of the sacrament;[40] by others as regrettable when they end up feeling frustrated by having welcomed and met the request;[41] and still by others as a chance to encounter young adults and "help them arrive at their own truth, even if only partially."[42] Chauvet's suggestion is clearly on the side of the third tendency. For him, the persistence of requests for the rites of passage is explained very well for psychosocial reasons, a matter that should not be ignored. Certainly this is not all, but "the theological logic, showing the discrepancy between the sacrament of faith that the church offers and what the parents in effect ask for"[43] cannot ignore them when it envisages the sacraments as symbolic mediations in their

---

[39] Chauvet, *Les sacrements, parole de Dieu au risque du corps* (Paris: Ouvrières, 1993).

[40] In some dioceses of France that offer baptism in stages, some pastors have imposed a simple welcome in view of a later baptism (possibly asked for by the child him- or herself) on those who do not openly profess faith in Jesus Christ.

[41] How many pastors express their frustration regarding baptisms that are never followed by catechization, feeling that they have "sold out" the sacrament?

[42] Chauvet, *Les sacrements*, 201. Chauvet, *The Sacraments: The Word of God at the Mercy of the Body* (Collegeville, MN: Liturgical Press, 2001), 185. Hereafter the corresponding page numbers for the English-language versions of *both Les sacrements* and *Symbole et Sacrement* will be indicated by "ELV, p." The reader may discern which work is being referenced from the French work cited.

[43] Ibid., 197. ELV, 181.

sensible dimension, "in the wake of linguistic and cultural mediations without which there would not be a human subject."[44] Chauvet's theological reflections concerning the pastoral meeting, following requests for sacraments, and the relationship between infant baptism and the faith of the parents,[45] have opened a pastoral field that has not yet been fully explored. The *Sacramental Pastoral Guidelines* for the sacraments of Christian initiation and marriage, published by the French Bishops' Commission on Liturgy and Sacramental Pastoral Care in 1994,[46] is greatly indebted to him in the following ways: the positive regard given to those asking and their motivation to ask for sacraments provides an anthropological condition favoring a possible conversion; the recognition of a reciprocity in the pastoral meeting that places the pastoral agent in a position of being the asker; the importance of the pastoral meeting prerequisite to the sacrament that opens a future promise to the degree that one doesn't fear the confrontation with the Gospel, and where that is done in an evangelical way, in truth and without excessive moral rigor, etc.

SACRAMENTAL PASTORAL CARE: THE PLACE OF EVANGELIZATION

In fact, one of the keys for this pastoral question resides in approaching sacramental pastoral care, such as infant baptism, as a place for evangelization, not an occasion of evangelization. The nuance is enormous: it marks the difference between sacramental pastoral care that rests upon the sacrament itself in its capacity for evangelization to the degree that it is accompanied, undergirded, prepared, and followed up afterwards . . . and sacramental pastoral care that is essentially a catechetical moment where the sacrament is the pretext. This latter has little chance to succeed in a secularized society where someone expects to remain master of what is good for him or her. Since the catechetical proposition does not correspond to the parents' expecta-

---

[44] Chauvet, "Une relecture de Symbole et sacrement," *Questions liturgiques* 88/2 (2007): 111–25.

[45] Chauvet, "Baptême des petits enfants et foi des parents," *La Maison-Dieu* no. 207 (Summer 1996).

[46] Commission épiscopale de liturgie, *Pastorale sacramentelle—Points de repère*, Liturgie, no. 7 (Paris: Cerf, 1996).

tion, it cannot reach them easily,[47] even if the psychosocial reasons that motivate them to make the demand for the sacrament, like their entire system of representation regarding the sacrament, the church, and God himself, need to be evangelized. In other words, it is futile to think that one can make these people happy in spite of themselves! The movement is in an entirely different direction when one considers the judicious and accompanied implementation of the sacrament itself as a place of evangelization in caring for people. Here it is a matter of recognizing their system of representation, granting the psychosocial reasons, and with this at the very center of these realities, to let them listen, see, smell, touch, and taste the grace that God gives to each person in every circumstance, and especially in the sacrament. The goal is not only to prepare for fruitful reception of the sacrament, but to open the process for a possible turnabout through the Pasch of Christ.[48] This will necessarily bear fruit, not always according to our own design, not always in first place for the immediate benefit of the persons encountered, but at least for the benefit of the entire church.

Four conditions are necessary for sacramental pastoral care to be a place of evangelization:[49] it presupposes an evangelical attitude, a process with stages, the celebration as not only the end point of a process but also the source of the life of faith, and an ongoing search for the happiness of the persons encountered.[50] "Here then are people, such as they are, with their requests more or less justified. How to evangelize them? How to make sacramental pastoral care a way of evangelization? More precisely, how do we advance with these people on the road where we ourselves are going to be evangelized? This

---

[47] This does not mean that every proposal on structured catechesis should be abandoned. Some are very good, while others become more interesting during the course of a later realization.

[48] A turnabout like what the Emmaus story tells us (Luke 24:13-35) when the two disciples recognize him: "That same hour they got up and returned to Jerusalem . . ."

[49] Commission épiscopale de liturgie, 17–29.

[50] "For you have to know the difference between the good and the bad shepherd consists in that the good shepherd cares more for the welfare of his sheep, while the bad shepherd cares only for his own welfare." St. Thomas Aquinas, *Commentary on the Gospel of John 10, 3* (*Liturgia horarum*, Roman Office of Readings, Monday of the 21st week).

presupposes a certain number of steps, with some attitudes to develop for each one of them."[51]

In other words, since evangelization is reciprocal by nature, sacramental pastoral care demands of its agents that they allow themselves to be evangelized by those whom they encounter. The Spirit also speaks through them! This first condition already has some enormous consequences: it determines the way we look at the other, qualifying the nature of the relationship and of the ensuing communication.

FOUR STEPS FOR FURTHER DEVELOPMENT

The steps envisioned are defined by the bishops' text as being fourfold: "Welcome," "favor growth," "celebrate the sacrament," and "care for what follows." Such an approach has the value of marking the "obligatory passages" of all sacramental pastoral care: if this seeks to be a place of evangelization, none of these steps can be omitted. Nevertheless, it has the drawback of introducing—without really wanting to—a successiveness. For these four steps cannot or should not be purely successive: the welcome is not only a prerequisite to any process but must be understood as a permanent attitude; the progression that it attempts to favor does not happen only in the initial preparatory period for the sacrament but at the heart itself of the celebration and of the time that follows; the aftermath has no chance of being effective if it was not already taken into consideration at the beginning of the process; etc. Furthermore, it is not enough to determine what the four steps are. You have to determine their content: the reflection depending upon Chauvet's theology must be extended. Let me offer succinctly some partial aspects.

"To welcome" truly means a fully disinterested welcome; that is, without calculation (not motivated by the desire to well dispose the interlocutor about what is to come next), without any falseness (mere appearance), and without expectation of some benefit in return. This welcome, often well executed in different pastoral places, is contrary to the logic of the marketplace. It is there that the language of offer and demand makes itself totally unseemly,[52] even deadly to the degree that it

---

[51] Commission épiscopale de liturgie, 19.

[52] Chauvet uses the marketplace vocabulary while noting its ambiguity: *Les sacrements*, 204; ELV, 188. The bishops of the Episcopal Commission on the Liturgy emphasize that this language traps us. *Pastorale sacramentelle—Points de repère*, 20.

leads inevitably to the commercial paradigm opposite the attitude of Christ in the Gospel and of sacramental grace. Let us go even further! If we designate those who want to receive the sacrament of baptism for their infant by the term "askers," (*demandeurs*[53]) it is suitable to call the pastoral agents by the same name as those who meet and celebrate the sacrament with them: they themselves also ask to make the experience of the encounter of God with Jesus Christ in the sacrament; they also ask of those whom they meet to accept being on the road with them; they also ask for the sacrament for the infant and for the church that has received the mission to give glory to God and to work for the salvation of all. Would it be best then totally to abandon this term "asker"? Words like "candidate," "catechumen," or "confirmand" are better adapted when the subject wants him- or herself to receive the sacrament. Concerning infant baptism, the correct term is not easy to find since it means the parents who are both "companions" and "confessors": "those who present." But if, according to linguistic content, we hold that the choice of words (symbols) are not without accident in communication, then a revision of language is necessary so that a change of attitude may have a chance to work. It must be admitted that a disinterested welcome does not pass by itself on a human level—it presupposes a permanent conversion.

"To favor growth" demands some work both in the way of favoring progress and all that can be the object of the progress. In other words, in the framework of infant baptism it is a matter not only of finding an adapted way to teach adults (andragogy),[54] to search for the means for discovery and the possible apprenticeship of the Christian life in relationship to the God of Jesus Christ, but to spot what is the potential progress for each person in a soteriological perspective. The first building site in progress has already become the object of much pastoral effort, namely, the organization of meetings with parents (documents, audiovisual tools, pedagogical methods), but perhaps less the second. What progress to propose? What Good News to give for tasting? Which possible crossing

[53] Translator's note: in the marketplace known for supply and demand, the term *demandeur* might better be rendered as buyer, but the subsequent play on words in French would not translate well into English.

[54] We deliberately use this sometimes-controversial term "andragogy" to mean the theory and practice of adult formation, considering that it is better used in a learning situation. Cf. Malcolm Knowles, *The Adult Learner: A Neglected Species* (Houston: Gulf, 1984). See our article: Office de Catéchèse du Québec, *Dossiers d'andragogie religieuse* (Ottawa: Novalis, 1982–85).

and what illumination can open the way to happiness for the parents encountered, as much as for ourselves? There isn't an all-purpose solution: the goal is truly found in the common search, by the pastoral agents and the parents, about what can constitute a way of happiness that renders credible the salvation brought about by Christ. A religious sister working in pastoral care for baptism in her diocese, wrote:

> When the Gospel speaks of encounters of Jesus with his contemporaries, it tells us that this entails something good, something new in their lives. What can we do in order that the encounter with the Church may be good news in the lives of the parents who ask for baptism for their child? The happy 20–30 year olds say that deep down inside there is worry because they know about the instability of couples today. Many of their friends experience the failure of their love within ten years of marriage. Some marital counselors think that one of the reasons for this weakness is the lack of dialogue that the spouses have. If the occasion for baptism is for some an occasion for a true dialogue as a couple, an exchange with other couples or with the priest, it is already the beginning of good news.[55]

To favor growth presupposes bringing up to date what it means for each person—parents, children, and pastoral agents—to enter into a perspective of salvation in the light of the Easter Christ. It is there that the Scriptures bear an irreplaceable witness: not first of all to give a sufficient understanding about Jesus and what he can do, or to allow to live better the celebration of the sacrament, but to bear witness to the possible way of salvation that others preceding us have taken through Jesus Christ, and that is available to us today.

"To celebrate the sacrament" presupposes working on the quality of the celebration. This has for some years become a leitmotiv: the famous *ars celebrandi*! In fact the celebration of the sacrament can only release all its potential to the degree that the rites are done artfully, as is appropriate in a noble and simple way,[56] with enough reserve so as not to be overdone and with enough truth so as not to appear as mere illusion. In short the *ars celebrandi* is the essential key to the encounter with the present Christ who turns us toward the Father and to the en-

---

[55] Sr. François-Marie Kester, "Le baptême des petits enfants," *Célébrer* no. 249 (April 1995).
[56] Cf. SC no. 34.

counter with our brothers and sisters with whom we form one people in the Spirit. This means that the *ars celebrandi* does not only concern the rites themselves with respect to rubrics and the required adaptations, but also involves the right place[57] and the bodily attitude of each person—ministers and assembly. The work in progress is always open: how to favor for each person the right posture that is suitable (taking into consideration history and culture) to live the encounter with Christ and to support brothers and sisters in the same process, all the while maintaining the unity of the ecclesial community. Pastoral sacramental care must take charge of the enculturation of the living tradition of the church, which is the liturgical celebration.

"To care for what follows" supposes that we work both on the conditions of what follows from the first meeting forward and the characteristics of a true contemporary mystagogy. The position of the bishops of France sought to make the pastoral agents feel less guilty and to restore the sacramental fruits to their proper place: "There is no scandal in the sacraments not producing all that we would like. Rather it is necessary to see in them a place of testing, which allows us to be realistic and to renounce control over both the action of God and the future of others. . . . It is the reception itself of the sacrament and its celebration that should direct a new existence in its various aspects."[58]

However, beyond this affirmation the work in progress remains largely open to imagine attitudes and pastoral strategies that allow the pursuit of the way already begun, and to open it to a wider ecclesial dimension.[59] The idea of a postbaptismal year dear to Chauvet proved to be a happy initiative, especially for those who did not belong to some kind of movement or ecclesial group. It is still necessary to work on the content so as not to limit the final celebration presided over by the bishop. The research is open. It is the way we watch over the aftermath of the sacrament that verifies sacramental pastoral care, some of whose characteristics we have tried to indicate here.

[57] Cf. J.-Y. Hameline, *Une poétique du ritual*, Liturgie, no. 9 (Paris: Cerf, 1997), chap. 3 "Observations sur nos manières de célébrer."

[58] Commission épiscopale de liturgie, *Pastorale sacramentelle—Points de repère*, 23.

[59] Cf. Conference of Bishops of France, *Texte national pour l'orientation de la catéchèse en France et principes d'organisation* (Paris: Bayard–Cerf–Fleurus, 2006).

A CONCLUDING OVERTURE:
PASTORAL CARE OF THE PASCHAL MYSTERY

Sacramental pastoral care, understood in the spirit of Vatican II and drawing upon Chauvet's sacramental theology, leads us to the following goal: first, it is a matter of opening and following a way, the one—for each person—of his or her own existence, in relationship with the God of Jesus Christ, especially encountered (symbolically) in the sacraments. We can readily appraise it: no one leaves this adventure unscathed, neither those welcoming, those being accompanied, and those accompanying. For the relationship that Christ himself introduced with humanity passes through the mystery of his death and resurrection. In other words, all sacramental pastoral care—to the degree it gives a place to the sacrament as "the fact of redemption that is turned towards us in such a way that we can really encounter there the living Christ"[60]—is called to make itself *pastoral care of the paschal mystery*, charged to restore tirelessly the Easter way opened by Christ, "wherein we agree to die in order to enter into life."[61]

If the great goal of our time is to open for people of this age the opportunity of discovering true happiness, if this happiness, we believe, is what God wants for every person, and if this is fulfilled in the death and resurrection of Christ, then there is nothing more urgent than to assist our contemporaries to go to the heart of the faith that constitutes the paschal mystery, such as the sacraments access for us. Otherwise, "it is for nothing that you have become believers" (cf. 1 Cor 5:1-11).

[60] E. Schillebeeckx, *Le Christ, sacrement de la rencontre de Dieu*, 55.
[61] John Paul II, cf. n. 23 above.

Chapter 6

"Is that your liturgical movement?":
Liturgy and Sacraments
in an Ecumenical Ecclesiology[1]

Gordon W. Lathrop

What place does the liturgy have in ecumenical thought and practice, and what place do ecumenical considerations have in liturgical scholarship? Or, said differently, how might the practice of the sacraments in a renewed liturgy shape an ecumenical conception of "church"? These are our questions. They are rightly questions to take up in honor of Louis-Marie Chauvet whose sense of sacraments as identifying communal events has already contributed so much to an ecumenical ecclesiology.

CONGAR'S REPORT OF CULLMANN'S QUESTION

Begin with an account of three liturgies. The first two are from the remarkable, honest, and closely observed account, written by the Dominican theologian Yves Congar in his personal journal from the time of the Second Vatican Council, but only recently published. The date is October 11, 1962, the opening day of the council. The place is St. Peter's Church in Rome:

> At 8:35 am one hears over the sound system the distant noise of a half military march. Then the *Credo* is chanted. I have come here in order to *pray*: to *pray with*, to pray *in*. I have in fact prayed a

[1] This paper, in a somewhat different version, was first delivered on October 27, 2006, in Paris, under the title "La question d'autre: la place de la liturgie dans la recherche œcuménique," as part of an international colloquium celebrating the fiftieth anniversary of the Institut Supérieur de Liturgie at the Institut Catholique.

101

great deal. Nonetheless, to kill time a choir intones successively everything and anything. The most well known chants: *Credo, Magnificat, Adoro Te, Salve Regina, Veni Sancte Spiritus, Inviolata, Benedictus* . . . At first one sings along a little, but then one lets it go. . . . My God, you who have led me by ways that I have not chosen, I offer myself to you to be, if it is your will, an instrument of your Gospel in this event in the life of the Church, the Church that I love but that I wish could be less "Renaissance," less "Constantinian.". . . Applause is heard on St. Peter's Square. The pope must be coming. He enters, no doubt. I see nothing, behind six or seven ranks of cassocks that have climbed up on the chairs. For some moments, in the basilica, there is applause, but neither cries nor words. The *Veni Creator* is sung, in alternation with the Sistine Choir, which is nothing other than an opera company. *It should be abolished.* The pope, in a firm voice, chants the versicles and the prayers. The Mass begins, chanted exclusively by the Sistine Choir: several morsels of Gregorian and some polyphony. The liturgical movement has not penetrated the Roman Curia. This immense assembly says nothing, sings nothing. They say that the Jewish people is the people of the eye, the Greeks the people of the ear. There is nothing here except for the eye and for the musical ear: no liturgy of the Word. No spiritual word. I know that soon enough a Bible will be installed upon a throne, in order to preside over the Council. *But will it speak?* Will it be listened to? Will there be a moment for the Word of God?[2]

The next day, Friday, October 12, Congar continues:

I get a taxi to the reception at the French embassy. . . . Oscar Cullmann, Hébert Roux, Max Thurian and Roger Schutz [four French-speaking Protestant observers at the Council] are there. I kiss all of them on both cheeks. . . . Then Cullmann [a Lutheran professor at the Sorbonne and at the University of Basel] says, *à propos* of Thursday's ceremony, "So is that your liturgical movement?"

It seems to have been a casual, offhand question. But it is a piercing question, nonetheless, worthy of our continued consideration. And Congar himself later wrote, by way of reflective response: "Alas! The movement has not gotten through the Bronze Doors!"[3] One year later,

---

[2] Yves M.-J. Congar, *Mon journal du Concile*, vol. 1 (Paris: Cerf, 2002), 106–7.
[3] Ibid., 111–12.

the bronze doors seem to have been only partially penetrated. Père Congar writes of the opening liturgy of the second session, on Sunday, 29 September 1963:

> I am not at all able to interpret ecclesiologically the very structure of the ceremony: between two ranks of mute, spectator bishops, the pontifical court passes, costumed as if in the 16th century, preceding a pope who thus appears, all at the same time, like a temporal monarch and a like a hierarch: *above*, only above. The Sistine Choir coos; the Fathers take up one or two lines of the *Ave Maris Stella*. Will the Church keep *this* face? *This* appearance? Will it keep on presenting *that* sign? It seems to me evident at this moment that the Gospel is in the Church, but captive.[4]

We do not know if Professor Cullmann again asked his question.

But anyone who knows the ecumenical fortune of liturgical renewal knows that these events are not alone. The muting of the biblical word, the obscuring of the central Christian signs, the absence of communal participation, and the appearance of leaders and choirs as rulers or performers have been found widely in all our churches. Indeed, a third example might be a liturgy that took place on a much smaller scale. It was held several years ago at a North American Lutheran liturgy conference, a conference intended to encourage the renewal of liturgical practice in the local parishes of the Lutheran churches of Canada and the United States. The liturgy was to be a celebration of the Word. The hope of the planners seemed to have been to model the possibility of a rich and deep, public and communal Christian ritual that did not have to be a full Eucharist, but rather a liturgy focused in the Bible as the source and center of our gathering, reading, preaching, singing, and praying. One problem was that there was not a Bible or lectionary or gospel book in sight. There were many banners. And very many vested clergy and blaring trumpets. But no Bible. The liturgy began with a procession and a considerable amount of marching about. Scores of vested clergy and burning candles were ceremoniously moved to their places. Trumpets blared. Banners were waved. But neither Bible nor lectionary book. When at last someone rose into the ambo to read the Scripture, he held before himself a loose half sheet of paper containing the reading. Just then, perhaps as a kind of justice in that too-large room, the sound system failed, and we could

---

[4] Ibid., 401–2.

not even hear what was read. And when someone rose to preach, it was, as Père Congar would say of one of the presiders at a conciliar Mass, *"mal et sans onction,"*[5] or, as Lutherans would say, "without the gospel."

Had Père Congar been there, he might rightly have asked, "So is that your liturgical movement, your Lutheran devotion to the Word of God?"

I do not tell these stories in order simply to make us laugh ruefully and certainly not to bring us to despair. Anyone who cares about pastoral liturgical work will come to have too many memories of bad examples. But what is important in these stories is Cullmann's question and Congar's openness to it or the imagination of Congar's *reprise* of Cullmann's question and the possibility of a North American Lutheran openness to it.

"Is that your liturgical movement?"

The question should not be heard as impertinent or mean-spirited. Rather, at least as in Cullmann's mouth and in Congar's report, the question profoundly respects core values of the other, separated community in the Body of Christ—profoundly honors the deepest *charismata* of renewal alive in that community—but then gently urges, by means of both affirmation and admonition, the realization of these values and gifts in actual, public, communal life. The question supports self-awareness and self-criticism, such as was already present in Congar the diarist at the council, for example. His own lively questions find company. Even more, questions like this penetrate to the central matters that belong to all Christians—the word and sacrament of Christ's gift, a fully participating assembly gathered around this word and sacrament by the Spirit of God, and ministers who humbly and lovingly serve this assembly in its vocation—and ask how these things that are both central and common to us all might stand forth in utter clarity.

LITURGICAL MOVEMENT, ECUMENICAL MOVEMENT

Indeed, in a certain sense the liturgical movement inevitably opens onto the ecumenical movement. Inquiry into renewed Christian ritual practice cannot help but notice the practices of all Christian communities. And hope for the manifestation of Christian unity must attend to the ways in which local Christian assemblies also visibly demonstrate

[5] Ibid., 402.

that concern for unity and common witness. If your definition of *ecclesia* includes a community enacting the presence of Christ in Word and sacrament, then a concern for the unity of that *ecclesia* must also include a concern for the clarity and centrality of that Word and those sacraments. Cullmann's question becomes, deeply, "Is that church?" Renewal, the recovery in the life of the churches of the centrality of Jesus Christ for the sake of the life of the world and that recovery through the resources of the Bible and the liturgy, can be seen as a common theme of both movements. If we take the definition of Père Congar, it might even be argued that a certain *catholicisme ressourcé*, alive in all the churches, can be seen as the goal of both movements—that is, a "catholicism recentered in Christ, a catholicism that is at the same time biblical, liturgical, paschal, communitarian, ecumenical and missionary," as Congar has written.[6]

In any case, the inquiry into the origin and meaning of central Christian liturgical practices has been, since the nineteenth century, an ecumenical undertaking. The studies of the Protestants Edward Pusey in Oxford, Johann August Neander in Berlin, and Philip Schaff in New York had effect in nineteenth-century Roman Catholic circles, at the very beginnings of the Roman Catholic liturgical movement, just as the twentieth-century work of Lambert Beauduin, Romano Guardini, Pius Parsch, and, in America, Virgil Michel also had a profound effect on renewal movements in many Protestant churches. Responsible histories of the liturgical movement need to tell of this mutual influence, though they have not always done so. But the mutual influence continues: liturgical scholarship, at its best, is an international and ecumenical conversation, a conversation carried on, for example, in the *Societas Liturgica*, but also in the North American Academy of Liturgy or in the recently formed Nordic society, *Leitourgia*. In fact, this conversation has proceeded so far and the mutual influence has been so strongly felt in the preparation of new liturgical materials in many different churches that one may rightly speak now of an "ecumenical liturgical movement." Furthermore, in recent years, historical, pastoral, and theological studies of liturgical practice have at least sometimes demonstrated a respectful, sensitive, and honest ecumenical awareness. And the important statements of the Faith and Order Commission of

---

[6] Yves M.-J. Congar, *Le Concile au jour le jour: Deuxième session* (Paris: Cerf, 1964), 45: *"catholicisme recentré sur le Christ, et qui est également biblique, liturgique, pascal, communautaire, œcuménique et missionaire."*

the World Council of Churches—especially, *Baptism, Eucharist and Ministry*—have included reflections on liturgical meaning and even counsel for liturgical practice, urging self-examination in the worship life of the churches.

The very goals of the liturgical movement can be articulated in ways that would be recognizable in many Christian communities. One could say the matter this way: In the liturgical movement, Christian communities continually inquire of themselves and of their neighbors whether the biblical Word and the preaching of the life-giving Gospel of Jesus Christ, the eucharistic meal and the prayers for and sending of help to the poor of the world are at the center of every Christian Sunday gathering. They inquire of themselves and their neighbors whether the assembly fully participates in these enacted signs, this very simple and basic *ordo* of Christian worship—*participates*, thus, in lively song and in ritual gesture, in a beautiful and accessible vernacular language, in serving each other mutually, in eating and drinking and in the gathering of gifts for the poor. They ask, furthermore, whether there is an open and clear process for anyone to come to and through the catechesis and the water-bath that joins us to this assembly. They ask whether the ministers who assist the assembly serve in a spirit of love and humility. And they ask whether all this is done in a way that respects and welcomes local cultural gifts. Or, said negatively, Christian communities inquire of themselves and of their neighbors whether secondary ceremonies, a display of rank and position, overly important musical choirs and professional music, a desire to entertain, an accent upon gender difference, or a spirit of religious individualism or religious consumerism or denominational exclusivity or local self-importance—to name only a few of the obstacles—are obscuring the central matters of Christian liturgy. Gently we should ask each other—about each of our local assemblies, not only our great councils and area-wide meetings—"So, is that your liturgical movement?"

I think that the counsel of the Ditchingham Statement, written by an international Faith and Order gathering in 1994, is quite correct:

> But the patterns of word and table, of catechetical formation and baptism, of Sunday and the week, of *Pascha* and the year, and of assembly and ministry around these things—the principal pairs of Christian liturgy—do give us a basis for a mutually encouraging conversation between the churches. Churches may rightly ask

each other about the local inculturation of this *ordo*. They may call each other toward a maturation in the use of this pattern or a renewed clarification of its central characteristics or, even, toward a conversion to its use. Stated in their simplest form, these things are the "rule of prayer" in the churches, and we need them for our own faith and life and for a clear witness to Christ in the world.[7]

But then the Statement continues with a small ecumenical celebration:

And we need each other to learn anew of the richness of these things. Churches may learn from each other as they seek for local renewal. One community has treasured preaching, another singing, another silence in the word, another sacramental formation, another the presence of Christ in the transfigured human person and in the witnesses of the faith who surround the assembly, another worship as solidarity with the poor. As churches seek to recover the great pairs of the *ordo*, they will be helped by remembering together with other Christians the particular charisms with which each community has unfolded the patterns of Christian worship, and by a mutual encouragement for each church to explore the particular gifts which it brings to enrich our koinonia in worship. This pattern or *ordo* of Christian worship belongs most properly to each local church, that is, to "all in each place." All the Christians in a given place, gathered in assembly around these great gifts of Christ, are the whole catholic church dwelling in this place.[8]

At its best, the liturgical movement in all the churches has called for the clear recovery of the Scripture at the heart of our meetings, of Eucharist, baptism, and healing ministry as the context in which we may understand Christ in the Scriptures, and of a consequent ethical testimony to Christ by mutual service and sharing. These marks of Christian identity, as Chauvet has called them,[9] are the very pattern of the life of the church—the way we may know a community is indeed

---

[7] "Towards Koinonia in Worship: Report of the Consultation," par. 7, in Thomas F. Best and Dagmar Heller, eds., *So We Believe, So We Pray*, Faith and Order Paper 171 (Geneva: World Council of Churches, 1995), 7.

[8] Ibid.

[9] Chauvet, *The Sacraments: The Word of God at the Mercy of the Body* (Collegeville, MN: Liturgical Press, 2001), 20, 28–29.

Christ's church—and, at the same time, their clarity in each assembly is the principal goal of liturgical renewal.

I think that all of this—the overlapping ecumenical and liturgical movements, the genuine hope for a certain *ressourcement*, the shared development of the liturgical renewal and its shared goals, the central matters of Word and sacrament, of assembly and ministry, the desire for a transparent, open, and humble witness and service to the world, the desire for each of our assemblies to be continually renewed, the mutual encouragement and the careful but willing mutual admonition—all this is hidden in Cullmann's question: "Is that your liturgical movement?" The very ability to ask this question implies an ecumenical-liturgical ecclesiology.

OBSTACLES TO AN ECUMENICAL-LITURGICAL ECCLESIOLOGY

Still, we have come to a time when many people have lost interest in both ecumenical and liturgical questions. Cullmann's question might now be understood to be impossible, it being assumed that we no longer have such access to each other. It is not simply that ours is a time marked by resurgent local identities of all sorts, by a fierce politics of identity-purity that has also come to expression in a new confessional and denominational rigor. But, even more, it is also a time when "renewal" of any kind will be questioned, with deep suspicions about the hidden exercise of power: "Whose renewal?" will be the question. "Who benefits from change?" It is a time when specific localities are important, even though some authorities have responded, often unsuccessfully, with a new insistence on uniform, so-called universal practices. Furthermore, it is a time when history itself is suspect: who is telling the story and for what reasons? And who has been silenced in the telling? And, as for ecumenism, who wants a larger ecclesial institution anyway? Is that what is meant by unity?

While I think that we should all resist the politics of identity-purity, these other postmodern themes should not frighten us. On the contrary, I think we can welcome them gladly as allies and old friends. Christians should indeed engage in a critique of power, calling always for the greatest transparency in any exercise of authority. In a liturgical-ecumenical ecclesiology, the only important authority is the authority to announce the mercy of God and call the community to service and love. Any other authority is apt to stray from the meaning of Jesus Christ. And locality is immensely important to Christian liturgical practice—the liturgical assembly is always a concrete local assembly—though also an assembly always in communion with the "more-than-local," as Edward Schillebeeckx has said.[10] Furthermore, a certain kind of history has indeed been overused and over-interpreted as the source for liturgical renewal. The Eucharist has a more diverse history than we have ordinarily told, though that ought not discourage our efforts at reform. Rather, the source of the Eucharist is Jesus Christ even now breaking into our symbolization and ritualization of meals and making the resultant open celebration to be the place of his self-giving in the Spirit for the life of the world. In thought about that present juxtaposition—Jesus and our own ritual meal practice—there are rich, current resources for an ongoing renewal. And, finally, the goal of both the ecumenical movement and prayer for Christian unity has more and more emerged not as a large, centralized institution of any kind, but as a communion of local churches, concrete local assemblies sending signs of recognition, encouragement, and support to each other, as a richly diverse *church-of-churches*, with our leaders and bishops as servants of this communion.

But the postmodern themes have discouraged us. It is easier to attend to scholarship without the complicated calls for reform, easier to do theology without pastoral implications, easier to rehearse old ways of telling history, easier simply to support our own ecclesial community without bothering about the others.

But it is not more faithful to do so. Nor is it more interesting.

Still, even more discouraging have been some of the official stances of the churches. On June 29, 2007, for example, the Roman Catholic Congregation for the Doctrine of the Faith, at the direction of the Bishop of Rome, published the document "Responses to Some Questions Regarding Certain Aspects of the Doctrine of the Church." It was a document intended to underscore anew several assertions that had been pointedly made in the declaration *Dominus Iesus* published by the same Congregation in the year 2000. Neither in that declaration nor in the more recent "Responses" do the central things of the ecumenical-liturgical movement, the "marks" of Christian identity that we have been considering here, play a major role. The ecumenical-liturgical insight that "church" is always at least a participating assembly gathered around Jesus Christ in bath, word, prayers, table, and

[10] Edward Schillebeeckx, *The Church with a Human Face* (New York: Crossroad, 1985), 55ff.

sending to the poor, remains unconsidered. Rather, ecclesiology is built out of the assertion of Roman primacy, making "unity" into a thing that can be seen rather than an article of faith, a "mark" that can be observed only in the Roman churches, leaving other Christian groups at least "defective" and, more likely, not "churches" at all.

Still, other Roman Catholic leaders have spoken with a different voice, recalling different "marks," ones more clearly evident in participating local liturgical assemblies. The Roman Catholic participation in the process of the so-called Lima Document and in a variety of bilateral dialogues, for example, joined in asserting our common baptism. If we are "incorporated into Christ" in baptism—and if the church is none other than that *corpus Christi*, always grounded in baptism—then the baptized are part of church. Furthermore, the Roman Catholic Church in October 1999 officially signed and proclaimed the following declaration, recalling the hearing of the word in assembly: "The Lutheran Churches and the Roman Catholic Church have together listened to the good news proclaimed in Holy Scripture . . ." (*Joint Declaration* 14). In this regard, we are especially helped by the kind clarity and godly dissent of another Roman Catholic archbishop, Rembert Weakland of Milwaukee, when he wrote about *Dominus Iesus*:

> In my opinion the documents of Vatican Council II made the role of baptism much more significant as entrance into the Body of Christ and thus into the church: "All who have been justified by faith in baptism are members of Christ's body and have a right to be called Christians, and so are deservedly recognized as sisters and brothers of the Lord by the children of the Catholic Church" (*Lumen Gentium*). The documents of Vatican Council II do not hesitate to use the word "churches" to characterize these communities of the Reformation (*Unitatis redintegratio*). Unfortunately, *Dominus Iesus* does not take into account the enormous progress made after Vatican Council II in the mutual recognition of each other's baptisms and the ecclesial significance of such recognition. What is disappointing about this document is that so many of our partners in ecumenical dialogues will find its tone heavy, almost arrogant and condescending. To them it is bound to seem out of keeping with the elevated and open tone of the documents of Vatican Council II. It ignores all of the ecumenical dialogues of the last 35 years, as if they did not exist. None of the agreed statements are cited. Has no progress in working toward convergence of theological thought occurred in these 35 years? Our partners have every reason to believe we

may not be sincere in such dialogues. We seem to be talking out of both sides of the mouth, for example, making agreements with the Lutherans on Monday and calling into question the validity of their ecclesial nature on Tuesday.[11]

Nonetheless, in such a climate, it seems to make little sense to ask Cullmann's question. Official opposition—in many churches, not only in the Roman Curia—has discouraged us.

RESOURCES FOR A MOVEMENT RENEWED

But, in the face of the postmodern discouragements, there remains, for example, the fascinating assertion of Patrick Prétot, reworking the thought of Michel de Certeau: "Christianity is the religion of which the characteristic is to think of itself under the sign of 'not without the other.'"[12] And, in the face of the official discouragements, there remain the remarkable words of Roger Schutz, one of those four ecumenical guests whom Congar kissed on both cheeks on the evening of Cullmann's question, words addressed to each of the new brothers of the Community of Taizé and still reaching out to all of us: "Never resign yourself to the scandal of the separation of Christians, all so readily professing love for their neighbor, yet remaining divided. Make the unity of Christ's body your passionate concern."[13] And these contradictions call to us, "whether the time is favorable or unfavorable" (2 Tim 4:2).

Of course, an ecumenical ecclesiology arising from and practiced by an ecumenical liturgical movement is not a full response to the continuing need for Christians to think of their religion under the sign of "not without the other" or for Christians to make unity their "passionate concern." But it is a modest, though clear beginning.

And there exist important resources for making that beginning again. The Constitution on the Sacred Liturgy of the Second Vatican Council is one such resource, especially in its remarkable seventh paragraph about the "presences of Christ" in the liturgical assembly. In its repetitions, the text nearly sings of Jesus Christ in the assembly:

[11] The Milwaukee *Catholic Herald*, September 10, 2000.

[12] Patrick Prétot, "Écritures et liturgie: Épiphanie d'une présence," unpublished paper, 2: *"le christianisme est la religion dont la particularité et de se penser sous le signe du 'pas sans l'autre.'"*

[13] Brother Roger of Taizé, *Parable of Community* (London: Mowbray, 1984), 13.

He is present with his power in the sacraments, so that when anyone baptizes it is Christ himself who baptizes. He is present in his word, since he himself speaks when the holy scriptures are read in church. He is present, in short, when the church prays and sings, for he himself promised, "Where two or three are gathered in my name, I am there among them" (Matthew 18:20).[14]

This basic assertion of Vatican II can also be recognized as a basic assertion of the liturgical movement and as a foundation for the ecumenical movement. It can continue to animate our local work for renewal and can be the grounds for our turning to neighboring churches, even churches separated from us, with respectful affirmation and admonition.

There are also resources in the ecumenically important work of Martin Luther. In his 1539 essay, *Von den Conziliis und Kirchen*,[15] Luther asked a pastoral question: how can a simple person tell when a gathered community is the church? How can a needy person find the assembly of God? In his answer, he brought his theology to work. You can know that an assembly is the church of Jesus Christ, he says, when at least seven marks or *Kennzeichen* or signs of life are present in strength. This assertion—and others like it from both Luther and his colleague Philip Melanchthon—is the very origin of the idea of *notae ecclesiae*, "marks of the church," in theological debate.[16] But here the discussion is not polemical. Indeed, it is rather a proposal of pastoral ecclesiology. For Luther, in this essay, the seven signs are these: the preached word of God, the sacrament of baptism, the sacrament of the altar, the use of absolution, the calling and consecrating of ministers, the public use of thanksgiving and prayer, and, nota bene, shared suffering. This list—including this last sign as well—is a pastoral-liturgical

---

[14] *Constitution on the Sacred Liturgy* (Collegeville, MN: Liturgical Press, 1963), 8: "*Praesens adest virtute sua in Sacramentis, ita ut cum aliquis baptizat, Christus ipse baptizet. Praesens adest in verbo suo, siquidem ipse loquitur dum sacrae Scripturae in Ecclesia leguntur. Praesens adest denique dum supplicat et psallit Ecclesia, ipse qui promisit: 'Ubi sunt duo vel tres congregati in nomine meo, ibi sum in medio eorum'* (Mt. 18:20)."

[15] *D. Martin Luthers Werke* 50 (Weimar, 1914), 509–653; see also "On the Councils and the Church," LW 41, 9–178.

[16] See Timothy J. Wengert, "A Brief History of the Marks of the Church," in Gordon W. Lathrop and Timothy J. Wengert, *Christian Assembly: Marks of the Church in a Pluralistic Age* (Minneapolis: Fortress, 2004), 17–36.

list. It is an encouragement toward renewal and, at the same time, a calling toward realism, humility, ethical consequence, and the abandonment of triumphalism. This little list can be an ecumenical treasure for mutual encouragement, for the asking of the question of Cullmann among each other in other words.

But there are more recent resources as well: the sacramental and liturgical statements of the World Council of Churches, the papers on liturgy and ecumenism read at the *Centro Pro Unione*[17] in Rome, and the work of Chauvet, to name only a few. These all call us to the work of Cullmann's question—to mutual affirmation and admonition that encourages among us a renewed clarity of word, sacrament, and responding ethics, of Luther's *Kennziechen* for the church or Chauvet's marks of Christian identity or the Second Vatican Council's places of Christ's presence.

The renewed movement, focused on the central things, might look something like this: We might recall that the three-year Lectionary, developed as *Ordo Lectionum* in Roman Catholic practice since the reforms of the Second Vatican Council, has—with certain adaptations—come to be used widely by many other churches, especially as the *Revised Common Lectionary*, used in North America, Great Britain, and widely elsewhere in the world. Pastors could consider meeting ecumenically, week by week, with other parish leaders from other, separated communities, to discuss the meanings of the shared texts in each place—to explore the possibilities in these texts for preaching and for catechesis in the present time. Then, recalling that in many language areas the shared texts of liturgy—the *Gloria* and the *Credo*, the *Sursum corda* dialogue and the *Sanctus*, for example—have been translated together, as texts we have in common, we might rejoice in these texts and resist any attempt to change them, unless the changes are made together, *"not without the other."* Further, even if it is impossible to celebrate Eucharist together at this time, we might consider inviting and welcoming ecumenical visitors to our Sunday liturgies as witnesses to hope. Then we might ask our visitors to tell us what they see in the celebration, what they would affirm and what they might question. If we have a catechumenate, we might consider welcoming the catechumens of other, separated communities to some common discussion of the meaning of Christian faith in the present time. Or, even

[17] James F. Puglisi, *Liturgical Renewal as a Way to Christian Unity* (Collegeville, MN: Liturgical Press, 2005).

if this is not possible, we might consider the possibility of some people from one parish being present at the baptisms being practiced in neighboring, separated communities, and vice versa. We might even consider this: all the Christians in a single place—in a village or a neighborhood—might come together to build a single, shared baptistery that would subsequently be used by them all, on the model of the ancient baptisteries of the Mediterranean and early European world.

And scholars themselves might also recall both the question of Cullmann and the openness of Congar to that question. They might, for example, consider the method of the former archbishop of Uppsala, Yngve Brilioth. In his *Eucharistic Faith and Practice, Evangelical and Catholic*,[18] as also in his *Brief History of Preaching*,[19] Brilioth made of "motif research" an intentionally irenic method. While studying those central marks of the church found in preaching and Eucharist, he saw that the historical diversities of Christian practice could be regarded as enriching the whole church and unfolding the whole mystery of Christ. At the same time, particular communities could still be urged to recover a fuller balance in their life, urged to let the central matters of Christian worship stand forth as central. It is a method worthy of emulation. A critically irenic method belongs to a spirit marked by "not without the other."

"Is that your liturgical movement?" I have imagined this question of Cullmann, reported by Congar, as the question of a friend, himself deeply involved in the pastoral and theological recovery of sacramental life in Christ in his own church. The question is one we rightly ask each other, still today, encouraging each other against despair and rejoicing with each other when the Word and sacrament of Christ's gift are set out clearly, in a local participating assembly in communion with the other assemblies—in the church—itself sign of the mercy of God for the life of the world.

[18] London: SPCK, 1965. Originally, *Nattvarden i evangeliskt gudtjänstliv* (Stockholm: SKDB, 1951).

[19] Philadelphia: Fortress, 1965. Originally, *Predikans historia* (Lund: Gleerup, 1945).

Part 4

Liturgy and Ethics

> The sacraments allow us to *see* what is said in the letter of the
> Scriptures, to *live* what is said because they leave on the social
> body of the Church, and on the body of each person, a mark
> that becomes a command to make what is said real in everyday
> life. . . . Only on this condition can the letter be vivified by the
> Spirit; only on this condition does it emerge as Word.[1]

As Bruce Morrill notes at the beginning of his chapter, Christians
from the very beginning surely were conscious of the split between the
mysteries celebrated and the way of life that flows from them. The result can be a feeling of guilt, at times deadly, which Nietzsche vigorously denounced in *The Genealogy of Morals*. In the light of pardon and
justification, however, this Christian consciousness of abandonment
can also become a formidable pointer for ethics. Still, the moral dynamic does not proceed only from faith. It exhibits itself so authentically in culture that Christian theology, especially in the Catholic
tradition, grants it a justifiable autonomy, not only of existence but
also of the call for Christ's disciples.

It is this that leads moral theologian Philippe Bordeyne to pay attention to the recent methodological developments in the ethical question. After the sudden interest in ethics that we experienced in the
second half of the twentieth century, we ask ourselves today, sometimes in a radical way, about the subjective and social conditions of the
possibility of ethics, from which arises the interest of contemporary
moral theology in the resources of moral formation contained in the
liturgy. This historical contextualization is important for a good grasp

---

[1] Louis-Marie Chauvet, *Symbol and Sacrament: A Sacramental Reinterpretation
of Christian Existence*, trans. Patrick Madigan and Madeleine Beaumont
(Collegeville, MN: Liturgical Press, 1995), 226–27.

of what Chauvet wanted to do, of those questions to which he tried to respond by evoking Scripture and the tradition. Sacramental theology permits him particularly to assert that action required by a lived and celebrated faith can be nothing other than the *sacramentum* referred to as the mystery of Christian existence summed up totally by the gift that Christ makes of himself to his disciples. Hereafter, ethics has no reason to allow itself to be instrumentalized by social imperatives that are supposed to impose on it the norm of efficaciousness, with the purpose of reducing the split between word and action. Such a vision, too simple to be true, contradicts the mystery of the Christian identity, paradoxical because it is paschal. Against these invading sirens of ethics, Chauvet mobilizes Christian liturgy to resist the schema of technical performance. Developing a perspective of fundamental theology and attentive to the lengthy mediations of salvation, he asserts that Christian faith assumes silence and the night, without reflecting the deceptive tomorrows that eclipse absence and mourning. Thus Chauvet places anew the paschal mystery at the heart of theological ethics, which had probably given excessive weight to eschatology due to its necessary debate with the secular eschatologies of Marxist inspiration (Ernst Bloch).

It is precisely on this paschal base that Morrill, as liturgical theologian, undertakes constructing a theological approach from Christian existence sensitive to the gestation of drama that is the cataclysm in the ethical conscience of our contemporaries. Successively questioning Scripture, the practical-fundamental theology of Jean-Baptiste Metz, and the moral philosophy of Edith Wyschogrod, he asserts the claim of Christian faith to traverse the dilemmas of our time in a liberating manner. The story of the life given by Christ, specifically transmitted in the eucharistic memorial through time, appears as formative in the face of the current challenges of morality. This story prohibits the nullification of a possible critique of the past by a culture that gorges itself on ephemeral images that just as quickly vanish into oblivion and are thus ruled out to orient the present and the future. Liturgical actions affect believers deeply by their persistence in time, lived by the community. The paschal memory works on the eruption of the divine into human space by a gift always reiterated by the very person of Christ, Savior of human history.

Just as Morrill insists with Chauvet on the capacity of the paschal mystery to receive the contemporary drama and to subvert it, Bordeyne stands more on the originality, in the very individualistic contemporary context, of a positive experience of grace that makes itself known to subjects as it acts in spite of everything when they enter into contact with a believing community. This "paradoxical encounter" with the divine majesty and its power of transformation, articulated in theological terms by the liturgist Jean-Yves Hameline, is capable of making the subjects stronger to confront the drama of ethics. Conversely, the Christian experience of liturgy allows us more calmly to assume in the light of the forgiving and transforming grace of God the aspect of failure and of passivity that transects the most noble ethical endeavors.

The common point between the two authors is their placing each other on guard against oversimplification about the relationship between ethics and liturgy, which would end up in a reciprocal instrumentalization. For this reason, they use terms that aim to maintain the "paradoxical" tension (Morrill) and the "horizon" of encounter (Bordeyne). In reading these two chapters, we remember that the relationship between the two fields implies an effort at attention, one to the other, rich with new insights. Such would appear to be the practical fruits of the dialogue between the two theological disciplines, ethics and liturgy, that deserve to know each other better and to face their common problematic.

Chapter 7

The Ethical Horizon of Liturgy

Philippe Bordeyne

The manner of introducing ethical inquiry into work dedicated to liturgy and sacraments has changed over the past twenty years. At the risk of forcing the connection, let us say that ethics is no longer only the "bad conscience" of liturgists careful to make Christian worship come out of the very restrictive framework of celebration and to open itself to practical considerations. As the liturgical movement never ceased to impress upon us, "we would misunderstand liturgy and religion if we isolate them from life. They are not actions that are sufficient in themselves, but on the contrary they are an appeal to witness that all our lives belong to God."[1] Louis-Marie Chauvet joined in this legacy when he examined "the uncomfortable tension between the sacramental pole of institution and the ethical pole of verification."[2] He presupposed on the one hand, contrary to all ethical skepticism toward worship, that the celebration of the sacraments was prone to transform daily life, and on the other hand that there was nothing automatic, whence the necessary verification. But then everything happened as if the critical pivot was in the hands of ethics, which aroused a lively admiration in the 1980s.

---

[1] Joseph André Jungmann, *L'annonce de la foi, expression de la bonne nouvelle*, trans. R. Virrion (Mulhouse: Salvator, 1965), 163.

[2] Chauvet, *Symbole et sacrement: une relecture sacramentelle de l'existence chrétienne* (Paris: Cerf, 1987), 234; Chauvet, *Symbol and Sacrament: A Sacramental Reinterpretation of Christian Existence* (Collegeville, MN: Liturgical Press, 1995), 228. Hereafter the corresponding page numbers for the English language versions of both *Les sacrements* and *Symbole et Sacrement* will be indicated by "ELV, p." The reader may discern which work is being referenced from the French work cited.

Today ethics is less sure of itself. On what grounds are the criteria of verification for the liturgy laid down when the plurality of norms and of systems of legitimation make the formulation of consensus about ethical priorities more hypothetical? The current crisis makes us become conscious that the rational faculties were held as givens in the normative structure conceived by the Enlightenment. At the dawn of the twenty-first century, the moral formation of subjects, the transmission of values, the acquisition of aptitude to lead one's life, have become the most important questions,[3] and moral theologians are in search of communitarian spaces for the training of ethics. Whence the perspective of this chapter: From the point of view of ethical theology, what are the liturgical resources for initiating subjects into the moral life?

We will begin by presenting the epistemological framework where the question about the ethical horizon on the liturgy emerges: the problem of identity and the renewal of the ethics of virtue, studies on the ethical potential of practical rituals, and attention to the power of renewal contained in the sacramental encounter with Christ dead and risen. Then we will reread Chauvet's contribution from the point of view of theological ethics. From the start let us say how indebted we are to him for having delved into the *thought* about the complex connections between ethics and liturgy in the philosophical and theological categories that burst from liturgy and sacramental theology. With the risk of the maze of "multiple languages of our time,"[4] Chauvet respects the true autonomy of ethical questioning. Typical of his age, the central category of "verification," however, gets in the way of access to the current questioning about the genesis of the moral subject. The final part of the chapter will demonstrate how we can depend on Chauvet to employ a fundamental anthropology about the subject seized by grace, taking into account the lived experience of the liturgy in the postmodern world and some of the current challenges this presents for moral formation.

---

[3] Volker Eid, hrsg. [ed.], *Moralische Kompetenz: Chancen der Moralpädagogik in einer pluralen Lebenswelt* (Mainz: Matthias-Grünewald, 1995).

[4] *Gaudium et Spes*, no. 44, 2.

LITURGY—
A NEW CHAPTER FOR FUNDAMENTAL MORALS

The place of liturgy in moral theology has evolved considerably. At the beginning of the twentieth century, participation in the liturgical life was among the "commandments of the church" inscribed on the first tablet of the Decalogue. A number of obligations toward God were taught as being in conformity with the virtue of religion. This approach embraced the exercise of virtue as a code established by the authorities of the church, which greatly reduced St. Thomas's perspective, and underestimated its teleological turn. In the midst of the twentieth century, the specificity of Christian morality led to the evaluation of the sacramental life as the place where the moral life of the Christian was fed.[5] Beginning in the 1980s the communitarian problematic appearing in the United States reached the communal liturgy as a privileged place where abilities to live morally following Christ were forged. This new focus must be studied in a social context including its theoretical explanation.

Renewal of the Virtues and Christian Identity in Moral Theology

Facing the redeployment of European universities in the nineteenth and twentieth centuries, Catholic moral theology sought to assimilate the normative system conceived by the Enlightenment, showing that it was not incompatible with the legacy of medieval theology. Confident in creation restored to its full dignity by redemption, did not St. Thomas have great respect for the faculties of practical reason formalized in the structure of natural law, the immediate norm of morality? These efforts permitted a passage beyond certain ideological oppositions between church and state and attenuated the image of obscurantism attached to the Catholic Church, giving it the conceptual tools to tackle the ethical problems connected to a changing society.[6] With hindsight it seems that this search for harmony with modernity concluded by masking the very original contribution of Christianity to the moral formation of subjects, especially through catechetical, liturgical, and sacramental practices, or through charitable works.

---

[5] Bernhard Häring, *La loi du Christ. Théologie morale à l'intention des prêtres et des laïcs* (Tournai: Desclée, 1955–59).

[6] See the importance of natural law in the social encyclical of Leo XIII, *Rerum Novarum*, 1891.

In a different way, depending upon region and school, moral theologians became aware of the problem of law and freedom that appeared with Nominalism and became central in the Enlightenment perspective. This problem should not hide the rich patrimony of virtues, known in ancient philosophy, and largely taken up by the fathers of the church, becoming central in the Thomist conception of the Christian life drawn toward the beatific vision.[7] But the renewal of the ethics of virtue simultaneously led their reformulation into narrative categories, by either drawing from the rich Christian patrimony and contemporary literary works[8] or underlining the capacity for the great Christian story of salvation to fashion the subjects in a preceding tradition.[9] Under the influence of philosopher Alasdair MacIntyre, notably, the Aristotelian virtues have been reinterpreted in the perspective of identity, the measure of the narrative character of all human life.[10] But other moral theologians have explored the path of identity in a more interdisciplinary way to elaborate an anthropology of moral dispositions.[11]

The ethics of virtue enlarged the spectrum of the questions likely to inspire subjects to aim for the good and to endeavor to achieve it.[12] In a world moving away from tradition, where respect for law is no longer interiorized, the problematic of identity appears to be able to give a taste for ethical adventure. This supposes that one learns to combine all the palette of virtues to achieve human identity in the competitive contexts where concrete lives are woven.[13] Moral theology takes into consideration these displacements to think about the connection that Scripture has with traditional sources. The lawyer in the Gospel of Luke, familiar with the normative universe, asks Jesus: "[W]hat must I

[7] Servais Pinckaers, *Les sources de la morale chrétienne. Sa méthode, son contenu, son histoire* (Fribourg: Éditions Universitaires de Fribourg, 1985).

[8] Dietmar Mieth, *Dichtung, Glaube und Moral. Studien zur Begründung einer narrativen Ethik* (Mainz: Matthias-Grünewald, 1983) (2).

[9] Stanley Hauerwas, *The Peaceable Kingdom: A Primer in Christian Ethics* (Notre Dame, IN: University of Notre Dame Press, 1983).

[10] Alasdair MacIntyre, *After Virtue: A Study in Moral Theory* (Notre Dame, IN: University of Notre Dame Press, 2007).

[11] Thomas Laubach, hrsg. [ed.], *Ethik und Identität: Festschrift für Gerfried W. Hunold zum 60. Geburtstag* (Tübingen: Francke, 1998).

[12] Vincent Leclercq, "La morale des vertus dans la formation des futurs prêtres," *Seminarium*, XLVI, no. 4 (2006): 895–921.

[13] James F. Keenan, "Vertu et identité," *Concilium* 285 (October 2000): 87–96.

do to inherit eternal life?" (Luke 10:25). Today entrance into Christian ethics proceeds from a different question, finely induced by the story of the Good Samaritan: "Who might I become if I walk in the steps of Christ?"

Formation of Character in the Community's Liturgy

The growing interest in theological ethics for the liturgy joins in a general questioning about the resources for a lived faith. The communitarian strain has forged the notion of character to translate the influence of motivations and of communitarian beliefs on the capacity to act.[14] The Christian community is founded on the collective decision to live the paschal mystery in faith and thus on the acceptance that everyone's identity is formed through the story of the life, death, and resurrection of Jesus. The community is not a reservoir of doctrines or visions of a predetermined world but, rather, the historical framework that enables the faithful to configure their own lives to the story of Jesus and from it to receive the potential for a moral imagination.

This insistence on the particularity of Christian ethics does not impede its opening itself to the universal. The structure of fulfillment of the Scriptures, which passes through the liturgy, impedes any exemplarism in the following of Christ. Just as Jesus is presented as the heir to the kingdom that he announces, so likewise Christians refuse to define the ethical sense of Jesus' story that continues to spread in the history of the world. Through the resurrection, Jesus is confirmed in "his vocation to announce the Kingdom of God and to make it present."[15] God stamps his seal on the promises transmitted through the prophets awaiting the end times. The liturgy, which replaces the story of Jesus in the hope of Israel, guarantees the tension of the community toward the future that exceeds it. Interest in the liturgy is at the heart of a communitarian ethic.

More recently, it places more light on the enrollment in the story of Jesus in some of the specific rites "that enable a discernment."[16] The

---

[14] Stanley Hauerwas, *Character and the Christian Life* (San Antonio: Trinity University Press, 1975). The Methodist theologian was the student of James Gustafson who began the retooling of moral theology in Scripture.

[15] Stanley Hauerwas, *The Peaceable Kingdom*, 79.

[16] Stanley Hauerwas & Samuel Wells, eds., *The Blackwell Companion to Christian Ethics* (Malden: Blackwell, 2004).

influence of Hauerwas's Catholic students,[17] who practice a stricter liturgical *ordo* than his Protestant students of the "low church" movement, is evident here. The enactment of the ritual holds all their attention: the assembly that becomes a body in the fraternal greetings, then in the entrance song, the confession of sins where they renounce violence, asking God's pardon, etc. This more concrete approach of the liturgy restores to communities the carnal aspect of faith and thereby of character. Restored to its place of honor are the following: the voice that proclaims, preaches, asks pardon and praises; the ear that listens to the Word and welcomes it; the hands that receive the Body of Christ that are lifted toward God and are joined with others in fraternal links; the foreheads that allow themselves to be washed in baptismal water in order "to find the true life in the life of Christ."[18]

Sacraments Offer a Transforming Encounter with Christ

These recent developments allow us to better grasp, *a posteriori*, the Catholic hesitations in the face of a certain Protestant way of posing the connection between ethics and liturgy.[19] To insist so much on the good attitudes forged through regular participation in worship, one runs the risk of communitary exemplarism, which Catholic authors do not fail to denounce. This focusing on the liturgical community seems incompatible with the ecclesiological renewal of moral theology since Vatican II and with the opening to the world. Even the medieval tradition of natural law was constituted in dialogue with philosophical and religious traditions on the subject of ethics.[20] In overevaluating faith in relationship to love and justice, the Protestant communitarians seem to neglect the principle of the correct autonomy of civil and political institutions.[21]

But Catholic theologians also fear liturgical exemplarism. The gap between ritual customs and the formation of character remains a complex epistemological problem, also studied very little even in Protes-

---

[17] Lisa Sowle Cahill, "L'éthique communautarienne et le catholicisme américain," *Recherches de Science Religieuse*, 95/1 (January–March 2007): 21–40.

[18] Stanley Hauerwas, *The Peaceable Kingdom*, 93.

[19] See the article "Liturgy and Ethics," *Journal of Religious Ethics* 7/2 (1979), with Margaret Farley's response to the contributions of Paul Ramsey and Don Saliers.

[20] Jean Porter, *Natural and Divine Law. Reclaiming the Tradition for Christian Ethics* (Ottawa: Novalis, 1999).

[21] *Gaudium et Spes*, no. 36.

tant theology.[22] It is even more acutely evident that the sacramental rites introduce a true discontinuity with ordinary life.[23] Nevertheless, the ethics of virtue opens a promising field for theological research and pastoral praxis in liturgy,[24] where Paul Ricoeur's moral philosophy can be stimulating.[25] The Catholic approach to virtues emphasizes subjects' capacities of critical resistance to the cross-influences of traditions. It devotes itself to equipping ethical subjects for personal discernment in line with a moral and pastoral theology with a more European trademark.[26] This insistence on the subjective means, almost independent of communities (even against them), draws from the spiritual tradition of discernment of spirits.

The work of the Catholic theologian William Spohn creates a bridge between the Protestant approach on virtues, more centered on the ethical potential of the community, and the Catholic approach, more sensitive to the subjective means contained in the practices of spirituality.[27] For Spohn, the sacraments make a *transforming* encounter with the risen Christ come alive, reactivating the strength of the narrative calling of Christianity. The eschatological tension running through the liturgy implicates the faithful in a dynamic of growth in Christ's body that mobilizes faithfulness to the ethical call of Jesus. The question of identity (Who might I become in following Christ?) appears as the true pedagogical motive of the story of the Good Samaritan, a motive unveiled in Jesus' invitation to dare to have an analogical imagination: "Go and do likewise" (Luke 10:37).

[22] Christian Scharen, *Public Worship and Public Work: Character and Commitment in Local Congregational Life* (Collegeville, MN: Liturgical Press, 2004).

[23] Lieven Boeve, "The Sacramental Interruption of Rituals of Life," *Heythrop Journal* 44 (2003): 401–17.

[24] Philippe Bordeyne, "La liturgie comme ressource pour la formation éthique des sujets," *Recherches de Science Religieuse* 95/1 (January–March 2007): 95–121; "La référence à la vulnérabilité en éthique de la santé: défis et chances pour la foi chrétienne," *Revue d'éthique et de théologie morale* 239 (June 2006): 45–75.

[25] David A. Stosur, "Liturgy and (Post) Modernity: A Narrative Response to Guardini's Challenge," *Worship* 77/1 (2003): 22–41.

[26] James F. Keenan, *Moral Wisdom: Lessons and Texts from the Catholic Tradition* (Lanham, MD: Sheed & Ward, 2004). Note the importance of authors such as Josef Fuchs and Gérard Gilleman in Keenan's thought.

[27] William C. Spohn, *Go and Do Likewise: Jesus and Ethics* (New York: Continuum, 2000).

CHAUVET'S CONTRIBUTION TO CLARIFYING
THE RELATIONSHIP BETWEEN ETHICS AND LITURGY

Chauvet's contribution is even more helpful if we can properly situate his own question in this story and are able to distinguish it from the current question about the ethical formation of subjects. Chauvet envisages relationships between ethics and liturgy in a context of the "devaluation of the liturgy" and of the "overvaluation of ethics, particularly in its militant version."[28] The results are implicitly indicated in the confrontation between spiritual and temporal involvement that marked Catholic Action in France beginning in the 1950s.[29] While noting the "appeasement" of this debate, Chauvet assessed that the tension remains and should remain between sacraments and ethics, that it is constitutive of the Gospel, and that it protects against a temptation to absolutize law. Chauvet's method consists in respecting the request for ethical verification of religious practices, while highlighting that Christian worship reverses this problematic in regard to the newness of salvific grace. Chauvet is correct to allow this unresolved tension, but the way in which he deals with it moves him further away from current ethical questioning.

Critical Analysis of Christian Praxis

Chauvet's remaining interest today is his concern to maintain a trusting relation with the social sciences in order to assume, in the liveliness of theological work, a critical reflection on the practices engendered by theology throughout history.[30] It is a matter here of *verifying* the ethical potential of Christian celebrations. But Chauvet explains little about his way of understanding ethics. He barely embraces the distinctions developed in ethical theory that, as we have seen, produce differentiated insistences, even divergences. Chauvet is more interested in language, body, and social mediations of acting, human mediations that the sacramental action needs to recognize. "The fact that there are sacraments leads us to say that *corporality is the very mediation where faith takes on flesh* and makes real the truth that inhabits it." He tells us this "with all the pragmatic force of a ritual expression that speaks by its actions and works through the word, the word-as-body."[31]

---

[28] *Les sacrements: Parole de Dieu au risque du corps*, 71–72; ELV, 54.

[29] Robert Wattebled, *Stratégies catholiques en monde ouvrier dans la France d'après-guerre* (Paris: Ouvrières, 1990).

[30] See hereafter Jean-Louis Souletie's contribution, Part 6, chap. 11.

[31] *Symbole et sacrement*, 385; ELV, 376.

Consequently, the theory of *speech acts* becomes the principal operator for verification. The clarification of the performative dimension of ritual words allows one to envisage symbolic actions as actions "really changing the position of the subjects."[32] In applying this theory to the language of symbolic exchange, we rearticulate sacramental gratuity and the ethical obligation: "Every gift received obligates . . . every word 'received' as such imposes an obligation."[33] However, the obligation to give in return, according to a countergift that is never equivalent to the initial gift, does not remain purely exterior: every act of language brings with it an illocutionary dimension in such a way that "it is always ultimately oneself that one gives" in the given word.[34] The relationship between ethics and liturgy thus escapes moralism. The language and symbolic analysis of Christian ritualization shows that the sacraments resist the Marxist and Freudian suspicion: they lead to an act that is not a pure projection of intrapsychic conflicts. Chauvet belongs to a generation of theologians who pay the price for the confrontation with the epistemology of social sciences and their quest for emancipation,[35] to clarify on what conditions "it is ethical to be Christian."[36]

Beyond this effort of reification of human mediations for acting, it is necessary to remember Chauvet's insistence on Christian identity given in the sacraments, even if he does not really underline the ethical challenge. "[W]ithout the return-gift of an *ethical* practice by which the subject 'verifies' what it has received in the sacrament, Christian identity would be stillborn."[37] The ethical horizon of liturgy is first of all Christian identity, which the sacraments nourish in favor of the process of symbolic exchange. Chauvet never departs from the Christian aspect when he summarizes the connection between ethics and liturgy in critical discernment. He pleads for a double "rereading,"

[32] *Symbole et sacrement*, 138; ELV, 131. Chauvet refers to J. L. Austin, *Quand dire c'est faire* (Paris: Seuil, 1970).

[33] *Symbole et sacrement*, 274; ELV, 267.

[34] Ibid.

[35] Chauvet, "Quand le théologien se fait anthropologue . . . ," J. Joncheray, ed., *Approches scientifiques des faits religieux* (Paris: Beauchesne, 1997), 29–46.

[36] Henri-Jérôme Gagey, "Xavier Thévenot et la question de la différence chrétienne," J. Doré and G. Médevielle, eds. *Une parole pour la vie: Hommage à Xavier Thévenot* (Paris: Cerf/Salvator, 1998), 257–75; here 266.

[37] *Symbole et sacrement*, 288; ELV, 281.

openly confessing: "Consequently, just as the liturgy itself must become the object of an ethical reinterpretation to become fully Christian (see chap. 6), so also, and conversely, an ethics which is not reinterpreted liturgically, that is to say, as a theological response to the initial grace from God—as generous as it might be—would lose its Christian identity (1 Cor 13:1-3)."[38] This *theological* definition of the liturgy emphasizes that the social sciences (here the study of rituals) should never have the last word for evaluating its potential ethic. The theologian claims responsibility for an object that exceeds the competence of the social sciences: faith that allows itself to unfold in all its human mediations. Consequently, the risk of critical verification of the liturgy through epistemology of the social sciences proceeds at the risk of the faith, and not the opposite.

The Primacy of Ethics as Worship

For this reason, while Chauvet proceeds to the critical evaluation of Christian practices, he upholds using Scripture as the highly original approach toward worship and ethics specific to Christianity. Ethics is envisaged as truthful worship that is fulfilled in the daily life of the Christian actively responding to the initiative of divine grace. But Chauvet is not content to *define* worship and ethics in their mutual relations. In restoring the movement of Christian revelation, especially the New Testament critique of the Law and the Temple as institutions of salvation, he shows that God himself in his Son *takes the existential and corporal risk* of the criticism of the ancient cult. The "paschal rupture" inaugurates the worship of Christians as the "*welcoming in their daily lives this grace of God through theological faith and charity.*"[39]

Consequently, the relationship of verification between ethics and liturgy is *reciprocal*. It involves an *existential and corporal* dimension that proceeds from the common household of worship and moral life:[40] the memorial of the paschal mystery. "Thus, the *ritual* memory of Jesus'

---

[38] Ibid.

[39] Ibid., 258; ELV, 253.

[40] In "reconciling oneself to the liturgical rites," theology agrees to retrieve the faith such as it came to us "at the risk of the body," and not to impose upon it a mode of rationality that crushes corporality. (Chauvet, "The Broken Bread as Theological Figure of Eucharistic Presence," L. Boeve & L. Leijssen, eds., *Sacramental Presence in a Postmodern Context* [Sterling: Peeters, 2001], 236–62.)

death and resurrection is not Christian unless it is verified in an *existential* memory whose place is none other than the believers' bodies."[41] This christological lever allows a critique of any instrumental reduction of the ethical potential of the liturgy. "For I have set you an example, that you also should do as [*kathôs*] I have done to you" (John 13:15). Relying upon Xavier Léon-Dufour's commentary that combines this word of eucharistic anamnesis, Chauvet interprets *kathôs* not as *exemplum,* but as *sacramentum,* that is, a gift on the part of Christ to act like him. The reception of filial adoption, which is at the heart of eucharistic memorial, protects ethics against the sacrificial or moralizing temptation. "As the sacrifice of freedom, the Eucharist gives us back to ourselves and to others (its dimension of reconciliation) in the very act where we as children give ourselves back to God in offering God our thanksgiving (such is its first dimension as a 'sacrifice of thanksgiving')."[42]

But whereas Chauvet proceeds theologically from one part to the next, he tends to overvalue the absence of God. "The liturgy is *the powerful pedagogy where we learn to consent to the presence of the absence of God, who obliges us to give him a body in the world.*"[43] Is this the price to pay for the theory of *speech acts,* which leads one to favor the interaction between two protagonists about the exchange (the church and Christians) in an examination of the relationship between ethics and liturgy? Is this the expression of a latent temptation in Christian theology, consisting in seeing the liturgy as a *lex agendi* through assimilation to the adage *lex orandi, lex credendi?*[44] In this case, the absence of God would be the opposite of an ethical exemplarism that would follow a sacramental exemplarism, dismissed by Chauvet. Prudently the French moral theologian Xavier Thévenot tackles the subject of the relationship between ethics and liturgy according to an analogy of

[41] *Symbole et sacrement,* 266; ELV, 260–61.

[42] Ibid., 321; ELV, 314.

[43] Ibid., 270; ELV, 265.

[44] This comparison is dubious since faith considers the Christian life as worship, unyielding to law. Furthermore, the adage does not connect the *lex credendi* directly to the *lex orandi,* since this was honored as an interpretive tradition of Scripture and therefore refers to it. (Enrico Mazza, "*Lex orandi et lex credendi*: Que dire d'une *lex agendi* ou *lex vivendi*? Pour une théologie du culte chrétien," *La Maison-Dieu* 250/2 [2007]: 111–33.)

structure,[45] proper to maintaining the tension between the two poles.[46] A member of a people accustomed to calling out to "those who act" (Isa 38:15; author's translation), the theologian cannot abandon thinking about *the act of God in the liturgy*, not only under the human aspect of received grace but also under the aspect of grace that *gives itself* and that is received *as such* through the believing subject. For the discovery of the first act of God is decisive in the apprenticeship of the worship dimension of the ethical act, where this is a response to God's loving initiative.

Maintaining a Respectful and Critical Rapport with Ethics

From the point of view of theological ethics and especially in the Catholic perspective that values the proper autonomy of secular institutions in charge of justice and equality (GS 36), the limit of Chauvet's process also comes from the fact that he views ethics in a general way, without taking into consideration concepts and currents that are allowed to develop in history as a science of practical reason. For this reason, this sacramental theologian participates, in spite of himself, in the process of idealizing ethics that, elsewhere, he questions with due reason. In order that the sacraments may exercise to the very end their critical function in the face of ethics, it is necessary to identify what needs to be corrected in ethics, which presupposes that one indicates reciprocally the ethical postures that seem the most appropriate, understood as the practices necessary to verify liturgical practices.

In a post-traditional society, the great ethical ideas such as the good, evil, freedom, law, virtues, judgment, discernment of conscience, and the moral universal, can no longer be held as givens. It is important to show how the liturgy is open to introduce believing subjects to them. Consequently, the examination of the relationship between ethics and liturgy cannot be satisfied with a theory about action, as the social sciences encourage. If attention to the anthropological mediations of

[45] Xavier Thévenot, "Liturgie, morale et sanctification," *La Maison-Dieu* 1 (1995): 105–18.

[46] Chauvet admits himself that "*Symbol and Sacrament* would have done better to balance the relationship between faith and reason, especially in the relationship of "homology" and "analogy." (Chauvet, "Une relecture de *Symbole et sacrement*," *Questions liturgiques* 88/2 [2007]: 111–25.) For the dynamic tension between ethics and liturgy, that he would like to maintain, refers to the fruitful tension between faith and reason.

ethics is necessary, it is fitting to show interest in properly ethical mediations of ethics, that is to say, to the *ethos* that is used in a diversified and often conflictual way in the history of cultures, through representations more or less thematized. These realities must be taken into consideration in theological ethics.

In summary, Chauvet's rereading in the light of contemporary ethical challenges encourages us to reinvest simultaneously in Christian worship in its specificity and the question of the ethical formation of subjects. As Chauvet has taught us, the sacraments gain by being envisaged first of all as liturgical actions.[47] But it is further necessary to characterize *that in which* the lived experience of transformation by grace, attributed to an Other who is present, acting, and who gives himself to be recognized in ritual space, reconfigures the subjects for ethics. To claim that the liturgy has this power is also to show how the experiences it makes possible serve as a critical analysis about certain reductive conceptions about freedom and ethics.

THE TRANSFORMATION OF SUBJECTS BY GRACE AS THE HORIZON FOR CLEAR DISCOURSE ABOUT ETHICS AND LITURGY

The direction of this last part will appear clearer if I situate it in the French ecclesial context and in my own experience as a priest of a diocese near Paris during four years in service to the catechumenate. In keeping with other European countries, the French practice of Sunday Mass attendance has diminished greatly, while the number of infant baptisms, as well as marriages and religious funerals, has declined. On the other hand, the number of adult baptisms and confirmations augments and incites pastoral renewal. The pointed demand for the rites of passage is not doused, but it is accompanied by a thirst for informed faith that requests the installation of a catechesis for the different moments of life.[48] In the large population centers, the powerful attraction of well-prepared Sunday Masses and Pentecostal or evangelical-like assemblies arouses traditional communities to new liturgical initiatives. Society in general no longer generates spontaneously Christian attitudes, with the result that many citizens no longer have a

---

[47] See the contribution of Patrick Prétot above, Part 1, chap. 2.

[48] Henri Derroitte, ed., *Catéchèse et initiation*, Lumen Vitae (Bruxelles: Pédagogie catéchétique, 2005).

lived experience of sacramental practice. On the other hand, contacts that are by chance or intentionally sought out with a prayer community are often the occasion of spiritual resurgence[49] that can lead to a strong ethical component.

Some Subjects Convert in Response to an Unconditional Welcome

In the collective experience of the catechumenate, there are many biographical stories attesting that some subjects in a liturgical celebration discerned a call to change one's life. They talk about having thereby received the strength for a fresh start. One such catechumen hears the call of Jesus to pardon and to reconcile herself with someone who has deeply wounded her, another renounces sexual straying, still another shares her resources with those less fortunate, yet another comes to overcome a character defect that poisons his or her social or family relations. For some, it is the whole of the celebration that moves them, but for others it is a precise moment like a passage of a reading or a homily, the signing of the senses at the moment of election in the catechumenate, the personal response to the bishop at the time of a decisive call of the catechumens, or the first glimpse of the assembly after receiving baptism. In the present context, where social spaces capable of giving an ethical incentive are rare, Christian communities can seek greater consciousness that they singularly fulfill this role without confusion or separation between the Gospel and morality.

We should not isolate the liturgical event from other communal moments of ethical formation because they favor liturgical experience of conversion and afterwards take over from it. The collective reflection at the edges of the rites of Christian initiation introduces one to the art of practical judgment, especially in the diocesan days around the bishop. Drawn forward by the desire to become Christian, the catechumens ask themselves about the identity they will receive with the bath of baptism. Questioning their Christian speakers on the lived examples, they want to know what kind of person they will become in

---

[49] Chauvet, whose theology is molded by a lived experience of pastoral care, admits that he became more "understanding" toward some very ambiguous questions about the church. He explains, "for example, instead of reacting to parents who ask for infant baptism, even though they never put a foot inside a church, saying to myself: "here they come; what stupidity!" [the theology of mediation] allows me to respond saying, "here they come; what an opportunity!" (*Une relecture de* Symbole et sacrement).

changing their way of living and renouncing certain behaviors. As they who live in community have seen, these questions in general come before the interrogation about norms and what they must do. The well-thought-out reflection avoids moralizing simplifications, and it introduces one to the ecclesial-communal character of discernment of the divine will, even if the ultimate decision is reached in the sanctuary of conscience. It is not rare in such gatherings that catechumens impress the community in return and form it by the acuteness of the demands of life in Christ.

It would be risky to limit the portion of the liturgical action where the transformation by grace can happen to the subject. It is in its integrity that the liturgy is a "school of faith" and through it a mediator of a Christian life more aimed at God.[50] However, attention given to the power for ethical calling in certain elements of the rite can help to evaluate them. Thus, through its layout and its enrollment in the salvific economy, the liturgy confers on each person a place in our world awaiting salvation, where charity is made possible through the action of Christ and the breath of the Spirit. Access to this profound meaning is of great ethical significance because it strengthens hope. Besides, it is easier to give someone else one's place when one has found oneself after having experienced an unconditional welcome. From then on, a liturgical community attentive to fraternal welcome has a greater chance to introduce the discovery of a new world, restored in Christ, where one does not give preference to anyone (Act 10:34).

A Grace That Did Not Necessarily Have to Be

Thévenot highlights the importance of communal liturgy for the formation of ethical subjects, but without minimizing the contribution of these latter for their own formation when they try to believe in spite of doubt and to act in spite of the possibility of nonsense. The Eucharist, especially, appears to him as a figure of ethical action that incites subjects to convert and supports them in this process throughout their existence.[51] In remembering the violent death of Jesus, the Eucharist integrates the absurd, all the while proclaiming the possibility of its

[50] Joseph André Jungmann, "Liturgie, école de foi" (1957), *Tradition liturgique et problèmes actuels de pastorale*, trans. P. Kirchhoffer (Lyons: Xavier Mappus, 1962), 271–82.

[51] Xavier Thévenot, "Liturgie et morale," *Repères éthiques pour un monde nouveau* (Mulhouse: Salvator, 1982), 145–65.

being overcome. It also redirects subjects toward concrete action and fights against their propensity to flee from reality in the name of a desire for the absolute. That human freedom may be graced is felt when it becomes possible to open themselves without anguish to pardon, which makes the conversion possible.

Like Chauvet, Thévenot is heir to a theological anthropology of which their colleague Jean-Yves Hameline was the precursor at the Institut Catholique of Paris. Thanks to the concept of "ceremonial site" in the liturgical layout and their "corporal investment" through the faithful, Hameline brought out the *ambiguity* of the ritual experience in which the subject him- or herself becomes a believing subject.[52] The coincidence between the liturgical framework and the personal investment of the subjects is always fragile; sometimes it lasts "no more than a glance, the repositioning of a body, the sign of the cross or a greeting." The feast of the liturgy is always only a "possible feast." Breaking the succession of a thousand repetitions of the rites, marveling before the fleeting appropriateness of what the church celebrates teaches the subject to receive ceaselessly from others and to receive oneself from Another. This is precisely what the liturgy introduces for recognition.

From the ethical point of view, it is decisive to be aware that this event *could have possibly never happened.* This avoids the fact that the liturgy may be instrumentalized as a space of ethical exemplarity. Moreover, what is produced in the rite on account of ethics survives in the margin of the rite when the subject is grasped by an ambiance, a facial expression, or the tone of a voice that gives him or her access to the deep meaning of the prescribed rites. Thus the warmth of the word of welcome from someone presiding, an exchange of glances with another person, or the joy of mixing one's own voice in the singing of the assembly permits the subject to take his or her place in the people summoned by God. To the degree that they are neither automatic nor foreseen, just such events introduce subjects into the sense of gratuity and of gift without which there is no possible ethic. At the heart of the

---

[52] Jean-Yves Hameline, "Le culte chrétien dans son espace de sensibilité," *La Maison-Dieu* 187 (1991): 7–45. Reprinted in: *Une poétique du rituel* (Paris: Cerf, 1997), 93–123. The author relies notably on the course of *General Linguistics* of Ferdinand de Saussure, on the *Phenomenology of Perception* of Maurice Merleau-Ponty, and on the report of Erwin Straus on the psychology of lived experience in space and time (*Vom Sinn der Sinne* [Berlin: Springer, 1935]).

liturgical proclamation of the Scriptures, the singing of the psalms assumes an essential place from the ethical point of view, because it actualizes in a corporal and social way the critical function of praise.[53]

Subjects Not Only Acting but Enacted

The liturgical experience of grace helps to form ethical identities under the register of passivity and not only of activity. It challenges exaggerated expressions of subjective autonomy. To the extent that it should concern the presider or various members who make up the assembly, liturgical participation is simultaneously an action and a passion, where each person waives his or her own will and makes the sacrifice of self.[54] Including the theatrical dimension, the lived liturgy exposes each of its actors—ordained ministers and lay faithful—like bodies of light as much acted upon as acting.[55] As Paul Ricoeur insists from one end of his moral philosophy to the other: freedom that establishes the ethical, between acting and suffering, is the "only human."[56] The subject "testifies" most adequately to one's own ethical identity when he or she consents to accept "oneself as another":[57] one does not hold the keys to one's own identity.

These experiences are crucial, for every truly moral decision must shoulder the part of powerlessness inherent in human action. This is particularly clear in the ethical problems related to biomedicine, where the body is at the center, as in the liturgy. In the rich countries, couples confronted with the failure of fertility experiment when their bodies

---

[53] Brian Brock, *Singing the Ethos of God: On the Place of Christian Ethics in Scripture* (Grand Rapids/Cambridge: Eerdmans, 2007).

[54] "Each one of us must know how to establish restraint; it comes from within. But, in leaving, it is not lost. On the contrary, life expands in freedom and richness." (Romano Guardini, *Vom Geist der Liturgie* [Freiburg i. Br./Berlin: Herder, 1934], [end of chapter 3]; Fr. trans.: *L'esprit de la liturgie* [Paris: Parole et Silence, 1929], 54.)

[55] "The actor is not someone who expresses him or herself, but a split, a person separated, one who assists him or her, a spectator of his or her body, a person who goes beyond the person. In the theater, it is always the actor's departure from the human body that one comes to see. We come for the offering of the body, a body carried, offered, a word carried before itself." (Valère Novarina, *Lumières du corps* [Paris: P.O.L., 2006], 20.)

[56] Paul Ricoeur, *Philosophie de la volonté. 1- Le volontaire et l'involontaire* (Paris: Aubier, 1950), 453–56.

[57] Paul Ricoeur, *Soi-même comme un autre* (Paris: Seuil, 1990).

do not respond to the desire for children, whereas they respond well to other subjective expectations in life—interpersonal, romantic, professional, social, charitable, athletic, leisure, etc. Medical assistance for procreation is prone to provide some technical responses to a question that involves different ranges of the human, unyielding to the instrumental: the biological, affective, and genealogical relation. But initiation into the liturgy forges an understanding to act that leaves a place for passivity as well as for the power of renewal contained in the complaint that sterile women entrust to God (1 Sam 1:15).

"Sacramental-liturgical life does not respond to all the subject's needs for ethical formation—far from it! The actors of the liturgy must consent to other formative practices as well." As we have noted several times, ethics requires a specific formation of freedom, of conscience, of the sense of the norm and of the moral universal, of the aptitude to aim for the good and to resist evil, thanks to the exercise of the virtues. Ethics also needs communitarian places where subjects torn apart between worlds by ethos competition can train themselves for evangelical discernment.[58] In the face of the complexity of reality, the unity of the liturgy, which gathers diverse people together under the authority of the Word proclaimed and preached, offers a highly valuable space for interior unification before ethical combat. But this simple beauty can become a refuge. As Chauvet saw well, the ethical horizon of the liturgy holds us in an endless tension that lays claim to the fact that we may aspire to an inestimable gift of wisdom.

[58] Christopher Steck, "Saintly Voyeurism: A Methodological Necessity for the Christian Ethicist?" William C. Mattison III, ed., *New Wine, New Wineskins: Key Issues in Catholic Moral Theology* (Oxford: Rowman & Littlefield, 2005), 25–44.

Chapter 8

Time, Absence, and Otherness: Divine-Human Paradoxes Bonding Liturgy and Ethics

Bruce T. Morrill

SOURCES IN SCRIPTURE
FOR THE ONGOING CHALLENGE IN TRADITION

The relationship between liturgy and ethics, in terms of their intrinsic bond, has proven a challenge for Christianity from its origins. The problem resides both in the human condition in general and the content of the biblical message of salvation in particular. So common across cultures are people's patterns of revering certain places, objects, or persons as powerful beyond the normal affairs of the world that social scientists and philosophers of religion theorize about religion in terms of the sacred versus profane. Religion concerns the cosmic ordering of time and seasons, but most often not the ethical ordering of people's lives. Fundamental to Christian revelation, however, is the insistence that in Christ just such a sacred-profane dichotomy is invalid. Still, this revelation, as found for example in the Synoptic Gospels' enigmatic parables about the reign of God, is so shot through with paradox that it is not surprising to find a tendency among believers, from the very beginnings of Christianity, to refashion the message into the sacred-profane parameters of religion. This constant temptation to understand faith as the "sacralization" of certain objects, places, and personages rather than the "sanctification" of daily life through practices of justice, liberation, mercy, and forgiveness, Louis-Marie Chauvet situates in a pervasive resistance to "the bitter scandal of a God crucified for the life of the world."[1] That the resistance is strong can be evidenced by a brief survey of selected New Testament passages.

---

[1] Chauvet, *The Sacraments: The Word of God at the Mercy of the Body* (Collegeville, MN: Liturgical Press, 2001), 63, 50.

At the heart of the First Letter of Peter, J.-M.-R. Tillard argues, is an explanation of the new life Christians claim by baptism as mere "empty word" if not lived according to the ideal of Christ: "a comportment marked by compassion, love of sisters and brothers, mercy, humility, refusal to render evil for evil or insult for insult, blessing (3:8-9), mutual submission, unity of spirit . . . hospitality (4:9) and mutual service (4:10)."[2] Such human living, manifesting freely given divine gifts bestowed in Christ, is what glorifies God (4:10-11). Likewise, in the Johannine tradition, life in Christ is a corporate act of worship in Spirit and truth (John 4:23-24) realized through the practical love of the members one for another (1 John 2:8-11). Walking (a biblical metaphor for ethical action) in the light glorifies the Father, whose twofold commandment is belief in the Son and love for one another, an abiding in Christ made possible by the Spirit (1 John 3:23-24). The author of First John is addressing a serious problem, the false belief among some members that their abiding in God is a matter of a disembodied knowledge indifferent to the material needs of their brothers and sisters (3:17). To follow such teaching is to live as liars (2:4), to walk in darkness (2:11). This instruction finds dramatic expression in John's account of the Last Supper. At the moment Judas takes the morsel of bread from Jesus and abruptly leaves, darkness descends: "And it was night" (John 13:30). To the disciples remaining with him Jesus gives the "new commandment" to love one another as he has loved them (13:34-35). Just as Jesus' obedience and departure to the Father will glorify God (13:31-33), so too the mutual love of the disciples, empowered by the Spirit (14:16-17), will glorify the Father (15:8-10).

The Johannine farewell discourse binds the meal on the night before Jesus' death with the mystical-ethical import of both his life unto death and the lives of believers. The truth of their ritual worship in the Eucharist is a function of their living according to the Spirit the Father has given them through the Son. Therein lies glory of God. The symbolic action in John's supper narrative is the foot washing, making the ethical import of Jesus' life and death for his followers utterly explicit, perhaps more than would seem to be the case in the Synoptic accounts of the Last Supper. Xavier Léon-Dufour, however, disabuses us of the latter assumption through a textual analysis of the Lukan account, which situates the cultic tradition of the bread and wine within the

---

[2] J.-M.-R. Tillard, *Flesh of the Church, Flesh of Christ: At the Source of the Ecclesiology of Communion* (Collegeville, MN: Liturgical Press, 2001), 20–21.

larger testamentary tradition of the Lord's farewell discourse. "The liturgical action has value only if it expresses its efficacy in concrete fruits: faith and fidelity amid trials, hope of promised glory, love brought down to earth in service to the brothers and sisters."[3] Both the cultic and testamentary elements of the supper set the time of the church in an eschatological perspective charged with the ethical mission of witnessing to the Christ now absent, but who will share the meal with them in the fulfillment of the kingdom of God (Mark 14:25; Matt 26:29; Luke 22:16). Both traditions "are indispensable for showing the deeper meaning of the new presence of Jesus after his death. Both give expression to the same divine mystery, namely, that the disciples are invited to become other Christs."[4]

Finally, there is Paul's admonishing of the Corinthians for making a sham of the Lord's Supper (1 Cor 11:18-20). Selfish feasting to the neglect of the poorer members betrays a character inimical to that of the Christ they claim to commemorate in their Sunday assembly. For this reason Paul gives a commentary on the supper account he has received, wherein Jesus, after giving the bread and the cup, commands his followers, in the corporate plural, "do this in remembrance of me" (11:24-25). The failure of some to recognize the ecclesial reality of Christ's Body results in their self-condemnation in the liturgical action. Their disregard for the Other in the persons of the poorer members is a failure in "discerning the body" (11:29) of the Christ whose very person, life, and mission they claim to share in the bread and cup. They think they know Christ in the moment of their cultic meal action, but their failure to engage in the anamnesis (remembrance) of his life is a judgment against themselves. Jerome Murphy-O'Connor explains how for Paul the death of Jesus was the consummate act of what was most characteristic of his life, a self-giving for others. Only with the "realism of Paul's approach" to the message of the Gospel in mind can one understand what Paul means when he says that partaking of the eucharistic meal is a proclamation of "the Lord's death until he comes" (11:26). No mere verbal recitation, the act of proclaiming that definitive event in history draws the participants into the content and character of the message itself.[5]

---

[3] Xavier Léon-Dufour, *Sharing the Eucharistic Bread: The Witness of the New Testament*, trans. Matthew O'Connell (New York: Paulist Press, 1982), 247.

[4] Ibid.

[5] Jerome Murphy-O'Connor, "Eucharist and Community in First Corinthians," *Worship* 51 (1977): 61–62.

TIME AS OF THE ESSENCE
OF THE LITURGICAL-ETHICAL PRACTICE OF FAITH

Time, in terms both of history as the arena of human suffering and salvation and of commemoration (anamnesis) as fundamental to Christian sacramental realism, is of the essence when it comes to apprehending the intrinsic bond of liturgy and ethics. Still, as David Power observes, it has been easier to introduce anamnetic practices into the churches' books of worship than to formulate a theology of what happens in the act of anamnesis—and how.[6] How we understand the ritual action of anamnesis, including its relationship to the ongoing disruptive events of history, has everything to do with the intentionality with which we do it and, therefore, how it is formative of us as ethical agents. Our reformed liturgical texts might well contain robust eucharistic prayers, blessings of water and oils structured in anamnetic-epicletic patterns, and calls for genuinely homiletic preaching. Promulgation of these texts, however, does not guarantee the extent to which liturgical assemblies engage them as performative utterances, experiencing them as manifestations of God's gracious desires for humanity, and, indeed, all creation. This presents an ongoing task for liturgical theologians. Biblical and historical research on the Jewish and early Christian texts and ritual practices of anamnesis has yielded evidence for the intrinsic connection between liturgical memorial and ethical life.[7] This scholarship, nevertheless, can only serve a living tradition of faith if theologians place the knowledge of "remembrancing" revealed in the liturgy in dialogue with the present social conditions that impact, both positively and negatively, on the human exercise of memory today—a formidable challenge.

The liturgical notion of memory has long inspired Johann Baptist Metz's argument for the practical, ethical implications of embracing the Christian faith as the dangerous memory of Christ's paschal mystery. In his later work Metz coined a neologism to capture the dynamic character of liturgical anamnesis, *Eingedenken*, "remembrancing," based on the German adverb *eingedenk*, "in remembrance of," the phrase used in the institution narrative of the eucharistic prayer.[8] Metz

[6] See David N. Power, *The Eucharistic Mystery: Revitalizing the Tradition* (New York: Crossroad Publishing, 1992), 19–20, 260, 304.

[7] See Bruce T. Morrill, *Anamnesis as Dangerous Memory: Political and Liturgical Theology in Dialogue* (Collegeville, MN: Liturgical Press, 2000), 139–205.

[8] Johann Baptist Metz, *A Passion for God: The Mystical-Political Dimension of Christianity*, trans. J. Matthew Ashley (New York: Paulist Press, 1998), 181, n.

140

argues that this cultic action constitutes the key way the church has preserved its distinctive form of memory.[9] Christian theology now needs to recognize this intrinsically historical way of remembering ("remembrancing") as "the fundamental anamnestic structure of mind and spirit" or a "remembrance-structure" that Christians can bring to the social-ethical arena.[10] Metz emphasizes the Jewish origins of this type of remembering, which entails a sense of absence, the refusal to forget the suffering and dead. He also notes that from its origins the eucharistic remembrance was meant to be celebrated in festive expectation of Christ's return, an anticipatory awareness long dormant in much of the church.[11]

Metz considers the lack of expectation in a definitive future the symptom of a deep malaise in mainstream Christianity. Ours is a time of "postmodern Godless Christianity," practiced without recourse to the unsettled, unsettling history of catastrophe and consolation that comprises the narrative of Judeo-Christian tradition. In place of this bounded history of suffering and salvation, in denial of the contradictions inherent to historical religious awareness, many postmodern Christians have undertaken a recovery of religious myths, seeking "to unlock the potential for consolation that slumbers in myths and fables."[12] As the legacy reaching back to second-century Gnostics demonstrates, whenever Christians lose the sense of time's urgency, the practice of faith cedes to a religion of timeless myths, hindering the practical-ethical demands of the Gospel's message. The socioeconomic conditions of late modernity, Metz argues, aid and abet this sense of apathetic timelessness.

To the extent people accept the rationality of capitalism's exchange-principle and technology's instrumentalism, the logic of inevitable human evolutionary progress amounts to "a new form of metaphysics"

---

10. See also, James Matthew Ashley, *Interruptions: Mysticism, Politics and Theology in the Work of Johann Baptist Metz* (Notre Dame, IN: University of Notre Dame Press, 1998), 161.

[9] See Metz, *A Passion for God*, 131. See also, Johann-Baptist Metz, "Freedom in Solidarity: The Rescue of Reason," trans. John Bowden, in Johann-Baptist Metz and Jürgen Moltmann, *Faith and the Future: Essays on Theology, Solidarity, and Modernity* (Maryknoll, New York: Orbis Books, 1995), 77.

[10] Metz, *A Passion for God*, 64, 131.

[11] Ibid., 85.

[12] Ibid., 102.

or "a quasi-religious symbol of scientific knowledge,"[13] often with negative social consequences. Far from generating the sort of optimistic view of history and nature that characterized the nineteenth century, the present valorization of technical reason has produced deep measures of fatalism and apathy. People find themselves part of an anonymous, inevitable, timeless technological and economic process: "There is a cult today of the makeable—everything can be made. There is also a new cult of fate—everything can be replaced. . . . This understanding of reality excludes all expectation and therefore produces that fatalism that eats away [the person's] soul."[14] The need to conform for success in these systems depletes people's imaginations, inhibits dreams for the future, and ultimately threatens the loss of their subjectivity and freedom. In its now near universality, the exchange mentality inherent to market capitalism integrally influences not only politics but also "reaches the foundations of our spiritual life," to the effect that "everything now appears to be exchangeable, and interchangeable, even interpersonal relationships and life commitments."[15] The strains on personal and social relations overlap. Frustrations, especially economic hardships, in the face of the inadmissible limits of the instrumental reason of technology, the market, and political bureaucracies, give rise at times to hateful fanaticism, for which Auschwitz stands as the haunting witness.

With that powerful symbol of modernity's disastrous turn Metz articulates the current danger to humanity, as well as the emerging social and political movements confronting the suffering that technological and economic processes have caused. Anonymous progress is interrupted by questioning *whose* progress it is and at what cost to the freedom of *other* human subjects and, with increasing awareness, the ecology. These movements alert believers to the Gospel's call all around them: "Danger and being in danger permeate every New Testament statement."[16] What Christians bring to social-political processes

[13] Johann Baptist Metz, *Faith in History and Society: Toward a Fundamental Practical Theology*, trans. David Smith (New York: The Seabury Press, 1980), 171, 6.

[14] Metz, *Faith in History and Society*, 170. Here Metz draws on Horkheimer and Adorno. For his engagement of Nietzsche on the mythical totality pervading modernity, see *A Passion for God*, 78–81, 172–73.

[15] Metz, *A Passion for God*, 166.

[16] Ibid., 48.

is a rationality challenging and interrupting instrumental reason's narratives of progress: the dangerous memory of the lost and ruined, which "resists identifying meaning and truth with the victory of what has come into being and continues to exist."[17] Christians are only able to make this social contribution, however, if they celebrate their faith as a remembrancing of the suffering, death, and resurrection of Jesus, embracing its scandal and hope, and with these, the apocalyptic dimension of biblical eschatology that reveals a God passionately engaged in the bounded time of history.

That Metz, for all his arguing for the emancipatory potential of the remembrance-structure of Christian faith, does not explain in detail *how* the liturgically enacted memory of Christ relates to the realities, issues, and vagaries of history should not, Power would warn us, surprise us. From the pre-Nicene church's logo-centric worldview forward, tradition provides no model for how liturgical memorial becomes a force in history: "The relation of the remembered event to the present and its continued influence on history is the crux of a current eucharistic theology."[18] Power wagers that language's expressive ability holds the key to a problem that has become more urgent in an era requiring greater sensitivity to suffering and injustice. The work of philosopher of religion Edith Wyschogrod provides insights into both Western philosophical and Christian theological struggles with time and memory as these relate to the ethical exigencies of the contemporary social and technological context.

THE ETHICS OF REMEMBERING

Wyschogrod argues that speaking of the past through narrative and image is an intrinsically paradoxical work, the task of eliciting the past from one's situation in the present. To take up the vocation of the "heterological historian," by which she means anyone called to speak for the voiceless dead others, is to enter into the realm of ethics. Ethics in this case does not concern narrow epistemological questions concerning the criteria of truth and their application, nor does it rely on theories of justice. Ethics is something prior to this "discursive space," pursuing a very different line of inquiry: "Whose truth is being told, to whom, by whom, and to what end?" These questions both concern

---

[17] Ibid., 40.
[18] Power, *The Eucharistic Mystery*, 305. See also 126–32, 291–92.

history and "bear upon" everyday life in "searing ways."[19] The vocation is thus also to a community, working to return to the community some aspect of its past. In the present context, the task is to refigure the community that has been disfigured by what Wyschogrod calls the "cataclysm," a name she purposely chooses for its "cosmological dimensions."[20]

The cataclysm constitutes the first of two governing conditions of the modern context. The cataclysm is the nadir history reached over the past century, "the void exposed by the event of the mass annihilation of persons within ever more compressed time frames, a void that remains indescribable and yet constitutes the unique moment, the entry of the nihil into time."[21] While by no means the only subject nor even the prolegomenon for every contemporary work, the cataclysm requires that alterity cut into any historical narrative in a manner comparable to (yet different from) Levinas's *il y a*.

The second governing condition of the modern context is the emergence of the culture of image and information. Visual and computer technologies have produced media wherein the object has become disconnected from materiality, resulting in a volatilizing of images in a hyperreality that the speaker cannot escape and must, therefore, engage negatively from within. While Western thought has continuously found the "unfettered" image threatening, as epitomized by "the Hegelian fear of the unfreedom of the image," the contemporary "universe of digitality," with its "simulations of the hyperreal," poses an even greater challenge to efforts at evoking the truth of events.[22] In a culture that presumes that anything can be simulated technologically, in which the distinction between the actual and the imaginary is blurred, it is difficult to communicate the truth about past events and persons (especially those of the cataclysm), and in a way that is not manipulative.

While the volatilizing of images presents new problems for the effort to make predicative and ethical statements about the past, the contemporary vocation of attesting to the past is also plagued by a long lineage of mistaken theories about language and image as *representa-*

[19] Edith Wyschogrod, *An Ethics of Remembering: History, Heterology, and the Nameless Others* (Chicago: The University of Chicago Press, 1998), 4.

[20] Ibid., xvi, xiii.

[21] Ibid., 14.

[22] Ibid., 178, 200.

tions of past realities. Wyschogrod argues that the "commonplace view" of our thoughts and communication as representing realities *as they exist independently* of our own perspectives is a conflation of "the major models of memory that have governed Western thought, that of inscription incising upon a surface, and that of a storehouse into which one can reach to fetch up some particular of the past."[23] Representationalist views fail to take into account the gap, the insuperable difference between the originating event and later occasions (acts of memory) relating to it. Structuralists and phenomenologists have produced a mounting number of arguments for how untenable is the thinking that the past can be "re-presented as if hypostacized in a perceptual 'present.'"[24] Such notions of representation fail to take account of, among other things, the constitutive role of language in all acts of cognition. The critique that Wyschogrod brings to the commonsense view of representation motivate her inquiries into the essential role of narrativity in the exercise of memory, as well as the need to acknowledge the challenge that time's passage poses to the paradoxical effort to attest not only to what happened in past events but also to the affective dimension of those events both for the people originally involved (and now dead) and for those presently remembering them.

The commonplace notion of memory as representation and the now pervasive culture of specularity and information require the development of a theory of time arguing against the assumption that a certain replication of a given event provides its meaning once and for all. The theory must nonetheless communicate the truth of the past in a way that accommodates specularity's framework, "in which reference is obliterated and images refer only to themselves."[25] These conditions require Wyschogrod (following Kant, James, Nietzsche, and Heidegger) to elaborate a theory of time's "doubleness" or bifurcation, a theory that holds two distinct views of time—time as stretched or flowing and time as punctiform—in a reciprocally challenging relationship. The first view envisions some block of time as a flowing of events through their pastness, presentness, and futurity. This stretched

[23] Ibid., 174. For Chauvet's critique of productionist schemes of representation in Christian sacramental theology, see *Symbol and Sacrament: A Sacramental Reinterpretation of Christian Existence*, trans. Patrick Madigan and Madeleine Beaumont (Collegeville, MN: Liturgical Press, 1995), 21–26.

[24] Wyschogrod, *An Ethics of Remembering*, 38.

[25] Ibid., 147.

view of time enables speaking about the relative distance of past or future events in relation to each other and the present. It thus provides a structure of discursive or visual narration that replicates the dynamics of that time period as actually experienced, yielding cognitive information. The other, punctiform, view of time supplies the framework for the ethical dimension of remembering. Whatever the time span between the before and after, "the after reflects a radical alteration in social, political, economic, and other cultural circumstances."[26]

Such an approach to time, with its expectation that the past can provide cognitive information and ethical implications for our present lives, invests time with a crucial, irreducible role in the quest for human freedom and redemption. Wyschogrod's cognitively and ethically productive view of time correlates with Metz's theological articulation of Christian faith as a praxis of memory, narrative, and solidarity engaged in the real history of suffering humanity (as opposed to the historicity of some abstract human subject).[27] Like Metz, Wyschogrod also recognizes an inclination toward timelessness in Christian theology. She recognizes in Christian Neoplatonism a view of "immobilized time, a static and changeless present or eternity as contrasted with the change, coming into being and passing away of time."[28] For Augustine, time is unreal. In the *Confessions* (XI, 13–15) eternity constitutes a presence that overcomes time's passing, a continuously shifting "now" in which any present moment ceases to exist as it gives way to past and future. With the present instant thus defying conceptualization, time cannot be punctiform. Yet Augustine's thought is shattered on the oxymoron of *time before creation*, which arises in his questioning what God was doing before that event. Wyschogrod argues that creation thus constitutes an epochal *moment* for Augustine. It is this recognition of time as punctiform, with moments after which affairs can never be the same, that is so important to an ethics of remembering.

In the contemporary context, the culture of virtuality generates its own tendency not to consider time real and, thus, not to perceive the persons and events of the past as exerting ethical pressure on the present. The current immobilizing of time is brought about by the fragmenting of the world into the virtuality of volatilized images that,

[26] Ibid., 148.
[27] See Metz, *Faith in History and Society*, 200.
[28] Wyschogrod, *An Ethics of Remembering*, 152.

in turn, are volatilized into information. In the face of this marginalizing of the stretched view of time, Wyschogrod proffers an important thesis: "[F]rom the standpoint of time's continuity, the question is not one of the reality or unreality of the past but rather of its hyperreality. The past is always already hyperreal, volatilized, awaiting only the technological instantiation it has now received."[29] Whereas the spatial world is comprised of material objects positively available to grasp, the only way one can grasp the past is by way of negation. To assert that something *was* is an "unsurpassable negation that breaks into the materiality of the world and volatilizes it." The past can only return to us as word and image, *"through its volatilzation in images."*[30]

The problem remains as to how those engaged in remembrance decide which images to choose and, moreover, how to relate them to each other and the present ethical context. Wyschogrod continues to exploit the stretched view of time, turning to Heidegger's theory of the future as the primordial mode of time, of human existence as an ongoing reach toward Dasein's nonbeing, that is, of life as anticipation of the nonbeing of death. The future's distinguishing feature is its relation to possibility, in that the future is anticipated as an annihilation of possibilities. Wyschogrod points out that the past is governed by this structure of futurity also. A past event exhibits possibilities for *its* future that it saw *then* but which now are annihilated. Present narration speaks both of what did occur as well as any number of scenarios of what could possibly have happened but did not occur. "If the past is to be retrieved, the not of that which can never be made present, the past's ungroundedness, its hyperreality, the field of images of that which could have but did not occur are intrinsic to that which is to be recovered."[31] Moreover, a further negation delimits the interpretative presentation of the past. The speaker is bound by the negative grounding of any historical narrative, namely, the assertion of what could *never* have been the case. This movement within the flow of time provides a "thick description" of the historical images in a narrative, resulting not in any absolute truth about the past but, still, a *"kind of certainty"* with which the historian can testify on behalf of the dead.

In addition to this cognitive yield from the stretched view of time, the punctiform view helps to establish the ethical significance of the

---

[29] Ibid., 166.
[30] Ibid.
[31] Ibid., 167.

passage of time, as found in an alteration of social, economic, political, and cultural forces. Matters of value are generated by a *moment* after which things must be considered differently. The change may be sudden or gradual, but the task is to assert that at some point "a new state of affairs has come about."[32] Wyschogrod's contemporary example is the phrase "after Hitler," not unlike political theology's argument for the changed state of the church's mission and, thus, theology "after Auschwitz."[33] The conclusions Wyschogrod draws from this dual engagement with time take on their own theological tone. Following Benjamin, she describes the vocation of those who speak for the voiceless others as messianic. Each generation must take up the responsibility of responding to the claim that previous generations have on it. Prior to writing narrative, the "heterological historian" considers the before and after that establish the ethical space of the enterprise. The narrativity of flow (past, present, future) provides the contexts of utterances, the particularities of subjects, the relations within and among images, and so on. Thus able to assert in indicative language the importance of a historical event, the heterological historian does so reflexively, personally attesting to the truth she puts forth.

LITURGY AND ETHICS: PURSUING THE REMEMBRANCE-STRUCTURE OF CHRISTIAN FAITH

Wyschogrod's philosophy of memory offers insights for any theology that defines (and thereby must serve) Christian faith as the praxis of word, sacrament, and ethics.[34] The open definition of the heterological historian lends her philosophical conclusions to the Christian theologian who, with the fractured image and narrative of the crucified yet risen Jesus at the center of faith, knows well that any effort at an intellectual articulation of that faith is characterized by only a "kind of certainty." While the proclamation of faith bears truth from which believers should never demur, that truth is only known in often perplexing and even tragic bodily and historical circumstances. That is, however, only a complex statement of what Paul put so directly:

---

[32] Ibid., 169. Wyschogrod notes Kierkegaard's theological concept of the momentous, the point at which eternity breaks into time as a person recognizes Jesus as the Christ, altering the believer's entire view of life.

[33] Metz, *A Passion for God*, 55–56, 121–32.

[34] See Chauvet, *Symbol and Sacrament*, 171–80; and *The Sacraments*, 20–39.

148

Gospel faith is practiced only in hope.[35] Moreover, the history of suffering is not the only contributor to the reserved certainty with which Christians live the truth they profess in faith. In addition to the fissured certainty with which Christian truth is known in social-ethical practice is the apophatic reserve intrinsic to all practices of mysticism, liturgy, and prayer. The trinitarian God of biblical faith reveals Godself *as* truth and *in* truth, yet certainty of our knowledge of this God is circumscribed by not only the human limits to our apprehending the divine mystery but also the perplexing revelation of the biblical God throughout the history of suffering to this very day.

Wyschogrod's demonstration of the necessity of not only image but also narrative for responsible ethical remembering in this age of specularity indicates both the redemptive and the emancipatory importance of Christians fully and actively participating in the liturgy's anamnetic enactment of the mystery of faith. The culture of specularity and information, with its volatilizing of images in hyperreality, indicates both a danger and an opportunity for those seeking to testify to the truth of the past. The danger lies in a diminishing of the value of people and events in the ever more rapid blur of passing images. The opportunity, however, lies in Wyschogrod's insight that the only way the past can return in the present is in the hyperreality that the past inherently *is*. Untethered to the material immediacy of the spatial world, recovering the past requires the volatilization of persons and events in word and image.

When believers remember the kenotic character of Christ in word and sacrament, they articulate not only what did happen in Jesus (decisions and actions resulting in his rejection and execution) but also the possibility that his story and future might have gone otherwise. Scripture and liturgy attest to this truth through language and imagery of the Son of God emptying himself into the human condition and suffering a tortured death for the sake of the many. Narrative (e.g., the Philippians hymn and eucharistic prayers, ancient and modern) indicates that the Son might not have done this at all and, thus, that his choice was made in both freedom and generous love.[36] Liturgical acts of anamnesis present anew the profundity of what Jesus decided and did, and thus, who he was and is. Thus does participation in the church's rituals of remembrancing affect believers, inspiring them to follow in service the Christ they encounter liturgically in word and sacrament.

[35] See Romans 8:22-25.
[36] See Chauvet, *Symbol and Sacrament*, 499–509.

Reflecting in this way on the liturgical action of remembering by no means implies that the anamnetic enactment of the paschal mystery can be reduced to the human processes of memory. *How* Christ is made present in anamnetic (and one must add at least parenthetically, epicletic[37]) action is a dual question concerning not only the human means and capacity for remembering but also the divine initiative and grace that make the liturgical event an epiphany of God's reign, a moment of redemption. Power draws an important lesson from Aquinas's dialectical understanding of the relationship between the causing and signifying that occur in sacramental action:

> Beyond the capacity to signify by use of the proper matter and form, to be causes of grace the sacraments of the New Law have to be endowed in act with a power that gives rise to an effect that goes beyond their native power to signify. Aquinas refers to this as a *virtus fluens*, operative only in the moment of sacramental action and not attributable to signification as such, even though operative through it. In fact Aquinas never says of sacraments *significando causant*, that is, he does not say that they cause by signifying.[38]

Power recognizes in Schillebeeckx's work a continuation of this view of cause and signifying action as distinct but related. Whereas Aquinas used the categories of sign and instrument within the analogy of being, Schillebeeckx engaged the interpersonal and symbolic in the more helpful analogy of an encounter with God. Léon-Dufour has pursued the personal-phenomenological approach through exegesis of the dominical command, "Do this in remembrance of me." At the conclusion to the image and words of bread and cup, Jesus' memorial command directs his followers to the presence of his person ("in memory of *me*"), to the presence of the one whose life of service unto death is becoming the source of their lives.[39] Jesus establishes a new, volatilized form of his presence that will sustain and be formative of his followers in his absence. The ritual action, through its symbolic imagery of words, objects, and gestures, makes present again the cognitive con-

---

[37] On the words of the supper narrative, anamnesis, and epiclesis as each articulating the power of the prayer as a whole, see Power, *The Eucharistic Mystery*, 136, and 90, n. 20.

[38] Ibid., 233–34.

[39] Léon-Dufour, *Sharing the Eucharistic Bread*, 67.

tent and affective power of encountering the one who died for sinful humanity, once and for all. The source of eucharistic grace lies in the divine mystery of the human person Jesus. The divine-human gift of his person is formative of Christ's followers through the human media of word and sacrament.

The dialectic of divine causality and human signification in the Eucharist demonstrates that ongoing philosophical reflection into the human phenomenon of remembering is not done with any intention of denying or minimizing the unique faith the church places in the divine mystery of its central ritual action. Still, the biblical content of Christian faith reveals both the human history of suffering and the unique personhood of every Other as constitutive of this ritual tradition. This irreducible role of history in human salvation and the vocation of Christ-like service to the Other situate the practice of faith in the "space" of ethics. Nearly two millennia of Christian practice bear witness that faith in Christ does not in some magical way, least of all "through" the sacraments, eliminate people's inclinations to shy away from the face of the suffering Other, despite Christ's teaching that this is the very place we can encounter the Lord whom we seek.[40] Likewise, the temptation to think that we know entirely who the Other is, that we can "write off" that person, for whatever reason, as unworthy of our efforts, betrays what Wyschogrod calls the "category mistake" of thinking that our language directly applies to (represents) the Other.[41] Herein arises the ethical necessity of narrative, which always *fissures* such totalizing illusions, such reductions of others to quick images, such as "homeless" or "foreigner." Apprehending the "narrative dimension of truth and value"[42] intellectually supports a faith practiced between word, sacrament, and ethics.

These explorations into ethics and remembering, memory and sacrament, provide insight into the "remembrance-structure" that Christianity can bring to the social processes of late modernity along two lines of inquiry: what this remembrance-structure is and how Christians can indeed bring it to the social arena. In making present the truth or reality of our salvation, liturgical anamnesis demonstrates both the punctiform and stretched views of time. Performance of the eucharistic prayer, for example, proclaims a definitive moment in

[40] See Matthew 25:31-46.
[41] Wyschogrod, *An Ethics of Remembering*, 9.
[42] Ibid., 32.

151

history, the death and resurrection of Jesus, which brought about a whole new way of conceiving God, the human condition, and the status of this world. This image in the moment, however, also needs the fluid sense of time, generated not only in the narrative of the eucharistic prayer but also throughout the entire liturgy. The reduction of the narrative dimension in the Mass, wherein for centuries the Liturgy of the Word cyclically touched a narrow scope of Scripture, homiletic preaching was lost, and the Liturgy of the Eucharist was performed silently by a priest who raised host and chalice above the back he offered to the people, cut out the human heart the act of divine worship was meant to sanctify. The meaning and, therefore, the symbolic impact of the eucharistic liturgy depends upon the anamnetic dimension of the proclamation of the Word in the readings and homily, of the assembly's response in the general intercessions, of the interplay of proclamation and response in the service of the Eucharist. Stripped of any of these remembrancing elements, the liturgy loses the very possibility of being an image of the glory of God and salvation of humanity in which the assembled people can take a full, conscious, and active part.[43]

As each enactment of liturgy, in word and image, reveals God's pleasure in being glorified through the redemption and liberation of people in history, its participants are formed in the remembrance-structure that is integral not only to the celebration of the faith itself but also to the pattern of seeing the world in the light of that faith. The remembrance-structure Christians thereby "bring" to contemporary society is a mindset valuing the narratives and images of the lost and dead and of those presently silent and marginalized as essential to decisions and actions taken in the economic, political, technological, and educational arenas. With the liturgy of the Lord's Day functioning as the source and summit of their lives, they find not only the courage and strength but also the desire and aptitude for joining fellow citizens in the ethics of remembering, opening up a space wherein the work for justice can move forward.

---

[43] See *Sacrosanctum Concilium*, nos. 9 and 14. Space limitations prohibit my elaborating examples from other liturgies of the church.

Part 5

Symbol and Sacrament: Theological Anthropology

> The symbolic element represents the whole of the world to which it belongs; better, it carries it in itself. This is why it *is* what it represents. Obviously, it is not "really" but "symbolically" what it represents, precisely because the function of the symbol is to *represent* the real, therefore to place it at a distance in order to present it, to make it present under a new mode. . . . From this point of view the symbol is no longer in the field of the unreal; on the contrary, it is in the field of the most significant and the *most real*. Only, the real we are speaking of here is not that of raw material; it is the real humanly (symbolically) constructed into a "world," of which we have spoken previously.[1]

Elbatrina Clauteaux asserts the original theological contribution that Chauvet has made in his ongoing linguistic and prelinguistic, phenomenological and ontological, argument for the inextricable relationship between symbol and reality in human experience. Chauvet's positive exploitation of the extralinguistic dimension of existence comes by way of his insistence on the bodily opacity of all human symbolic activity, including that whereby God comes into real-symbolic (sacramental) presence in the risen Christ "under a mode of absence." It is precisely its function of joining related yet truly different participants in a relationship (contract) that indicates the "meta-function" of all symbolizing, that is, the human mode of constructing a world of meaning is a function of the "always beyond" dimension of all such activity.

[1] Louis-Marie Chauvet, *The Sacraments: The Word of God at the Mercy of the Body* (Collegeville, MN: Liturgical Press, 2001), 72–73.

153

Drawing upon the seminal theories of such French theorists as P. Ricoeur and S. Breton, Clauteaux explicates the profound theological implications—both sacramental and anthropological—that open out from the recognition that the world-creating power of every particular symbol rests on the principle of a universal interdependence ontologically constitutive of reality. One must keep in mind, nonetheless, that the ontological reality of the world of symbolism always occurs in ontic specificity. Symbol occurs in the interplay of *logos* and *bios*, its noetic yield always emerging at the juncture of the linguistic and the semiotic, thinking and sensing, the rational and the physical, the spiritual and the bodily. Clauteaux closes by recovering for theology done in league with Chauvet a positive return to the doctrine of the hypostatic union. The revelation of God in the symbol-sacrament of Jesus Christ (and now, his ecclesial body in the world) brings salvation to humanity "from beyond" by joining the utterly different dimensions of the divine and the human on the symbolic terrain of our corporeal existence.

Judith Kubicki likewise highlights the world-constructing function of human symbolism, as well as the "beyond" dimension in this for Christians. She does so, however, with a view not to the ontological grounding but, rather, the ethical implications of sacramental anthropology. Kubicki builds on Chauvet's identification of the sacraments' power in the presence and action of the Spirit of the risen Christ and purpose as none other than the raising up of a "new humanity" to flesh out something of the eschatological, indicative-imperative tension inherent to the life of faith. Whereas Clauteaux ends with reference to the incarnation, Kubicki (with Chauvet) starts from the paschal mystery to argue for how the church's sacramental celebrations find validity only through ethical engagement with the world. In our own time, she observes, this world is fraught with violence, demanding of Christians their commitment, grounded in the grace of the paschal mystery, to work for justice and reconciliation.

Rather than argue abstractly, Kubicki demonstrates the function of symbol in world-construction by analyzing one particular Christian liturgical unit, the *Exsultet*, as disclosing the universal vision of the church's sacramental faith. The performance of the prayer asserts God's desire for and beginning of a new creation as the source of humanity's hope for its realization in a world whose darkness is the very medium for embracing and carrying forth the light of Christ.

Chapter 9

When Anthropologist Encounters Theologian: The Eagle and the Tortoise

Elbatrina Clauteaux

Once upon a time, a lonely Tortoise was walking on the earth, her eyes fixed on the road, minutely counting every little pebble, every twig, attentive to the least rustling of leaves, to the birds singing, to human conversations. From time to time she timidly stretched out her neck to better feel the caress of the wind, the heat of the sun, or the freshness of raindrops.

During this time, an Eagle in rapid flight was traveling through the sky, taking in the horizon at a glance with his piercing gaze. Nothing escaped his ever-awakened senses. It was thus that he saw down below on the level of mother earth something that resembled a rock, yet moving. Intrigued, he sharpened his glance just at the moment when "the thing" exposed its pointed head. A tortoise! Amused, the Eagle spoke to the Tortoise, and the Tortoise, who sensed and understood so well that she had to protect herself in her shell so as not to succumb to sensation, listened.

It was on that day that the Eagle and the Tortoise decided to go on a trip together. The Eagle-theologian, who one day became an anthropologist, discovered things old and new in the company of the Tortoise-anthropologist. The Tortoise-anthropologist could, thanks to the Eagle, develop and unfold her very recent theological knowledge and practice the philosophy of her youth. The Eagle amused himself and the Tortoise lost a bit of her shyness; she dared to stick her head out more often to look at the sky with the hope of seeing from time to time the flight of her Eagle-friend in the sky of theology.

It was like this that I first met Louis-Marie Chauvet, who directed my master's degree in theology. Later he became the director of my doctoral dissertation, and together we have presented a seminar entitled "Ecclesial Mediations of the Relation with God in the Writings of Barth, Rahner, and Balthasar"—at once a theological feast and a boiling over of thought. For Chauvet is not about making disciples. He teaches a whirlwind of reflections in the stream of convictions born of long theological practice. He evokes untiring questioning, as if what he said demands to be deepened further, drawn further out, or protected. He does not make disciples because he succeeds in extracting from his students the expression of what they have that is most original in them. He throws himself into a fruitful dialogue with his interlocutor. For four years, in this two-hour-long weekly seminar, he brought his enthusiasm, his pedagogical experience, and his openness to a triangular conversation with anthropology, philosophy, and theology. As for me, I brought my sensitivity and the curiosity of a tortoise, along with my love of wisdom and my young theology's naiveté of a Metis, whose interests were situated on the margins of philosophy, anthropology, and theology. The students did not escape from this *ebullitio*. I understood that those who see were able to see; those who were able to feel, felt; and those who search were able to seek. Chauvet taught me the secret of passing it on. I became a teacher. Our seminar let us navigate between epistemologies because the theological concern was always there as a beaming lantern, because we had sympathy for the social sciences and a common empathy toward philosophy. Chauvet doesn't do theology arising from the social sciences and philosophy. He theologizes *with* them, without confusion, without separation, in fraternal company and fruitful conversation. Thus we, teachers and students together, in an *open* exercise in the past, the present, and the future, created this work of thought in theology. Our seminar was always a game, a theological game where one teaches and learns by playing. I can assure you, we were never bored! For nothing is more serious than play, as Gadamer explained: "play has with seriousness an essential relationship which is proper to it . . . a sacred seriousness. So that the game is wholly a game, it is not its relationship that turns it away from seriousness. It is the seriousness in the game. Whoever does not take the game seriously is a killjoy."[1] The game precedes us, holds us, and captivates us. It also goes beyond us. Chauvet sometimes began to sing, and the discussions in the seminar turned into a kind of dance in the primary sense of a word game. The coming and

[1] *Vérité et méthode*, tr. française d'Étienne Sacre (Paris: Seuil, 1996), 119–20.

going of a *disputatio* was thus entered into, sometimes between two or three participants, sometimes between two faculty members, who sought to lead on the same foot, even though they were radically different, and at other times with everyone together like a dance company.

"The Eagle and the Tortoise" . . . A symbolic language for relating the encounter of anthropologist and theologian, who, in the work of Chauvet, make recourse to the symbolic: *Du symbolique au symbole* (1979), *Symbole et Sacrement* (1988), *Quand le théologien devient anthropologue . . .* (1997).[2] The symbolic in his theology is like a red thread whose color simultaneously characterizes humanity. For what is more "human" than the symbol whose paradigm is the body? If I could summarize his way of doing theology, I would say that it is *symbolic* in the etymological sense of *binding together, of creating connections* between the disciplines. It is in this vein, in a spirit of research and of recognition, a spirit that always animated our relationship as Eagle and Tortoise, that I would like to offer the following remarks: I offer you the fruit, not yet ripe, of my research on the symbolic, for as E. Jüngel used to say regarding his teacher Karl Barth, "a thinker you honor by thinking."[3] Here is what symbol gave me to think about.

First, I will present two symbols in a work found in American Indian wisdom. Further on will be the question of the symbolic in Chauvet. Then, the symbolic will submit itself to questioning about the "meta-function," this demanding energy that pushes beyond and toward abandonment. It proffers a critical exponent to our theoretical acquisitions and impedes the bringing of reality under control. We will see how the "meta-function" both allows taking account of the opaque side of the symbol from the anthropological point of view rooted in the real and, from the point of view of Christian liturgy, constitutes the thickness of the *real* presence of the sacrament. The real-symbolic interests theology in its efforts to understand the foundations of Christian identity, for in the sacrament-symbol we receive the grace to become what we are, sons and daughters in the Son.

---

[2] Of these three titles, only the middle one had been translated into English.
[3] Eberhard Jüngel, ". . . Pas de Dieu sans l'homme," in *Karl Barth. Genèse et Réception de sa théologie* (Genève: Labor et Fides, 1987), 195.

THE WORLD-TIME OF PEMON:
AN IMMANENT TRANSCENDENCE

All my research comes from my ethnographic experience working with the Pemon Indians in the Amazon of Venezuela. My husband, three children, and I have lived for ten years with these Amerindians, whose symbolic wisdom has left its mark on us. For fifteen years I recovered the sense of orality from these indigenous peoples in an interpretation that is itself symbolic. I came to propose the revival of some Pemon myths and tales in the form of story as a hermeneutical tool with a view to the theoretical interpretation of their wisdom. This work of philosophy of religion has led me to a fundamental consideration of the symbolic mentality, very much present in biblical religious language, and in liturgical expression, and thus present also in the theology that reflects these.

We are going to start with Pemon wisdom. Before dwelling on two symbolic figures of this wisdom, however, we will need to clarify some vocabulary, for if the reflection on symbols is to interest diverse disciplines (mathematics, linguistics, sociology, psychoanalysis, history, phenomenology, theology), it will require an initial understanding of the meaning of these terms. Let us distinguish *the* symbolic from symbolic science and symbolism. Symbolism is the functioning of symbolic figures in a determined field, while symbolic science is the science concerned with symbolism. *The* symbolic is taken in the present case as a symbolic order as such. It is the object of a phenomenological-hermeneutic approach within the theological endeavor.[4] Here are two symbols gathered during my ethnological observation with the Pemon people.

Pata Pemonton, the Land of Men, the country of the Pemon Indians,[5] is a living and vital place, symbolically located in World-Time, whose two mythical columns are *Pia Daktay, the First-Time,* and *Serewaray, the Now.* The *Waïpa,* the large common house of the village, symbolizes this World-Time. Its circular or oval form rests upon two poles: *Pia* and *Serewaray.* During the festivals the Pemon *Men* dance the *before* and the *now.*

> . . . *The common house is Waïpa-Toukouchi-pan, the image of the World of the Pemon! And Teriteri-pan is round! For Teriteri-pan, round is her*

---

[4] Cf. Chauvet, *Du symbolique au symbole* (Paris: Cerf, 1979), 13–19.

[5] *Pemon* means *Man. Pata* means *inhabited place.*

earth! Teriteri-pan, round is her sky. Her sky, her roof that rests upon two good and beautiful trees in order to recall the two poles of the great Waïpa of the World. The two poles, Pia Daktay and Serewaray, the two legs of time . . .[6]

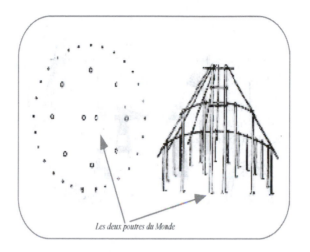

Les deux poutres du Monde

These two poles, these two trees, *waki mori, good and beautiful*, symbolize the fundamental myth of *Pata Pemonton, the Land of Men*, summarized in the Pemon formula: *Pia-to daktay tukaray-ray Pemon-pay epuetipue: In (that time) That-Time, everything of the World was like men.*

The Pemon do not tell whence they come, nor whence they descended, nor how they began *to become Pemon*, that is to say, "men," nor even if there was or was not anything before them. They only speak of the First Time, itself a beginning, defined as an "era" when the entire world was *Pemon-pe*, like men, to such a degree that people, animals, and things were able to *speak together* and thus have little ones *together*. What we call "humanity" was thereby an attribute of all inhabitants of *Pia Daktay*, of the *First Time*, on *Pata Pemonton*, on the *Land of Men*.

> . . . *Tauron Panton Pia-Daktay, the Tale says that in That Time, before the World lost its colors in the mud of Pia-Konok the Great Rain, Men spoke with Things, and Things spoke with Men, and they could have*

---

[6] Elba Este-Clauteaux., "La Maison du Monde," appeared in the street paper *L'Itinérant*, no. 111.

*their little ones together. Wana-the-Blade-of-Grass had often had a child
with Katourou-the-Cloud, the wind carried their love, a Waïra-Tapir
could marry with Paranka-the-Majestic-Cedar, the color carried their
love, a Pemon could have a little one with Wadamori-the-Tortoise, the
land carried the two of them to each other. The World was with Aouka-
the-Joy-of-Things, because Things and Men could speak together . . .
Tauron Panton, thus spoke the Tale.* [7]

Pia-Daktay, the First Time,[8] is thus primordial Time, a time that was
not yet totally there but would return if man, the only one to watch
over "humanity," ritually relived this time, *sereware*, now. An *immanent
transcendence* is at work in ritual mediation. Leaving neither the flesh
of symbol nor the robe of myth, the Pemon transcend toward That-
which-goes-beyond-us, horizontally and vertically.

We have here the symbol of the symbolic, that is, the universal communication here and now mediating symbolic actions, which is to say
what *holds a place* of this World-Time, a World-Time whose sole human
being is capable of re-presentation. An ordered world, rendered cosmic by myth, in the rite, governs the existence of the Pemon, as this
second example will demonstrate.

*Tauron Panton Pia Daktay, the Tale says that in That Time, when Things
of the World spoke pemon with the Pemon and they could have little ones
with each other, it was Waremba-the-Great-Liana who explained mar-
riage to Men.*
I am Waremba-Chinak,
I am Waremba-the-Liana,
I embrace my tree without suffocating it,
I lean against him to ascend toward the light.
At times, after many years, I am stronger than him,
But if a storm kills him, it kills me,
If the wind lays him on the ground, I lie on the ground,
If he dies, I die.
I am Waremba-Yey.

[7] Este-Clauteaux, "Karan-Piasan, le Voyage-du-Sorcier," *Panton Pata Pemonton, Histoires de la Terre des Hommes. Contes, Mythes et Légendes des Indiens Pémon
du Venezuela* (Paris: L'Harmattan, 1997), 91f.
[8] *Pia* means tree roots, ancestors, authority. *Daktay* means weather, time,
season.

I am Waremba-the-Marriage-Tree.
Toukouy toukouy, let us dance, let us dance.[9]

Waremba, The Marriage-Tree, a tree always accompanied by a liana, teaches the human couple the particularity of the bond that unites them—asymmetric, reciprocal, and alternating: man and woman are *symbolically* liana and tree, each by turn. In this symbol the rootedness in the real is evident. It is a matter of a tree that exists in the forest that they often encounter, and that produces in a Pemon spirit the figuration of another reality, one of conjugal union. It is a matter of reaching symbolically the reality of marriage without leaving the reality of the tree. From that point transcendence, horizontal and vertical, is present in the immanence of life.

Let us remember by our reasoning that in this religious cosmos, given rhythm through myths and rites, we have access to a real and symbolic presence of an immanent transcendence, what configures identity and life.

FROM SYMBOL TO THE SYMBOLIC: THE OPAQUENESS OF THE SYMBOL

Keeping in mind this anthropological account, let us remember the theological activity of Chauvet. In the linguistic watershed of the 1970s, he thought about the sacraments, which "are for humans" according to the question of the human-real, that is to say, in the problematic of language as mediation coming from Heidegger.[10] In a risky position for that time, Chauvet defended his revolutionary dissertation, *Du symbolique au symbole-sacrement.* The sacraments in this perspective are understood no longer in the logic of sign and cause but, rather, in the symbolic order of gap and exchange. Chauvet maintains vigorously that it would be "folly" to pretend *"that we can somehow pull ourselves out of the necessary mediation of symbols,* situate ourselves outside of discourse, and apprehend reality directly . . ."[11] The symbolic is the milieu wherein the real happens *for* us, and symbol is "the

---

[9] Este-Clauteaux, "Waremba, l'Arbre-Mariage," *Panton Pata Pemonton. Histoires de la Terre des Hommes. Contes, mythes et légendes des Indiens Pémon du Venezuela* (Paris: L'Harmattan, 1997), 138–43.

[10] Cf. Chauvet, *Du symbolique au symbole,* 9f.

[11] *Symbole et Sacrement. Une relecture sacramentelle de l'existence chrétienne* (Paris: Cerf, 1988), 86; English trans., 82.

161

witness of the vacant place."[12] He explains in a conceptual way what we observed with the Pemon people: the symbol is contact with a living reality. But in insisting upon the effects of the revealing and operative dimension of the symbol for sacramental theology, he emphasizes the linguistic dimension.[13] From there he brings about an invaluable contribution to fundamental theology while also introducing new questions.

The prelinguistic dimension of the symbol, more ontic than linguistic, is always presupposed to be at the point of becoming language in the broad sense: "For there is no human reality, however interior or intimate, except through the mediation of language or quasi-language that gives it a body by expressing it."[14] But this opaque face never totally absorbed by speech, this "flesh" of the "word" that we call the symbolic-real, has not been sufficiently considered. In order to think about it one must find adequate metaphysical words, whereas at the time of Chauvet's *Du symbolique au symbole* we were at the tail end of traditional metaphysics, and the "grafting" of hermeneutics onto phenomenology, postulated by Paul Ricoeur, was still recent.[15] It only resides there as a *"witness* to a vacant place," the symbol holding the real by means of its flesh. Like an ambassador who re-presents his country in speaking and acting in its name, the symbol makes present what it refers to and, through what is physical, its corporal opaqueness (action, gesture, object), it conveys toward and in what is symbolized.[16] For this reason, by this positive realization of the extralinguistic, there is no more vacant place, no more absence, so that the presence "under the manner of absence" of the Risen One becomes sacramental presence, that is, *symbolic-real.*

These presuppositions, always affirmed in sacramental theology,[17] demand attention, thanks to the vigorous resurgence of the endless metaphysics that we practice under the name of "meta-function." It is

[12] Ibid., 125; English trans., 117–18.

[13] Cf. ibid., 441–54; English trans., 425–38.

[14] Ibid., 95; English trans., 90; cf. *Du symbolique au symbole*, 20, 56ff.

[15] Cf. *Du texte à l'action, Essais d'herméneutique II* (Paris: Seuil, 1986), 39–73.

[16] Cf. Dominique Dubarle, "Pratique du symbole et connaissance de Dieu," *Le mythe et le symbole. De la connaissance figurative de Dieu,* (Paris: Beauchesne, 1977), 210–28.

[17] See the essays in this volume by Jean-Louis-Souletie and Philippe Bordeyne.

under its demanding grasp that we are forced to envisage the conditions for the possibility of this symbolic-real that comes into language without being reduced by it. For if the symbol gives such considerations to think and speak about, it is because lived reality, in its being and its appearance, *is* symbolic: "Before constructing a text (a culture, a religion) at the literary level (ethnological or liturgical), symbols offer a significant *texture*."[18]

I understand this symbolic *texture* as the condition for the possibility of the symbol and, moreover, as the attachment of the symbolic to the real so strongly defended by Chauvet: "*the symbol touches the most real aspect of ourselves and our world. It touches us to the quick.*"[19] Thus in his work and his teaching he invites us to move further and to think about the symbolic as the condition for the possibility of the symbol and thus for sacrament. For although he cannot return to the metaphysics of onto-theology, we must rediscover "another beginning" of the eternal metaphysic thanks to the force of questioning the "meta-function," in order to articulate the phenomenon and the foundation.[20] This "meta-function," often found in Chauvet's numerous writings, is a pointer that activates it as a "concern" to go further. It testifies that for theologians reality is greater than our theories, "because the metaphysical, although overcome, does not disappear."[21] Let us recall what Chauvet said most recently at Louvain when he gave a lecture on the occasion of receiving a doctorate *honoris causa*:

> Language requires that we think about it as an "ontophany." Without doubt *Symbol and Sacrament* should have emphasized more the "onto" of this ontophany, especially in the development of the importance of that which S. Breton calls "*the meta function*" understood there and even beforehand in *metaphysics*. What indicates this function? It is indicated as a function of openness of permanent displacement, that the truth is always "meta," in the sense of

[18] Paul Ricoeur, "Poétique et symbolique," *Initiation à la pratique de la théologie* (Paris: Cerf, 1987), 42.

[19] *Symbole et Sacrement. Une relecture sacramentelle de l'existence chrétienne* (Paris: Cerf, 1988), 130f.; English, 123; (emphasis in original French and translated English version).

[20] Cf. John Paul II, encyclical *Fides et Ratio*, no. 83 (Paris: Cerf-Bayard-Centurion-Fleurus-Mame, 1998), 107f.

[21] Martin Heidegger, "Dépassement de la métaphysique" *Essais et conférences* (Paris: Gallimard "Tel" 52), 82, cited by Chauvet, *Symbole et Sacrement*, 53.

"beyond," and thus that its articulation can only be (literally) "meta-phorical."[22]

Let us take Chauvet at his word and try to accomplish his wish by providing some working hypotheses with an eye to later theological developments. If as Ricoeur says, "to show something leads to saying it,"[23] let us look at what is given in the symbol. Let us, in a postmetaphysical age or "meta-physic" of reason, work on a meeting between phenomenology and metaphysics in an "ontophany" of the symbol.[24]

THE WORK OF THE "META-FUNCTION": ONTOPHANY OF THE SYMBOL

The idea of the "meta-function" took shape at the beginning of the 1980s among a group of exegetes, philosophers, psychoanalysts, and historians who, over the course of several years, met in Paris at the Jesuit-run Centre Sèvres. Since that time thinkers such as Stanislas Breton, Paul Ricoeur, and Jean Greisch have used the concept in the development of their philosophy.[25] Starting from the argument that metaphysics does not have a monopoly over the prefix *meta*, since it is a surpassing force proper to the human spirit seeking to go beyond the questioning characteristic of all scientific endeavors, these thinkers in the age of hermeneutical reason believed in the "maybe," the "maybe" and the "as if" . . . because the human person no longer understands the self only as "existing" or "possessing" but also as "becoming," that is, as a historical human person.[26]

---

[22] Chauvet, "Une relecture de *Symbole et sacrement*," *Questions liturgiques*, 88/2 (2007): 111–25. Cf. "Le pain rompu comme figure théologique de la présence eucharistique," *Questions liturgiques* 82/1 (2001): 11ff.

[23] "Parole et symbole," in *RSR Le symbole* (janvier–avril 1975): 156.

[24] Cf. Jean Greisch, *Le cogito herméneutique*, (Paris: Vrin, 2000), 190–95; Hans-Georg Gadamer, "Phénoménologie, herméneutique, métaphysique," *Revue de Métaphysique et de Morale* 98/4 (1993).

[25] Stanislas Breton, *Poétique du sensible*, (Paris: Cerf, 1988), 35–55; Paul Ricoeur, *Réflexion faite: autobiographie intellectuelle* (Paris: Esprit, 1995) 88ff.; Greisch, *Le cogito herméneutique*, 173–248.

[26] Cf. Clifford Geertz, "Comment nous pensons maintenant: vers une ethnographie de la pensée moderne," *Savoir local, savoir global, les lieux du savoir* (Paris: PUF, 1986), 183–204; and Gadamer, "Phénoménologie, herméneutique, métaphysique," 483f.

To exercise the "meta-function" is to question so as to exceed, displace, or rediscover, because it opens the spirit to the possible of the other and the elsewhere.[27] Thus the work of this function consists of reinterpreting the traditions of thought in favor of a possible meaning that abides in the shadow, thanks to the intercultural dialogue of our third millennium. For us who have departed phenomenologically from another and an elsewhere with the Pemon Indians, it is a matter of theorizing again from the lived symbolic.

The Symbolic-Real

What do we mean by the symbolic? I am not going to give a definition. Others are accustomed to study symbol from the perspective of linguistics, ethnology, sociology, psychology, or mathematics. These multiple definitions that make claim to the polysemy of the symbol, and thus its constitutive plurivocality, all start from a discussion of *symbolon*, a sign of recognition constituted by two halves of a broken object. The etymology of *symbolon*, from the verb *sym-ballo* (to throw *together*), indicates the idea of recreating a unity and presupposed harmony. In fact, if in the original meaning *symbolon* meant an object cut into two parts of which two persons each keep a half, it is because the two fragments served to make known the bearer and to prove an economic, familial, or friendly relationship that existed beforehand, allowing hospitality and recognition. Each fragment refers symbolically to both the unity and the breaking. It is by thus departing from this primary experience, of which the etymology preserves the trail, that I envisage the symbolic as this structure of the human spirit that makes it possible to enter into relationship with the world, but also as the fabric of relations that form the world. The symbolic *is* as such *the agreement with,* and in this sense we can speak about transcendental value. Whereas the concrete symbol is the crystallization of this agreement realized by humans, the symbolic is the condition for its possibility.

If the tree surrounded by a liana is the symbol of marriage among the Pemon Indians of the Venezuelan Amazon, in France or elsewhere this means nothing. This tree-liana is not only a symbol *inasmuch as it is among these Indians* but also inasmuch as, in a symbolic logic that obeys the ontological correspondence of orders, this relationship of the tree and the liana is also a "bond" whose "bond" is the relation between a man and a woman. It is a matter of a well-determined link, a

[27] Cf. Gadamer, "Phénoménologie, herméneutique, métaphysique," 483–87.

165

link that takes the form and shape in the reality of a certain tree as of marriage. If "bread" symbolizes food in the Western world, like "corn" in America or "millet" in Africa and "rice" in Asia, it is because before everything else, bread, corn, millet, and rice are food. The symbol "refers to nothing more than is already present in itself."[28] It is a mediation of participation. It is because of this that, in a genealogical effort, we attach our symbol to the experience that etymology recalls for us, but also to the logic that undergirds it phenomenologically and that gives an account of an ontological reality. The ultimate reason for the *symbolon* is to signify and to show that there is a fractured unity to be reunified, that of the reality, because without real presence there is no symbol. It is in revealing the fracture of a harmony and the harmony behind the fracture that the symbol re-presents.

Therefore, departing from a particular example, if *a* symbol as such can only function in a cultural, ritual, and contextual collection, this does not mean that its foundations may be only particular. A particular symbol refers of course to a particular world that it crystallizes, but its *symbolic virtue*, its symbolizing power, does not come to it from this world but from a principle of universal interdependence, ontologically constitutive of reality. We will therefore speak of a symbolic principle and of "pretension" to the universal from the logic generated by it.[29] If *a* symbol introduces us in *a* given order, *the* symbol, inasmuch as it is a phenomenon that manifests itself from itself, gives an account of the harmony of the world in which we participate.

The fundamental hypothesis of the epistemology of Feyerabend,[30] explained by Jean Ladrière, says "that there exists a real objective world, which contains the observer and which is of such a kind that between our sensations and the events of the world there exists a high degree of correlation. The sensations and perceptions are simply indicators: They therefore have a role that is totally analogous to that of the physical instruments." Extrapolating from this thesis I would say that language and symbol are the expression of the interpretation of the world that humans make in and through these sensations and per-

---

[28] Gadamer, *Vérité et méthode*, 172.

[29] Cf. Dubarle, "Pratique du symbole et connaissance de Dieu," 214f.

[30] "Problems of empiricism," Robert G. Colodny, ed., *Beyond the Edge of Certainty*, (Englewood Cliffs, NJ: Prentice Hall, 1965), 145–260; *L'articulation du sens I. Discours scientifique et parole de la foi* (Paris: Cerf, 1984), 38.

ceptions that are, in my opinion, much more than physical instruments, instruments for "interpreting" music.

Ernst Cassirer with his notion of "symbolic form" had some intuition in this regard. The human person has the power and the need to create symbols. People have always used certain perceptible phenomena, certain things from everyday life and from ordinary language, to evoke, convoke, cite, replace, denote, signify, represent, reveal, to symbolize other phenomena, other things that are not observable, not verifiable here and now. This is a creative process, and the "symbolic form" comes to be "the condensation in the facts of language of an activity that does not refer to a sense already constituted, but which to the contrary shapes it in the course of a process."[31] Indeed, if by the "symbolic form" we mean "the universal energy of the mind through which a content of spiritual meaning is placed side by side with a sensible concrete sign and is intrinsically adapted to this sign,"[32] it is because it deals with a creative activity in the sense of conforming itself, from a transcendent point of view, to what gives a framework a priori to thought and to do right humanly by such a framework.[33] This framework is the ontological reality of the world in which the symbol participates.

The Play of Symbol: Between logos and bios

To think about symbol by itself is to try to take in the totality of its shape. It always appears to us as something "mixed," difficult to discern, because constitutively it is made up of the linguistic and the prelinguistic, two dimensions that it assimilates concretely, like the interplay of gear pieces. The symbol signifies, shows, and operates simultaneously since it balances between the noetic, the ontological, and the ontic. It makes us participate in all these orders and thus becomes a different order that creates a system.[34] The symbol is not limited to the sphere of the *logos*. "For it is not its meaning which connects it to another meaning, it is on the contrary its own proper being, manifest,

---

[31] Jean Lassègue, "Note sur l'actualité de la notion de forme symbolique," *Methodos* 2 L'esprit, CNRS, 2002, p. 157.

[32] Ernst Cassirer, "Le concept de forme symbolique dans l'édification des sciences de l'esprit," *Trois essais sur le symbolique, Œuvres* VI (Paris: Cerf, 1997), 13.

[33] Jean Lassègue, "Note sur l'actualité de la notion de forme symbolique," 157.

[34] Cf. Dubarle, "Pratique du symbole et connaissance de Dieu," 210–17.

that has 'meaning.' When you encounter it, it is that by which we recognize something else"[35] because it puts us in contact with it.

Paul Ricoeur, who reflected about symbol, is confronted in his work with its complex nature. If the symbol gives rise to thought, it is first of all because it gives rise to a "semantic nucleus" that delivers its interpretation. Through this "semantic nucleus" the symbol is similar to language and may be enlightened, thanks to the theory of the living metaphor. It is the living metaphor that institutes the similitude to language, thanks to an impertinent prediction that, rather than substituting one meaning for another, establishes a tension between the ordinary and the extraordinary. Consequently, metaphor is the model of transference of meanings present in all symbolism. This productive imagination enables "seeing like," that is, to perceive the resemblance. We know that knowledge is never achieved directly; rather, we need what Kant called "over simplicity" in order that the productive imagination gives an image to the concept and thus realizes some new syntheses. The metaphor and the schema produce some semantic innovation and, like the symbol, show a second meaning through a primary meaning. But metaphor and schema keep a distance regarding the similarity apprehended by the predication and the conceptualization. *Articulating* in tension the two meanings, the symbol *assimilates* the resemblance and reunites two levels (for example, the engagement ring as a symbol of marriage). For this reason, there is a more real presentation in the symbol than in metaphor and concept, for it is not simply a matter of "sense." Still, only the metaphor can clarify the symbolic meaning, and only *the work of the concept* can witness to the excess of meaning of metaphor and of the excess of the symbolic-real: ". . . the symbol assimilates rather than apprehends a resemblance. Much more than assimilating some things to each other, it assimilates us to what is thus signified. . . . All boundaries recede, between the things and between us and the things."[36]

This means that the symbol does not reduce itself to its linguistic dimension, not because it can situate itself outside language or interpretation, but because it is the opaque origin, rooted in life experience and its effects, confounded in the hubbub of the world, situated in the lived experience. Thus, while the "metaphor holds itself in the already purified universe of the *logos*, the symbol straddles the line between

[35] Gadamer, *Vérité et méthode*, 89.
[36] Ricoeur, "Parole et symbole," *RSR Le symbole*, 150.

bios and *logos*. It witnesses to the original rooting of the Discourse on life"[37] while keeping all its opaqueness in the thick meaning.

The symbol, as linked to the prelinguistic soil, is not limited only to some sciences of language. The "dream," a phenomenon studied in psychoanalysis as a representative paradigm of psychological situations, is the entanglement of desire, drive, and language. Consequently, the terms accounted for are symbolic and situate themselves at the crossroads of the lived and its expression, working on a transposition of meaning: repression, displacement, condensation, transference. These terms are neither purely metaphorical nor purely ordinary. They want to account for the work realized in and through dreams; they refer as much to life as its representative interpretation. The example of a dream shows well that the symbolic does not express itself totally in the linguistic, that it is between discourse and what produces it.[38]

Another interesting example of this excess of the symbolic in relationship to the linguistic is myth. Philosophy of religion shows how myth is not of the order of the pure interpretation of reality or of its transmission. Myth inscribes itself in the rite, with belief giving the efficacious power to the word, but there is something else in the myth that arises from its connection with the world to be ordered, the cosmos. The logic of the symbolic correspondences present in the myth makes it something else than a metaphor whose life belongs to discourse; the life of the symbolic or myth goes beyond the discourse. It feeds itself on the capacity of the cosmos to show its order, to be "cosmetized." Of course, it is the word that mediates this, but this is presupposed. It is also the real presence that allows for the symbol. A myth is a story, certainly, but a religious story, connecting the human world to the divine world by the rite that repeats and realizes the mutual implication.[39]

Poetic activity also falls into the "more" symbolic since the experience that comes from language in the poem goes beyond the words, all the while remaining suspended to the word. It is as if the aura of the lived reality floats around the metaphor, raising it to the level of word-symbol.[40]

[37] Ibid., 153.

[38] Cf. Ricoeur, "Poétique et symbolique," *Initiation à la pratique de la théologie. l'Introduction*, 51–53.

[39] Cf. ibid., 53f.

[40] Cf. ibid., 54.

Thus we cannot separate the metaphorical word and symbol; we can barely distinguish them. Since in the metaphor there is the possibility of becoming a symbol, thanks to the genius of the poet, there is in the symbol a metaphorical process of translation of meaning, even if, as we have attempted to say, the symbol is the conveyer of the real to the real. The category of "play" would be the most appropriate to account for the nature of the symbol. Thus the play between *logos* and *bios* allows us to understand that the symbol is more than language yet requires it constantly and dances with it.

CONCLUSION

The anthropological and philosophical approach to symbol can go beyond its ever-open frontier toward a theology of sacrament. For if the God of Jesus Christ is the Totally Other, he is also the Totally Near, and he is really in symbolic and sacramental relationship with us. Thus, it seems that the symbol is, according to its etymology, this concrete mediation, metaphorical and anaphoric, that allows us to navigate between worlds. *When the theologian becomes anthropologist,*[41] this symbol-sacrament rediscovers its human roots, and when the anthropologist becomes theologian, passing through philosophy, the symbol-sacrament ontologically returns to its divine aim. For the symbol-sacrament is the witness of the "hypostatic union" of the divine and the human in Christianity.

People inhabit this earth symbolically. Spirit in the world: it is in the play, the back and forth between the sensible and the intelligible, between the *thinking* sense and the *sensing* thought, that the human person deploys his or her humanity.[42] This "way of being" is therefore symbolic, as *symbolic* is the encounter of God and humans in the symbol-sacrament of which the body is the archi-symbolic place.[43] "The most spiritual takes place in the most corporal": this is the heart of Chauvet's theology. This "more spiritual" is God himself in this mystery of his self-communication, coming really "at the risk of the body" in sacrament.[44]

[41] Chauvet, *Approches scientifiques du fait religieux* (Paris: Beauchesne, 1997), 29–46.

[42] Cf. Heidegger, *Le principe de raison* (Paris: Gallimard, 1962), 126ff.

[43] Cf. Chauvet, *Symbole et Sacrement*, 158f.; English, 151ff.

[44] Chauvet, "Une relecture de *Symbole et Sacrement*," leçon academic lecture given at Louvain, March 7, 2007, p. 12; *Les sacrements, parole de Dieu au risque du corps* (Paris: Ouvrières, 1997). Cf. Karl Rahner, *Traité fondamental de la foi* (Paris: Le Centurion, 1983), 139–50.

Chapter 10

Sacramental Symbols in a Time of Violence and Disruption:

Shaping a People of Hope and Eschatological Vision

Judith M. Kubicki, CSSF

INTRODUCTION

The classic novel, *A Tale of Two Cities*, by Charles Dickens, opens with the following lines:

> It was the best of times, it was the worst of times, it was the age of wisdom, it was the age of foolishness, it was the epoch of belief, it was the epoch of incredulity, it was the season of Light, it was the season of Darkness, it was the spring of hope, it was the winter of despair.[1]

In penning this paradoxical description of France on the eve of the French Revolution, Dickens likens his own time, the mid-nineteenth century, to the earlier epoch he is describing. Many might think these words just as aptly describe our own twenty-first century. On the one hand, advances in technology, science, and medicine have paved the way for unprecedented opportunities for improving life and solving problems. On the other hand, threats of random violence perpetrated through terrorism and street violence undermine the ordinary citizen's sense of security, not only in war-torn countries, but in every corner of the globe.

---

[1] Charles Dickens, *A Tale of Two Cities* (USA: Modern Library, 2000), 3. Originally published in 1859.

But the violence we inflict on each other is only a part of the story. Environmentalists have identified humankind's exploitive, wasteful, and destructive relationship with the earth as the direct cause of growing environmental ills. Such woes threaten not only the well-being of life on the planet, but also the integrity of a sacramental system that speaks through the various elements of creation. Industrialized nations pursue strategies that put profit before conservation and squander the planet's resources for the benefit of a powerful minority. Such policies have also been identified as the root cause of human strife on every level of existence. Indeed, most of the world's conflicts spring from religious bigotry, greed, and fear of the stranger. Controversy continues unabated regarding the ways in which we deal with immigrants, illegal aliens, gays and lesbians, and others perceived to be living outside the boundaries of traditional cultural or social norms. On a more local or personal level, threats to security also include sudden loss of employment or health, natural disasters, and the day-to-day challenges of providing for one's family, including elderly parents.

Even a superficial knowledge of history, however, reminds us that disaster and violence of every imaginable kind have been a part of the human story from the very beginning. Indeed, pain and suffering are an intrinsic part of the human condition. But what perhaps makes the twenty-first century different from former times is that never before has it been possible to be aware so vividly and so instantaneously of the pain and struggles occurring not only in our own homes or neighborhoods, but also in places thousands of miles away. This is part of the price we pay for technological prowess and expertise. The pain both across the globe and across the street is accessible to our everyday awareness.

Nevertheless, within such a world of strife, fear, and disruption, Christians continue to celebrate God's promise of healing and reconciliation won for us by the death and resurrection of Jesus Christ. We do this in a particular, though not exclusive, way through rituals called sacraments. Much has been written about the sacraments, including their theological and pastoral significance for the life of the church. In the past, the task of traditional Roman Catholic sacramental theology has been to explain how the seven sacramental rites of the church celebrate the grace of Christ bestowed on persons of faith who receive one or more of the sacraments worthily. Focus was on the action of Christ, the role of the minister, and the faith of the individual believer and church community. All this is still within the purview of sacramental theology. However, significant shifts have occurred as a result of the Second Vatican Council. This is particularly evident in the two council documents on the church. Article one of *Lumen Gentium* speaks of the church as "a sacrament—a sign and instrument, that is, of communion with God and of the unity of the entire human race . . ."[2] This same description of the church is repeated in article 9 of *Lumen Gentium* and again in article 42 of *Gaudium et Spes*. In other words, the council's first definition of church is church as sacrament, more specifically "as a *sacramentum mundi* ('sacrament of the world'), the visible sign of the 'saving unity' that embodies God's will and intention not only for humankind, but for creation itself."[3]

Such a vision of church suggests that what Christians do when they celebrate the sacraments is of critical importance, not only for the church's own self-realization, but also for a world torn by violence and disruption. Indeed, those who engage in the symbolizing activity we call sacraments are in some very real way being called to celebrate what Rahner has called "the liturgy of the world,"[4] not in isolation from, but in communion with the global community and the cosmos.

The work of Louis-Marie Chauvet has contributed significantly to the post–Vatican II task of understanding the role of sacramental celebrations within the context of life in the contemporary world. And while his contributions are many, this essay will consider only two aspects of his thought. The first is his theological anthropology of symbol, and the second, related to it, is his focus on the paschal mystery as the starting point for developing a sacramental theology.

A THEOLOGICAL ANTHROPOLOGY OF SYMBOL

In his highly influential *Symbol and Sacrament*, Chauvet posits an understanding of the human person as both shaping and being shaped by symbolizing activity. His anthropology of symbol begins by looking at the root meaning of the Greek word *symbolon*. Its literal meaning meant "to throw together." It could also be translated as "gather

---

[2] Dogmatic Constitution on the Church (*Lumen Gentium*) in *Vatican Council II: Constitutions, Decrees, Declarations*, gen. ed. Austin Flannery, inclusive language edition (Northport, New York: Costello, 1996), no. 1.

[3] Nathan Mitchell, *Meeting Mystery: Liturgy, Worship, Sacraments* (New York: Orbis, 2006), 253.

[4] See Michael Skelley, *The Liturgy of the World: Karl Rahner's Theology of Worship* (Collegeville, MN: Liturgical Press, 1991).

together," "hold in common," "exchange," "meet," or "converse."[5] Chauvet explains it this way:

> The ancient *symbolon* is precisely an object cut in two, one part of which is retained by each partner in a contract. Each half evidently has no value in itself and thus could imaginatively signify anything; its symbolic power is due only to its connection with the other half. When, years or even generations later, the partners or their descendants come together again to "symbolize" their two portions by joining them together, they recognize this act as the expression of the same contract, of the same alliance. It is thus the agreement between two partners which establishes the symbol; it is the *expression of a social pact based on mutual recognition* and, hence, is a *mediator of identity*.[6]

Today, Chauvet observes, the semantic field of the word "symbol" has been expanded to include every element (e.g., object, word, gesture, or person) that, exchanged like a password, enables either groups or individuals to recognize one another and identify themselves. In this same way, the many symbols celebrated in the sacraments—bread, wine, oil, fire, water, altar, crucifix, among others—mediate Christian identity and hence also the relationships within the community we call church.[7] Celebrating sacraments by means of symbolic activity enables the Christian community to weave and reweave relationships and to negotiate both individual and communal identity. Another way of describing this dynamic is to say that by means of sacramental activity, individuals and/or groups of Christian believers are reconciled with one another and with God.

Furthermore, Chauvet makes it clear that the significance of a symbol does not lie in the object, word, gesture, or person understood as such. Rather, it is by means of an activity by which human beings exchange some object, word, gesture, or person that they are able to recognize one another and discover their own identity. In other words, there is no meaning hidden in a symbol waiting to be discovered. Rather, it is by means of the exchange between persons that a symbol

---

[5] Chauvet, *Symbol and Sacrament: A Sacramental Reinterpretation of Christian Existence*, trans. Patrick Madigan and Madeleine Beaumont (Collegeville, MN: Liturgical Press, 1995), 112.

[6] Ibid.

[7] See ibid.

mediates meaning. Gathered together in coherent patterns, multiple symbols provide a symbolic order that enables human beings as subjects to "build" themselves as they engage in building their world.[8] The task of the contemporary church is to discover what the activity of "building our world" might actually look like, given the challenges facing us today.

THE PASCHAL MYSTERY

A second contribution Chauvet offers the study of contemporary sacramental theology is a method that begins with a consideration of the Easter mystery rather than the Incarnation. This may not at first seem unusual or surprising since the church has always celebrated Easter as the first among all feasts. In fact, in the early church, it was the only feast celebrated. However, as Chauvet points out, the gradual fragmentation of the paschal mystery into a multiplicity of feasts observed throughout the liturgical year created a situation that made it easy to forget the eschatological "today" as a memorial. Instead, multiple liturgical feasts came to be viewed as the observances of an anniversary of one of the events in the life of Christ. This approach tended to weaken the faithful's appreciation of liturgy's innate sacramentality.[9]

By beginning with a consideration of the paschal mystery, Chauvet breaks with the traditional approach formulated by Scholastic theology. The point of departure for the Scholastics was the mystery of the Incarnation. By placing the treatise on the sacraments after the treatise on christology, this approach characterized the sacraments as "the prolongation down to us of the 'holy humanity' of Christ."[10] Chauvet proceeds differently. He builds his sacramental theology on the paschal (Easter) mystery rather than the hypostatic union in order that he might challenge our presuppositions about God and about the sacraments. He poses the radical question: "What sort of God are we then speaking about if we are able to maintain, in faith, that God offers God's very self to be encountered through the mediation of the most material, the most corporeal, the most institutional of the Church's actions, the rites?"[11] In Chauvet's schema,

---

[8] Ibid., 86.

[9] Ibid., 484–85.

[10] Chauvet, *The Sacraments: The Word of God at the Mercy of the Body* (Collegeville, MN: Liturgical Press, 2001), 155.

[11] Chauvet, *Symbol and Sacrament*, 498.

the sacraments appear not as the somehow static prolongations of the incarnation as such but as the major expression, in our own history, of the embodiment (historical/eschatological) of the risen One in the world through the Spirit, embodiment whose "fundamental sacrament" is the church visibly born at Pentecost. The sacraments are thus situated in the dynamism of a secular history reread as a holy history. The theological affirmation of sacramental grace is understood in the wake of the church's faith in the power of the risen One continually raising for himself, through the Spirit, a body of new humanity.[12]

This "new humanity" is the corporeal manifestation of God's presence in the world. For this reason, we call the church a *sacramentum mundi*.

These two key aspects of Chauvet's methodology—developing a theological anthropology of symbol and starting with the paschal mystery rather than the Incarnation—provide pathways for discovering new insights into the celebration of the sacraments in a world torn by violence and disruption. For by focusing on symbol as the negotiator of identity and relationships and by highlighting the paschal mystery as the starting point for interpreting liturgical celebrations, Chauvet lays a foundation for retrieving a key understanding of Christian sacraments as symbolizing activity that shapes a people who can be instruments of reconciliation and signs of eschatological hope.

RECONCILING RELATIONSHIPS

On the anthropological level, symbolizing activity is about weaving and reweaving human relationships and thereby coming to know one's identity. On the theological level, sacramental activity is also about weaving and reweaving relationships in order to discover one's identity. But in the case of the sacraments, those relationships have an important theological dimension. The relationships negotiated include individuals with themselves, individuals with the community (church), and the church, thus constituted, with God and all creation.

Genesis tells us that before the Fall, our first parents were in right relationship with God, self, each other, and all creation. The New Testament tells us that the rupture that resulted from the Fall has finally been repaired or reconciled by the death and resurrection of Christ. Our participation in all the sacraments is fundamentally directed toward a lifetime response to God's invitation to be reconciled with

[12] Chauvet, *The Sacraments*, 160.

God—and hence with each other and creation. This response is ritually enacted through the sacraments and involves an ever-deepening participation in the paschal mystery of Jesus Christ.

Thus the reconciliation of humankind with God and all creation is primarily a response that takes the forms of the slow and halting journey toward the wholeness lost with the Fall and ransomed by the death and resurrection of Christ. Biblical wisdom refers to this wholeness as "justice," a justice that brings human beings into right relationship with God, self, others, and creation. John R. Donahue provides a succinct definition of biblical justice when he explains:

> In general terms the biblical idea of justice can be described as *fidelity to the demands of a relationship*. In contrast with modern individualism the Israelite is in a world where "to live" is to be united to others in a social context either by bonds of family or covenant relationships. This web of relationships—king with people, judge with complainants, family with tribe and kinfolk, the community with the resident alien and [with the] suffering in their midst and all with the covenant God—constitutes the world in which life is played out.[13]

Donahue speaks of a "web of relationships." Using Chauvet's framework, we would say that this web is constituted by the symbolic network that weaves and reweaves the individual and communal life of Israel. Fidelity to relationship is a necessary component of living a life of justice.

Walter J. Burghardt offers a telling description of what that justice looked like in daily life in Israel:

> They were just when they were in right relation in all aspects of their life: properly postured toward God, toward other men and women, and toward the earth, God's material creation. Love God above all else; love every man, woman, and child like another self, as an image of God; touch God's nonhuman creation, all that is not God or the human person, with reverence, not as despot but as steward.[14]

[13] John R. Donahue, "Biblical Perspectives on Justice," *The Faith That Does Justice: Examining the Christian Sources for Social Change*, ed. John C. Haughey (New York: Paulist Press, 1977), 69.

[14] Walter J. Burghardt, "Worship and Justice Reunited," *Liturgy and Justice: to Worship God in Spirit and Truth*, ed. Anne Koester (Collegeville, MN: Liturgical Press, 2002), 36.

Burghardt's description makes clear that biblical justice includes four components: God, self, human persons, and creation. All four need to be in right relationship for justice to prevail on the earth.

It is this Jewish understanding of justice out of which Jesus spoke when he described his ministry in the synagogue in Nazareth; "The Spirit of the Lord is upon me, because he [the Lord] has anointed me to bring good news to the poor. He has sent me to proclaim release to the captives and recovery of sight to the blind, to let the oppressed go free" (Luke 4:18). This theme—struggling to make all relationships right—runs throughout Jesus' ministry. His miracles are not so much proofs of his power, but gestures that return the ostracized to society and restore the sinner to God's friendship.[15]

Note, however, that biblical justice is radically different from other philosophical notions of justice such as commutative justice, distributive justice, and even social justice. Rather, biblical justice is linked with qualities such as mercy, steadfast love, and fidelity. The usual dichotomy between obligations of charity and obligations of justice is foreign to the Bible. In other words, biblical justice is about making things right rather than championing human rights. Furthermore, it gives priority to those most affected by evil and oppression. These are symbolized in the Hebrew Bible by widows, orphans, the poor, and strangers. It was embodied by Jesus' ministry to those who lived on social and religious margins.[16]

In the same way, the Christian journey is about being in right relationship with God, self, others, and creation. A commitment to work to build right relationships is rooted in the covenant initiated at baptism. This sacrament plunges the Christian into participation in Christ's paschal mystery. It is the point of entry into that lifetime participation that eventually comes to fruition in the fullness of God's kingdom at the end of time. As a result of baptism, the Christian lives out the paschal mystery of Jesus Christ as the way to weave and reweave right relationships. Sacraments become the church's primary means by which those relationships are initiated, healed, or reconciled. In other words, the symbolic order that constitutes sacraments provides Christians with the means by which that commitment to right relationships is communicated and nurtured. Expressing and shaping this commitment is possible because, as a complexus of language and quasi lan-

---

[15] Ibid., 37.
[16] Ibid., 38. See also Donahue, n. 13.

guages, sacramental symbols not only enable Christians to speak, but they also enable Christians to be spoken. What is spoken is Christ's word of healing and reconciliation.

Nevertheless, a very real tension exists between the Christian vision of the fullness of God's reign initiated by the death and resurrection of Christ and the world of darkness and sin that is our daily experience. This tension between the "already/not yet" of Christian existence reminds us that what Christ has accomplished is still an object of hope and desire. This desire is at the heart of Christian sacraments. For through sacraments, Christians experience the healing and reconciliation that enables them to become a people who can be signs of eschatological hope in the face of evil, violence, and despair. A study of any of the sacramental rites might be used to demonstrate how this dynamic is set in motion in the celebrating (handling) of Christian symbols. However, in the interest of space and time, only one paradigmatic moment will be examined in order to discover how the interplay of symbols can both express and shape reconciliation, and therefore, eschatological hope.

PROCLAIMING THE *EXSULTET*

There is perhaps no liturgical event richer in dense symbolizing activity than the Easter Vigil. For that reason, it is a prime example of the power inherent in the sacraments to proclaim the paschal mystery in such a way that the assembly hears God's word of reconciliation and is challenged to live in eschatological hope. The Easter Fire, the extended Liturgy of the Word, the Initiation Rites, and the Eucharist all involve a complexus of symbols that function as an archetype for all sacramental celebrations. To demonstrate how the symbolizing activity of sacramental liturgy can function in this manner, just one small component of the Easter Vigil will be considered. That component is the singing of the *Exsultet*, otherwise known as the Easter Proclamation.

The Easter Vigil begins with the blessing of the Easter fire. In the midst of actual darkness, the paschal candle is lit and Christ is proclaimed the light of the world. The fire is shared and the assembly, lit candles in hand, listen as the opening lines of the *Exsultet*[17] are intoned:

[17] English trans. of the *Exsultet* taken from the *Sacramentary* (New York: Catholic Book Publishing Company, 1974), 182–84.

> Rejoice, heavenly powers! Sing, choirs of angels!
>   Exult, all creation around God's throne!
>   Jesus Christ, our King, is risen!
>   Sound the trumpet of salvation!

Unbounded joy is the tenor of these lines, a joy that bursts into song from the firm conviction that Jesus Christ has risen from the dead. Furthermore, this cry of joy calls upon heaven and earth to join in celebrating this event. The text describes a world in which heaven and earth and all creation are united (in right relationship) because Christ is risen. This reference to creation is rooted in a biblical understanding of the cosmos as infused with the loving and active power of the Spirit's creative presence (see Gen 1:1).[18] The call for a royal trumpet fanfare complements the reference of Christ as king and underscores the significance of this earth-and-heaven-shaking event. The royal metaphor expresses the belief, common in the medieval world in which this text originates, that all is well in the realms of heaven and earth when the king (in this case, Christ) is victorious.

> Rejoice, O earth, in shining splendor,
>   radiant in the brightness of your King!
>   Christ has conquered! Glory fills you!
>   Darkness vanishes for ever!

The text is filled with images of light. Together, the four lines proclaim that the darkness of the earth is vanished in the shining splendor of Christ's victory. That is, creation reflects in its own radiant beauty the moral beauty of Christ's victory over sin and death. Indeed, in the glow of countless candles around the imposing paschal candle, light indeed appears to have conquered darkness. The text announces something more, however, when it claims that darkness vanishes *forever*. It is the first intimations of an eschatological thrust to the text. Our sights are set on a future that is being celebrated as already accomplished in the present. A little later on, the text continues:

> Most blessed of all nights, chosen by God
>   to see Christ rising from the dead!

---

[18] See also John Hart, *Sacramental Commons: Christian Ecological Ethics* (New York: Rowman & Littlefield, 2006), xviii.

Of this night scripture says:
> "The night will be as clear as day:
> it will become my light, my joy."

In this section, light and darkness are more broadly juxtaposed. The darkness of the night is declared blessed because it is out of that darkness that light and life erupt by the power of Christ's rising from the dead. The paradox of the resurrection, the paradox of life emerging out of death, is expressed through the paradox of night appearing "as clear as day." The text equates darkness with death and sin, and light with salvation and life. The vision of light provides a sense of well-being and happiness. What follows describes that sense of well-being even more specifically when it says:

> The power of this holy night
> dispels all evil, washes guilt away,
> restores lost innocence, brings mourners joy;
> it casts out hatred, brings us peace, and humbles
> earthly pride.

> Night truly blessed when heaven is wedded to earth
> and man is reconciled with God!

The message is expressed in the present tense. The claims are bold. This night dispels all evil, washes guilt away, casts out hatred, brings joy and peace. Finally, such a state of affairs among human beings signals an even deeper reality: all humankind is reconciled with God. Notice that the text does not say that the *light* achieves this state of perfection or reconciliation (biblical justice), but that the *night* achieves these wondrous things. The night of sin and evil, the night of Christ's suffering and death, result in a world where joy and peace prevail. This paradox is captured by the exclamation:

> O happy fault, O necessary sin of Adam,
> which gained for us so great a Redeemer!

An eschatological tension exists within the language of the *Exsultet* because the "future" (a reconciled world) is described as present in the "now" (a time still beleaguered by evil, disruption, and violence). Because of the construction of the text and its interplay with the symbols of darkness and light, the healing and reconciliation proclaimed so boldly in the song is envisioned as already achieved.

It is this ability of sacramental language to name the sources of both the darkness and the light that shapes the Christian community and enables them to discover the reason for their hope. This language is expressed not only as text, but also as movement and gesture, music and silence, darkness and light. In this way, the interplay of symbols in the text with the symbols of candle, fire, song, procession, and posture serves both to express and shape the Easter faith of the community. Repeated year after year on this night, this sacramental action mediates the transformation of those who participate. Such sacramental events empower Christians to be for the world a "sacrament" that speaks a vision of hope and contributes to building a world where reconciliation is possible through the power of Christ's resurrection.

The *Exsultet* closes with the following petition:

> May the Morning Star which never sets find this flame still burning:
>> Christ, that Morning Star, who came back from the dead,
>> and shed his peaceful light on all mankind,
>> your Son who lives and reigns for ever and ever.
>> Amen.

The eschatological theme that runs throughout the *Exsultet* is reiterated in these final lines. Christ's resurrection from the dead is humankind's source of hope and peace. That hope and peace are symbolized by the tangible, bodily experience of light conquering the darkness of night. Basking in that light, the assembly prepares for what will follow: the proclamation of the Scripture readings, the Initiation Rites with water, oil, and candle, and the eucharistic sharing of the bread and wine.

THE ESCHATOLOGICAL LANGUAGE OF HEALING AND RECONCILIATION

If symbolizing activity is about weaving and reweaving relationships, the *Exsultet* makes clear that a fundamental aspect of all the sacraments is the reconciliation of relationships—individuals with themselves, individuals with the community, and the community with God and all creation. Several verbs in the text signal this reconciliatory role: ransomed, freed, restored, wedded, reconciled. This pattern is constitutive of all sacraments since they are the means by which the church celebrates the gift of redemption won for us by the death and resurrection of Christ. It is by negotiating right relationships that sacraments, as language, speak Christ's word of healing and reconciliation. In other words, the sacramental rites are the means by which a healed and/or reconciled world is spoken. Furthermore, in speaking this word of healing and reconciliation, the thrust of this language is clearly eschatological. This is particularly the case with the Eucharist. As Bruce Morrill explains:

> The Church realizes itself as the body of Christ through the symbolic words, objects, actions and, moreover, through the overall shape of the structure of the eucharistic liturgy. This shape, however, is based on the eschatological principle that the liturgy is the one way that the Church, situated as it is in the old world, can experientially know, can envision, the new world to which God has ordered all things in Christ.[19]

The *Exsultet* is an example, par excellence, of the way in which the symbolizing activity of the sacraments enables the church to face the darkness of the present (old) world and yet envision a future (new) world where evil, guilt, and hatred are cast out and joy and peace prevail on earth. Sacraments proclaim that the salvation won for us in Christ is bestowed in superabundance on those who accept Christ's gift. This salvation, this grace, heals and reconciles us to God, self, each other, and all creation. The eschatological character of the sacraments enables Christians to live in the present world without despair or cynicism, facing the darkness of evil with the firm hope that the salvation not yet experienced in its fullness will be enjoyed at the parousia. The language of the liturgy reflects the tension of this already/not yet situation. In other words, while the liturgy speaks a vision of a world in right relationship, it also acknowledges that the world has not yet achieved that state for which it ardently longs.

NEGOTIATING RELATIONSHIP, TRANSFORMING A PEOPLE, AND OVERCOMING BOUNDARIES

Chauvet reminds us that since sacramental rites are a form of symbolizing activity, the sacramental symbols we celebrate, like all human symbols, mediate identity and relationships. This mediation of identity

---

[19] Bruce Morrill, *Anamnesis as Dangerous Memory: Political and Liturgical Theology in Dialogue* (Collegeville, MN: Liturgical Press, 2000), 112.

involves not only individual identity, but also the identity of the community, in this case, the church. Certainly we live in a world of violence, fear, disruption, and despair. Regularly celebrating the sacraments does not provide Christians with rose-tinted glasses that block out the stark reality of these times. Rather—as the example of the *Exsultet* powerfully demonstrates—regularly celebrating the sacraments over time transforms us into a people who put on Christ and commit ourselves to participating daily in the paschal mystery. Celebrating sacramental symbols is the way in which that transformation occurs because symbols are the means by which we negotiate our identity as Christians and our relationship to the ecclesial community we call church. The symbolizing activity forges and strengthens that identity and those relationships over time. By our daily, weekly, yearly commerce with God and with each other by means of such symbols as bread, wine, water, oil, and fire, we are able to name the violence and hate that pervades our world, not only as a reality "out there," but also as a reality present in every human heart. The transformation, healing, and reconciliation of the world begin with the transformation, healing, and reconciliation of a people into the Body of Christ. For as Chauvet points out, the symbolic order itself designates the system of connections that form a coherent whole, allowing us to situate ourselves in our world in a significant way.[20]

Sacramental symbols, therefore, signal Christian identity and constitute the church. In doing so, however, they also set up boundaries. Some belong and others do not. There is a paradox here, one that is inherent in a sacramental system that contains both human and divine elements. For while the sacraments point to the particularity of God's grace within an institution we call church, nevertheless the universality of God's reign crosses out those boundaries and reminds us that the Spirit is in the church so that the church may be sacrament for the entire world.[21] Such a realization has serious implications for the way Christians relate, not only to each other, but also to the world for which we are sign of God's healing and reconciliation.

This is what biblical justice requires of the Christian community and what we commit ourselves to when we celebrate the sacramental rites. As people living out the paschal mystery in their very flesh, Christians are called to cooperate with the Spirit in the healing of relationships,

[20] Chauvet, *Symbol and Sacrament*, 84–85.
[21] See Chauvet, *The Sacraments*, 169.

not only within the church, but with all humankind and all creation. It involves not only the poor and the disenfranchised, but also the stranger, the alienated, members of other faiths or religions, those who do not believe in God, and every element of the created world. When finally the reign of God is fully revealed, all our relationships will be righted. The God whom we encounter through the most material, most corporeal action of Christian sacraments is the God we also encounter in the building up and healing of our broken world. In celebrating the sacraments we commit ourselves to becoming that sacramental sign, that Body that God inhabits in order to reconcile a world that longs for the peace and joy promised as its inheritance.

Part 6

Sacramental-Liturgical Theology and the Human Sciences

> One stumbles, then, on the sacrament as one stumbles on the
> body, as one stumbles on the institution, as one stumbles on the
> letter of the Scriptures—if at least one respects it in its historical
> and empirical materiality. One stumbles against these because one
> harbors a nostalgia for an ideal and immediate presence to one-
> self, to others, and to God. Now, in forcing us back to our corpo-
> rality, the sacraments shatter such dreams. . . . They thus indicate
> to us that it is in the most banal empirical details—of a history, an
> institution, a world, and finally, a body—that what is most "true"
> in our faith thrives.[1]

Jean-Louis Souletie provides a highly informative, comprehensive short history of the relationship between modern theology and the so-cial sciences, describing the alienation of the two disciplines that re-sulted from each having assigned the other a subordinate role in its own methodologies. Among the original contributions Chauvet has made through his fundamental theological project, Souletie argues, is his demonstrating a way to overcome that impasse in a way that opens into a new, fruitful conversation between the two. The key lies in Chauvet's theological commitment to escaping the imaginary illu-sion that humanity has some immediate access to God, a fundamental conviction proper to Christian faith that nonetheless requires theology to take seriously on its own grounds the social-historical-psychological frameworks in which human practices of belief function.

[1] Louis-Marie Chauvet, *Symbol and Sacrament: A Sacramental Reinterpretation of Christian Existence*, trans. Patrick Madigan and Madeleine Beaumont (Collegeville, MN: Liturgical Press, 1995), 154.

Souletie demonstrates how social sciences, especially French psychoanalytic philosophy, contribute to practical theologies, both fundamental and "clinical," through a dialogue between these disciplines' distinct yet related pursuits of truth as intersubjective wrestlings with the Other. Chauvet's sacramental theology has placed fundamental theology on a new, postmodern threshold that seeks to establish foundations not within the second-order activity of academic theology itself, but on the primary theological terrain of liturgical practice. Souletie concludes with an insightful account of how H.-J. Gagey, Chauvet's colleague at the Institut Catholique de Paris, has advanced the methodological argument by proposing a "clinical" approach for a theology that sees its contribution to the pursuit of truth less in terms of foundations in themselves than rectifications of communal practices of tradition according to the truth revealed in the sacramental disclosures of genuine (and thus redemptive) otherness in both God and humans. Theology practiced in the style of clinical intervention, then, undertakes the ongoing task of discerning the holiness, the rightness (one thinks here of D. Tracy's "adequacy") of spiritual attitudes and ecclesial practices in a given time and place against the horizon of Gospel faith.

Nathan Mitchell likewise frames his contribution in terms of otherness or difference, exploiting Chauvet's replacement of the long-regnant instrumentalist sacramental theology of cause and effect, mired in the idolatrous "totalizing pretentions of metaphysics," with a linguistic, symbolic theology better suited to the revelation of God's grace. Theology does better by abandoning descriptive discourse, in which predications claim to capture causes and meanings, for doxological speech, whose forms are rhythmic and performative of growth and change. Doxology *de-nominates* God by addressing the divine as outside all proper naming, articulating the distance, the absence, the difference between God and humanity that permits genuinely transformative proximity. The predicative discourse of divine presence thereby cedes to conversational openness and reception of the gift of God's grace. The Catholic understanding of sacramental signification must be in terms of the poetic, symbolic, fragmentary, and, thus, generative languages of apophasis (incomprehensible difference) and apocalypse (generative rupture), genres native to both Judaism and Christianity. In Mitchell's estimation, Chauvet has made a singular contribution to sacramental theology by advancing the apophatic and apocalyptic qualities inherent in forms of ritual symbolism that genuinely open up space for God's revelation amidst humanity.

Chapter 11

The Social Sciences
and Christian Theology after Chauvet

Jean-Louis Souletie

INTRODUCTION

The French expression *sciences humaines* (social sciences) existed already in the seventeenth century. For Pascal and Malebranche it was the opposite of the "divine sciences." At the beginning of the nineteenth century came the opposition of the "observation sciences" from the "traditional sciences," opening the way for the new "positive sciences." It is in that mental space of Galileo that the social sciences took flight, so to speak, in naturalizing human nature, a naturalization beginning with R. Descartes, P. Gassendi and T. Hobbes. It is thus far from religion and even willingly at a distance from it that the social sciences operated, as the work of the French sociologist P. Bourdieu has suggested.

The first period in which the social sciences were born (1730–75) corresponds to the affirmation of the social theories, like that of Montesquieu and Jean-Jacques Rousseau, who broke with the religious and unitary visions of the human communities. The second period, fully documented between 1775–1814, is when the social relationships were not simply subjected to examination by reason, but thereafter they were subjected to proof by empirical observation. The last period, dominated by the figure of Auguste Comte, ran from 1814 to the second half of the nineteenth century. Social theories gained notoriety, the points of view differentiated themselves, and the terrain of professionalization began to be tilled. Thereafter psychological theories took leave of religion as *The Future of an Illusion*, as Freud's title suggests. In the second half of the twentieth century, however, Christian theology sought in these sciences a resource that would help the abandonment of Aristotelian metaphysics. The Gospel sometimes appeared as a paraphrase for that which the social sciences, like psychoanalysis, brought to light henceforth correctly: that the self-involving language of faith was understood as first and foremost referring to the subject and thus to the unconsciousness of the subject. The difference that D. Evans had established between the expression of an affect by the subject and the information relative to this affect was not always maintained rigorously for the term.[1]

In the field of theology Louis-Marie Chauvet reached an important supplementary and analogous stage to that put forth by the Belgian J. Ladrière in philosophy to found a concept of linguistic performativity within the confines of Anglo-Saxon pragmatism and Continental hermeneutics. The theologian from Paris thus engaged in a fertile conversation that leaves to each of the sciences its own capacity to know, and to theology its own field of expression. He had recourse to the social sciences not to construct with them a new scholasticism but to analyze the subject of ritual and liturgical practices. In this way he gave theology greater latitude for its own intelligibility, to envisage the manner in which the rites of the social and ecclesial body were constitutive of the human but also mediators of the divine. New conversations are now foreseeable along this line, but, I would argue, with more emphasis on a "clinical" style of theology as care for the ecclesial body.

First I will analyze this new field in which the social sciences and Christian theology could meet one another in a productive way. Then I will study the transition whereby the social sciences went from being an ancillary to the practices of theology to a "clinical" status, whose meaning I will unfold in the last part.

THE WOLF IS NO LONGER IN THE SHEEPFOLD

Conflicted Relations Between Theology and the Social Sciences

Theology and the social sciences do not engage in conversation except from a position of total heterogeneity. Every science, in fact, since it desires a way of knowing, possesses a conception of reality, a vision of the world and of humanity; in summary, a certain belief. This is the

---

[1] D. Evans, *The Logic of Self-Involvement. A Philosophical Study of Everyday Language with Special Reference to the Christian Use of Language about God as Creator* (New York: Herder and Herder, 1969), cited by J. Ladriere, *L'articulation du sens I. Discours scientifique et parole de la foi*, Cogitatio Fidei 124 (Paris: Cerf, 1984).

reason why they require that everyone think about and objectify the link between their "believing" position and the type of elaboration that they produce, as much in the field of theology as in their own in social sciences.

The two disciplines equally share a common hermeneutical dimension because they presuppose that their intelligibility comes from a historical understanding of objects produced by practices they analyze: religious beliefs or human behaviors. There are always reasons to decide on one interpretation rather than another, whatever the science may be that manages the hermeneutic. Every science describes its objects starting from certain presuppositions and according to an interpretation relative to the questions proper to the researchers of an era and their institutions. It follows that the multiple visions of the world lead to different epistemologies and methodologies. This is not any lesser among the sociological theories of Simmel and Parsons or the psychological theories of Jung and Lacan than among the theologies of the German J.-B. Metz and the Englishman J. Milbank.

Third, theology and the social sciences have in common that they consider human practice in general as the place for a discernment that leads to a permanent interpretation rather than as the quasi-mechanical application of a doctrine, whether it be sociopsychological or theological. Just as sociology analyzes practices of social actors and psychology analyses the psychic functions of historical subjects, Christian theology undertakes to describe, to evaluate and to think about God beginning with the experience of subjects who engage their faith in ecclesial and social behavior and practices.

This epistemological relationship has not always been envisaged so clearly, so that the history of their conversation reveals in large part the attempt of each of the partners, theology and social sciences, in its own turn, to annex the other. Sociology of religions in the first generation thus placed itself at the service of pastoral care, forging its criteria based upon doctrinal and magisterial givens of the Catholic Church.[2] The hopeful ecclesiastic took steps in favor of objective inquiry, which hindered him from truly taking account of religious identity's innovations in the order of expression. The same risk could exist today through a kind of instrumentalization of psychoanalysis by theology.

[2] Cf. Preface by G. Lebras for F. Boulard, *Premiers itinéraires en sociologie religieuse* (Paris: Ouvrières, 1954) and G. Le Bras, *Études de sociologie religieuse* (Paris: PUF, 1955).

191

It is not right in fact to subject the reading of the great Freudian themes (interdiction of incest, difference of the sexes and of the generations) to a theological reading of natural law. In the second part we will address different models of potential conversations between Freudian or Lacanian analysis and Christian theology.

But inversely theology finds itself sometimes annexed by the social sciences. The task of the social sciences would be to analyze reality by qualifying it, including the reality of belief, to impose afterwards constraints upon theology. But the diagnostic of resistances that reality poses to the projects of theologians and, conversely, the constraints that it imposes upon them does not mean a fatal destiny, nor does it therefore imply any indisputable orientation. An example can clarify this point. When we analyze the crisis of contemporary conjugality in sociological terms it is not possible for the sociologist to conclude by affirming that life today no longer permits long-term commitment and total commitment. A sociologist has no competence so to pronounce in a definitive way and thus to speak dogmatically. His task, more modest, is to analyze which constraints make it so difficult, even apparently impossible, for a long-term commitment, as had been the rule. Thus, he leaves the field free for a systematic theological analysis about the reasons for which the Christian faith remains so attached to this type of long-term commitment that it doesn't believe it has to renounce it. It is in this sense that theology starts from further on, and it is only according to this point of departure that its encounter with the social sciences will be productive. Therefore theologians find themselves directed to their own responsibility: to decode, according to their interests in the possible realities that come to light in the present, discerning where are the appeals, the promptings likely to mobilize the forces available in the church, by virtue of the mission that establishes it and conforming to the faith that animates it. They cannot simply submit themselves to the available belief of a defined era through a social science under a sentence that makes impossible the prophetic and eschatological range of their work.

A Productive Conversation

Beyond these regimes of submission, the conversation can become fruitful, as Chauvet has demonstrated.[3] The theologian from the Insti-

[3] Chauvet, "Quand la théologie rencontre les sciences humaines." In *La responsabilité des théologien. Mélanges offerts à Mgr J. Doré* (F. Bousquet, H.-J. Gagey, G. Medevielle, J.-L. Souletie dir.) (Paris: Desclée, 2002), 401–16.

tut Catholique de Paris has suggested a way to overcome the two impasses that we have just mentioned. The first risk in fact is to dismiss the social sciences after instrumentally using them. This reduces the results of the social sciences to illustrating and justifying theological opinion. Another trap would be the inverse, to eliminate theology to the benefit of a new scholastic of social sciences reportedly capable of discoursing on God and humans, all the while with the argument that God is spoken about in human languages. The place left vacant by the neo-Thomist would then be occupied by these discussions about humans. Anthropology thus becomes the place of an interrogation that takes shape between these two risks incurred through the confrontation of theology with the social sciences. But the reflection on humanity shapes itself as that which should renounce every foundation suspected of being submitted to the imaginary illusion of the immediacy between God and humans.

Thus symbolic exchange in the sacramental theology of Chauvet is the image of this relationship that escapes, according to the author, the resurgence of an ontological view dependent upon the notions of presence or reference. Symbol, unlike sign, leads into an order of which it itself is a part. It is grasped at the point where it is generated and takes form there where it emerges. It is "not primarily a function of *representation* of objects, but of *communication* between subjects."[4] The relationship of humans with God in *Symbole et sacrement* is made explicit in the symbolic exchange that operates in the ecclesial action. It is the exchange that is found favored here through a rapport with what is exchanged. The symbolic relationship to God effects itself at Easter through the withdrawal of the absent. God is made present in the exchange when the church reads the Scriptures, celebrates the sacraments, or practices charity.

The Contribution of Social Sciences to Theology

Like every other experience, that of faith admits to an analysis through the disciplines that have acquired their autonomy and their principles of validation. They have learned to thwart their own dogmatism by integrating the "undecidability," the impossibility to prove

[4] Chauvet, *Symbole et sacrement. Une relecture existentielle de l'existence chrétienne*, Cogitatio Fidei (Paris: Cerf, 1987), 128; Chauvet, *Symbol and Sacrament: A Sacramental Reinterpretation of Christian Existence* (Collegeville, MN: Liturgical Press, 1995), 121.

the logical completeness of a formal hypo-theoretical-deductive system. In the same way French bishop G. Defoix writes that theology, to be recognized as a science, must "include the practice of its theory in the field of its investigations."[5] Before such an injunction, theology asks itself about its function. Neither can it want to reduce itself to a critical theory about ecclesial life, nor resign itself to merge itself into a foreign discipline, whether it is history, ethnology, linguistics, or sociology. It cannot reduce itself, moreover, to the analysis of the subjectivity of the believer. The paradox is then at its height: on the one hand theology has to think about faith according to its own logic, and on the other hand it knows that it is connected to the experience of the human believer in the historical-social framework that is its own and that deserves to be analyzed for itself.

Mediation—Interface Between Theology and Social Sciences

The contribution of the social sciences is concerned with practical theology. This describes, evaluates, and reflects upon the events and the formation of subjects in the order of faith at the heart of their socio-psycho-historical experience. There is only a human subject, states Chauvet, in the linguistic mediation of an "I" in rapport with a you, a "you" that is the reversible of the first. This is equally true on the psychological level, where the "I" (ego) happens in language, as the "that" (id) had in Freudian terminology.[6]

For Chauvet it is thus impossible to think about the subject other than a body, as word, because it is always already spoken, that is, desired by another and spoken about through the culture that preceded it. The author explains that this human subject considered as a body-word assumes the characteristics of a triple body that determines its succession: "ancestral body of tradition, social body of culture, and cosmic body of nature."[7] In the sacramental rite it is the mediated character of all relationships to God that finds itself signified in the

[5] G. Defoix, "Le pari chrétien de l'intelligence: une tâche pour les Instituts catholiques," *Revue Études* no. 344 (1976): 253.

[6] "Wo es war, soll Ich weren," S. Freud, *Nouvelles conférences d'introduction à la psychanalyse*, 1933, trans. R.-M. Zeitlin, Connaissance de l'inconscient (Paris: Gallimard, 1984), 110.

[7] Chauvet, "Quand la théologie rencontre les sciences humaines," *La responsabilité des théologien. Mélanges offerts à Mgr J. Doré*, 404.

personal body, the social body of the church, the ancestral body of Tradition, and the cosmic body of creation in the metonymy of bread and wine. It is precisely through these mediations that everyone comes to pass as a subject in modern culture. The most spiritual therefore comes into play in the most corporal.

The status of truth changes in this approach. If truth always exceeds the discourse that one has about it, it seemed to Chauvet that it should verify itself through the passage of these long mediations by which the human comes about. The theological task is obvious. Ritual mediation is not an anecdote. It gives access to the truth of faith and participates in the construction of the believing subject in its linguistic, material, psychic, and political ambiguities. The social sciences have no other ambition here than to eradicate illusions of immediacy that lodge themselves in these corporal mediations where the human and believer become. But positively they help sacramental theology to think about itself further in the register of grace understood as "God who makes profitable the symbolic field that is the believing subject."[8]

This notion of mediation does not fail to bring into question the debate of some theologians with Chauvet's enterprise, as Dean H.-J. Gagey has demonstrated.[9] Thus the French Jesuit theologian Joseph Moingt questions our author in the following way: "[I]s it in virtue of the Cross, to recover an ancient formula, that the Christian sacraments, and they alone, hold an efficacy that is proper to them, or do they benefit, no matter what other rites, by the performative power common to all religious symbols?"[10] Alternatively, the efficacy proper to the sacraments would only owe somewhat to the ritual efficacy, and we can therefore be satisfied with the scholastic position that strives to uncouple symbolic efficacy and sacramental efficacy. Or further still, the efficacy properly sacramental would be intimately connected to symbolic efficacy: but how can these be articulated without separation or confusion? As the Swiss Protestant theologian P. Gisel has

---

[8] Ibid., 408.

[9] H.-J. Gagey is honorary dean of the Faculty of Theology and Religious Studies at the Institut Catholique de Paris; see his article "La responsabilité 'clinique' de la théologie," in *La responsabilité des théologien. Mélanges offerts à Mgr J. Doré*, 716.

[10] J. Moingt "Récit et Rite," Les sacrements de Dieu," *Recherches de Science Religieuse* 75/3 (1987): 338.

emphasized,[11] "the properly theological limit of the symbolic enterprise holds the risk of dissolving theology into anthropology by not
emphasizing enough that if the sacramental effectively falls within the
jurisdiction of the symbolic register, all the symbolic nevertheless is
not sacramental."[12]

FROM AN AUXILIARY CHARACTER TOWARD
THE SOCIAL SCIENCES TO "CLINICAL" THEOLOGY

Chauvet's theology allows us to situate the social sciences in an ancillary position in relation to the liturgical practices that theology
wants to reflect upon and not in relation to sacramental theology.
Therefore, challenging the regimes of submission in which the relationship between the social sciences and theology were able to fall,
Chauvet thus opens a new stage in their complex relationship. We can
distinguish three other approaches to this relationship that all point
toward what we might call "clinical" theology.

The Approach of M. Bellet

For Bellet, the goal of the debate is no longer that of the polemic between theology and psychoanalysis, whereby it is a matter for theology, for example, to critique Freud's theses in *The Future of an
Illusion*.[13] It is not even a matter of knowing how theology would be
capable of integrating the contributions of psychoanalysis, nor even to
ask why Freud the atheist needed Moses. The thesis of M. Bellet is that
psychoanalysis is a propaedeutic or preparation for theology, or at
least for philosophy that thinks about religion.

The practice of psychoanalysis is the quasi-propaedeutic place from
which Bellet reflects upon the interactions between theology and the
social sciences. Psychoanalysis fits into this experience, this relation-

---

[11] P. Gisel, "Du symbole au symbolique," *Recherches de Science Religieuse* 75/3
(1987): 357–69.

[12] Gagey, *Recherches de Science Religieuse* 75/3 (1987).

[13] "An illusion is not the same thing as an error. An illusion is not necessarily
an error. . . . That which characterizes an illusion, is it is derived from human
desires. . . . Thus we can call illusion a belief when, in the motivation of it the
realization of a desire is prevalent, and we do not take into consideration, this
happening, the relationship of this belief to reality, just like illusion itself that
foregoes being confirmed by the real." S. Freud, *L'avenir d'une illusion*, Biblio-
thèque de psychanalyse (Paris: PUF, 1971), 44–45.

ship with the Other, in that it tells us where the illusions of the subject come undone so that he may become the subject of his word and his desire. It is at this level that psychoanalysis meets theology. The analytical effect resides in the experience that the "theologian sets out to understand in a different manner his theology, as if he were to set out to speak about it what he did not mean there; and as if he were to open himself in the margins and the faults of discourse, another space of speaking, coming from the unknown."[14] Bellet holds that this does not only apply to the theologian in analysis. The disconcerting experience of analysis is also that of the subject in the Christian faith who finds himself as thrown out of the place where this faith seems to have its dwelling, particularly with respect to thought.

The experience of faith is also for the theologian a work of truth and disillusionment that the Bible illustrates through combat against the temptation of idolatry. This work of truth does not operate in the cultivated and gratifying zones of understanding. It operates from below, in the admission of what one is. It is the collapse of the "as if," this all too frequent "as if." "Let us think as if we truly have faith that God loves us." We go from disillusionment to disillusionment. Faith itself seems attained at the heart. The God of Jesus Christ and Jesus Christ himself seem to exhaust themselves to lose this intensity of power and presence that we give to them. They belong to this universe that we discard like a dead skin.

But the meeting of psychoanalysis and theology can open again the field of theology in a direction of its most original space. Since the eighteenth century theology was subjected to the judicatory authority of criticism in a way that obedience to faith, placed in the face of critical judgment, is in the deadly alternative of putting a limit on the free search for truth or of dissolving itself in this critical fire. "But there through analytical experience another leading place of humans and of human thought announces itself: this place, the word and hearing, is

---

[14] M. Bellet, unpublished orientation session for the Master in Theology at the Theology Faculty of the Institut Catholique de Paris (ICP) in October 2001. The author is a Catholic priest born in 1923, psychoanalyst, philosopher and writer and he has influenced numerous intellectuals in France. He authored more than forty works among which four are relative to psychoanalysis: *Foi et psychanalyse* (Paris: Desclée de Brouwer, 1973), *Dire ou la vérité improvisée* (Paris: Desclée de Brouwer, 1990), *Le Lieu perdu: De la psychanalyse du côté où ça se fait* (Paris: DDB, 1996), *L'Écoute* (Paris: Desclée de Brouwer, 1999).

the original relationship where humanity comes to itself in the primordial exchange: the work awakens the world and gives each thing its
name, its being-there."[15]

The first theological task introduces itself from that very moment for
Bellet as listening (obedience) to the Gospel, in this essential speaking
that coincides with the Logos having become human life. But he immediately emphasizes that it would be an illusion to believe that we
are in the pure hearing of this Word. The subject-theologian thus also
has to hear as the Word mingles in everything in him, even the bad.
Here concerns the other aspect of the theological task that dislodges
discourse from its apparent certitudes, that brings the critique upon
theology itself in the name itself of what it would speak. The theologian must constantly toil to overcome this confusion, in him and for
the other; his desire, "it is the positive disillusionment, that is to say
the discovery of all that his God has to compromise with humanity,
too human, that it may be for him an occasion to approach God, that is
to say, also, to discover Him farther away."[16]

The analytical space also opens for Bellet the practice of theology for
an encounter with God[17] for a believing subject who tests himself as
such in the unending work of disentangling the web of confusion.
From this point of view the psychoanalyst refers theology back to the
defense of the freedom of God and that of humans.

The Relation of the Social Sciences and Theology
in the Writings of R. Lemieux[18]

In an article entitled "The Wolf in the Sheepfold: Theology and Psy-

---

[15] Ibid.

[16] Ibid.

[17] "Non terminatur ad enuntiabile, sed ad rem," declared St. Thomas Aquinas (*ST* II–II, q. 1, a. 2, ad 2): that which is stated is not an end in itself; the purpose of the statement is the reality itself, a reality that is above everything
declared and above every human concept.

[18] Pioneer in social sciences in the Québec region, Raymond Lemieux has
contributed to the original development in religious thought. His work
marked by an interdisciplinary methodology situates itself at the crossroads of
sociology, history, psychoanalysis, linguistic studies and ethics of knowledge.
Consequently, it has radiated well beyond the field of religion to touch all the
social sciences. Attached to Laval University since 1965, first as a researcher in
religious sociology in the Center for Sociological Research, then as

choanalysis Exposed to the Field of the Other,"[19] R. Lemieux, for his part, has used his own understanding of the relationship between social sciences and theology, beginning with the Lacanian notion of the Other. Theology and psychoanalysis converse, according to the author, with the relationship with the Other as the condition for the possibility of word and truth.

The term Other refers as much for psychoanalysis as for theology

> to an organization of the mind, that is to a *method* that aims at reaching that which we do not know. In each case, it means an instance that escapes them and for which discourse tries to tinker with a consistency, with the intention of being able to live. Whence their misleading resemblance: for one and the other the sense is not found right away, it is not discovered, but one must invent it, tinker with the meanings from the materials that supply culture, materials hereafter scattered, that which does not facilitate the matter. The instance of the Other is first that of an absence. It refers to the experience of separation, of the placing in the abyss of desire in the space between two desiring subjectivities: an *ab-sense*, that is to say a sense that only conceives of itself in being other. The mystics gladly recalled this placement in the abyss that sustained their desire: until one takes the risk to damage their life, then nothing— they know it as their dark night—can guarantee it.[20]

For Lacan, the Other is an instance, a space in which it is a matter of discovering that the truth is the motor of analysis. This is a space to occupy, but that can only be if the subject occupies it. The process

---

professor in the Theology Faculty, Lemieux in 1980 founded the group of researchers in the religious studies at Laval University, which he still directs. He was also one of the founding members of the Cahiers de recherche en sciences de la religion. In 1974 he participated in the creation of a research group that would become the Groupe interdisciplinaire freudien de recherches et d'interventions cliniques (GRIFIC), of which he is president. The scale and originality of Lemieux's work has gained him recognition as a researcher worldwide. He is the author of some two hundred publications, almost half of which are published in the juried scientific journals internationally. He is also active in the midst of numerous organizations such as the International Seminar on Clinical Ethics and the International Association of Sociology.

[19] Lemieux, "Le loup dans la bergerie. Théologie et psychanalyse exposées au champ de l'Autre," *Théologiques* 10/2 (2002): 25–53.

[20] Ibid., 52.

operates through and in a questioning that does not train itself except in the measure of a word free of all seduction and without debt.[21] As we understand it, the status of truth here corresponds neither to the *adequatio eri et intellectum*, nor to the exactitude of observations methodologically constructed, but in the response by which the subject becomes himself. The insistence on the Other demands this perspective of truth because, as Lacan says: "[W]e go from the field of exactitude to the register of truth. But this register—we dare think that we do not have to return there—situates itself totally elsewhere and may be properly at the basis of intersubjectivity. It situates itself there where the subject cannot grasp anything except subjectivity itself, constituting an Other in absolute necessity."[22]

But the Other thus defined in its insistence, therefore, means neither God nor the gods. It is an Other without a face, never reducible to traits by which we claim to know it. It is an insistence, that is to say a logical place, empty, a space without image that cannot be picked out in the way of the surface of a body. It does not establish in it any less the exercise of the word, but this as coming from the Cartesian subject who is conscious and rational.

Lemieux rejects that we can assimilate the two discourses one from the other, that of theology and that of psychoanalysis. Still, the interchange of the two can be productive. The point of contact is surely the job of theology and of psychoanalysis. They do an impossible job because each lives by the prohibition to "benefit" from the other. The theologian constructs an intelligence of faith to manifest a meaning revealed in the eschatological mode that proceeds from the risk taken with the Other by the theologian himself.[23] The difference between psychoanalysis and theology is that, whereas the former encounters the urge of death and wants to know what there is to know about this Other that operates, the latter, without denying this urge—which would be to refuse this confrontation—attends to life. The act of faith that makes him take part in life is the motor for this theological act. Here the truth lies ahead for whomever engages with faith, but with

[21] J. Lacan, "L'instance de la lettre dans l'inconscient," *Écrits*, v. 1 (Points 5), (Paris: Seuil, 1966), 284–85, and Lacan, "Position de l'inconscient," *Écrits*, t. 2 (Points 21), (Paris: Seuil, 1971), 205.

[22] Lacan, "Le séminaire sur 'La lettre volé,'" *Écrits*, v. 1, 29.

[23] K. Barth expressed his wish in *Introduction à la théologie évangélique* (Genève: Labor et Fides, 1962).

the necessity of a backing, what gives meaning to a tradition, to be able to imagine what is ahead and ceaselessly overtake the character that is precisely imaginary.[24]

In this quest to name the Other in truth, the theologian is called to the risk of the other that his conversation with psychoanalysis makes him hear. He makes language happen, that is to say in a contingent manner, under the analogical mode of this reality that escapes him.[25] Theology therefore will unfold itself as *fides quaerens intellectum* in order to try to name life while attempting to arm itself against corruptions of his *intellectus*, of his desire to know not the Other but the relationship with the Other that he set in motion.

In his study Lemieux thus distinguished the two ways that the psychoanalyst and the theologian mean the Other: either the power of death to seek what one is, or the power of life on which one unreasonably relies. Is it not appropriate that in each case it deals with an instance, with the theologian representing it according to an analogy of faith that makes unavailable the mastery of the Other, while reaching out for it nevertheless? Is it only a matter in theology of a method that aims at reaching what is unknown? Is it only a matter of an absence, of a meaning that only conceives itself as being other when the incarnation and sacramentality seek to speak of presence? Is the way of the mystics maintained by the author sufficient when it "willingly evokes this abandonment (*mise en abime*) that supports their desire, until one takes the risk to damage their life since nothing—they know it as their dark night—can guarantee it?"[26]

"CLINICAL" THEOLOGY

In order to remain in this kind of conversation between the social sciences and theology, we consider the field of psychoanalysis a

---

[24] Lemieux, "Le loup dans la bergerie," 46: "truth that manifests itself therefore in the in-between, dazzling, in the present, that is to say the actual choice, always to recover, to go towards the unknown before us but which imposes upon the believer."

[25] Ibid., 50: "To name the Other, is to make happen the possibilities of the human. But at the same time, this naming is a forceful strike at the real, because to name the Other, indeed, is to give it a place, a habitation; it is also to assign an abode, that is to say to imprison it in the concepts and to reduce it in one swoop to the state of an idol."

[26] Ibid., 52.

201

privileged conversation partner in the same way Chauvet himself wanted to maintain it. Bellet found in psychoanalysis a propaedeutic for the theologian-subject who is invited into this conversation with the psychologists to seek the proper resources of faith and the *intellectus fidei* to dislodge the idols from his discourse. Lemieux tried to find in an insistence on the Other the present meeting point for theologians and psychoanalysts despite each one's different preference in using this Lacanian term. This, however, only provided him a negative theology that is not, in my opinion, sufficient to name the God who became not only life but also flesh. Let us see if a "clinical" style theology, as it has been called by Paris theologian H.-J. Gagey, provides a profitable understanding of the relationship between other theologies and social sciences, beginning with the approach inaugurated by Chauvet.[27]

The author depends for the invention of a "clinical" style on the psychoanalytical practice that can become, according to him, "a knowledge about the subject," a global hermeneutic of existence. In any event it is a "clinic" of libidinal investments of the subject within a given culture; a culture whose viability can only be postulated by a therapist, without it belonging to him—at least in the framework of transferential relations—to be made the judge or advocate. Psychoanalytical competence consists only in allowing the one analyzed to visit the psychopathological drifts of his investments, having to come to a conclusion in theory consist with the specifics of the invested objects. Can the same thing not be said, asks Gagey, of the social sciences in the assistance they bring to the constitution of theological discourse? A detour through the critical historical sciences of biblical exegesis allows him then to establish how they constitute a correction or rectification of dogmatic discourse that always is at risk of imaginary constructions. It is in this that the critical historical sciences analogically would have a corrective function to psychology: "to describe thus the task of theology is to signify that its responsibility is less the "foundation" than the "rectification." Indeed, theology did not invent its foundation, nor does it have anything to invent. It finds it there, where it is quite simply given to it: in the Christian tradition, as in the tradition of communal life, in the midst of which the believer is brought back in thanksgiving to his creator according to the logic of the incarnation and the paschal mystery. On the other hand, it returns

[27] Gagey, it is the intention of the article: "La responsabilité "clinique" de la théologie," *La responsabilité des théologien. Mélanges offerts à Mgr J. Dore.*

to them ceaselessly to rectify the manner by which the foundation is put into play.[28]

Gagey finds a good example of such an operation of revision still happening today in the work of Chauvet's sacramental theology. According to his diagnosis, the encounter with history and the other social sciences has led Chauvet to find in them the means to escape from systematic sacramental theology as well as the pastoral practice of "anti-ritualism" in the French church of the 1970s. Against this reduction in the church from Christianity to a kind of humanistic ethic,[29] theological work has shown the necessarily ritualistic character of the Christian faith. To do this it was indispensable to provoke the meeting with those social sciences concerned with rituality; it established convincingly that the symbolic is the good *analog* for thinking about the efficacy of the sacraments.[30] Something new then appeared as the fruit

[28] Ibid., 12: "To speak of "correction" is not in reference to an operation of re-establishment in the right path of the "theologically correct," starting from a position claimed by Sirius. It means a complex process in which, in the interface of rationality of the contemporary social sciences and theological rationality, the theological forum organizes the field of mutual questioning." The patristic period therefore seemed emblematic of this practical effort by which the councils depended upon the tradition without needing to create them in order to protect the mystery of the faith against the diversions for which they were made vulnerable, among others, the new conditions of intelligibility that created the Law in the Universe in the midst of which it was necessary to attest. This protection of the mystery worked in a critical way according to an operation of constant recasting according to the terminology of H. Urs von Balthasar: "all tradition must always be based on the historical moment and formulated again to correspond to it," cited in *Qui est chrétien*, (Salvator: Mulhouse, 1968 [orig., 1967]), 43.

[29] It is against this reduction that A. Vergote wrote: "The rite is in fact the only true expression of the faith. Through the ethical engagement, it realizes a work separated from it, but in which it recognizes its hope on the move. Prayer is for the most part the wild life that faith leads in us. It weaves between humans and God the multiform network of daily relationships and pushed it to the primal cry or the wonderful blessing, attention flying or human rumor punctuated by some revealing words. Only the rite gives faith the internal mediating form where it creates for itself it's carnal, cultural and communitarian image." A. Vergote, *L'interprétation du langage religieux* (Paris: Seuil, 1974), 211, cited by Gagey, "La responsabilité "clinique" de la théologie," 713.

[30] "If the object of sacramental discourse is the practice of ritual language in the midst of what is given and received by God, in return for faith, grace,

of this conversation between the social sciences and theology: it was the possibility to think about sacramental action on the concrete grounds of Christian rite, without needing to imagine a divine action passing for, so to speak, human ritual action. On the contrary, we therefore emphasize that, in the real, carnal, material effectuation of the liturgical action (the word liturgy contains the Greek root *ergon*— action) grace is communicated.

"Clinical" theology according to Gagey thus gives itself to the task of discerning health, the correctness of spiritual attitudes and of ecclesial practices. It first of all attempts to heal or to warn of the risk of an idolatrous reference for the realities of faith in order to reopen the way for a renewed attachment to the received tradition. Let us ask the question here about whether recourse to the human sciences has been determinant in the material, or whether the proper resources of revelation as the theological critique of idols in the Old and New Testaments were not sufficient. "Clinical" theology also seeks to hear and to warn about the risk of an absorption of human activity in worldliness. For these two tasks, recourse to the social sciences in theology has worked as a corrective. It has been in the matter of supplying the procedures of objectivity to the *intellectus fidei* from these Christian practices such as the liturgy of the sacraments that it tries to understand the field of modernity. These analogous working procedures that function by the demands regarding dogmatic theology have not nullified the question of truth in theology.

CONCLUSION

Theology and the social sciences have a shared place in modernity since they constitute themselves, one in relation to the other, after the decline of Scholastic philosophy. For a long time ignorant of their relatedness, polemics exhausted them in mutually unfruitful attempts to take one another over. In his theological reconstruction of a theory

---

salvation, if therefore, in other words, the *res sacramenti* does not happen other than in the mediation of the *sacramentum* and according to the mode of expression proper to this type of particular language that is rituality, how would the discourse of the *"intellectus fidei"* be able to avoid the gathering of new resources that anthropology, philosophy of language offer to it, even if certain ones still remain problematic?" "Ritualité et théologie," *Recherches de Science Religieuse* 78 (1990): 141, cited by Gagey, "La responsabilité "clinique" de la théologie," 713.

about sacraments beginning with symbol, Chauvet established a new threshold for a renewed conversation between them beginning with the notion of mediation that reunites them in a sustained distinction. The example of the connections that diverse authors have established between psychoanalysis and theology reinstate, however, the debate about the compatibility of these epistemological fields. If Bellet finds in psychoanalysis a permanent propaedeutic for the subject-theologian, he does not always arrive without it himself. Lemieux, on the Lacanian side, finds the Other as a meeting point, but it is at the price of introducing the wolf of psychoanalysis into the sheepfold of theology. "Clinical" theology that tends to the health of the ecclesial body in postmodernity finds in the social sciences some procedures of reification that protect the mystery of God, for which the theological discussions need to take responsibility. In each of these cases, the question about the truth of theological discourse is posed: neither *adequatio rei et intellectum* alone, nor exactitude, is produced by the subject alone. The meeting of the social sciences and theology thus clarifies the fact that it is less a question of method(s) than a question of truth.[31] Indeed, the

---

[31] Here the remarks of M. De Certau in *La faiblesse de croire*, (Paris: Seuil, 1969, 2003) reprinted in *L'étranger ou l'union dans la différence* (Paris: Desclée de Brouwer); new ed. established and presented by Luce Giard, 1987, 1991: "To believe is not to adopt a program: it is first of all to find the word. Believers speak about their lives in a new way when it becomes their response to someone. They perceive in themselves what they had never known without the mysterious questioning that reveals it to them, or still (what wells up by itself) they recognize the quality of the Stranger for the newness that it brings as a voice still unsuspecting in them and henceforth so essential that, except for it, to live would no longer have meaning for them. If faith is true, it is an interior truth connected to the encounter that made it come to being and whose resonance remains. For the believer, every layer still obscure of his or her life takes in this word, which is addressed to someone and it finds itself to the degree that it becomes someone who responds. The hearers of the first sermon proclaimed in the church already had this experience that is ours: 'To hear this, they had hearts transpierced and they spoke to Peter and to the apostles: Brothers, what should we do?' (Ac 2, 37). To render faithfully the text, and in particular a word used also in the Gospel for the 'piercing' of the side (Jn 19, 34), it is necessary to translate: 'This gave them a blow to the heart.' A shock opened for them the heart. The truth that reveals itself in them corresponded to that which presented itself to them, strange, and this spiritual communion was immediately a language that was addressed to the brothers and responded to them." (204–5).

object of theology, God as revealed in Jesus Christ, never ceases to call into question the presuppositions of those who engage it. It possesses the necessary resources for the critique of what is used for understanding. The image of God in the Incarnation is thus in the first place an image "in trial,"[32] a trial that aims at Jesus himself according to which he is confessed as Lord, or denied and executed, a trial that aims at the believer him- or herself, each declared in turn judged and pardoned. It is this trial that the liturgy restages through the paschal mystery that it unfolds. By invitation to the adoration of the living and true God, the *lex orandi* takes subjects into the trial of Jesus, inviting them to find their true place. Making them the adorers of the one true God, the liturgy unveils for them ceaselessly the idolatry from which they escape if they let themselves emerge in these rites through the Word that mediates them. The subjects are therefore in a position to go live what they have celebrated: *lex orandi, lex bene vivendi*.

If the social sciences under the aspect of "clinical" theology were in time to establish true procedures of objectivity regarding Christian discourse, they would not, however, be able in the process to excuse anyone from taking a position that opens the reading of the Gospel story with the same authority Jesus had and that is henceforth conferred upon the church in its practices, striving to be faithful to the Gospel.

---

[32] "Speaking about the trial of Jesus, we do not mean his trial in the strict sense before the Great Counsel or Pilate, but the controversy about the truth of God in which it comes as a witness, and on the other hand the trial about the subject of Jesus 'in the interior of the trial about the justice of God in which his witnesses intervene for him.' The expression thus explodes with numerous meanings, but it is also due to this that it is fertile. Behind its use there is the idea that history is better understood in the categories of juridical process and of debate about justice, life and freedom, than in the natural categories."
J. Moltmann, *Le Dieu crucifié*, Cogitatio Fidei (Paris: Cerf, 1974), 131.

Chapter 12

Rituality and the Retrieval of Sacrament as "Language Event"

Nathan D. Mitchell

> Rituality, by way of the non-utilitarian use of objects, places, language . . . which is proper to itself, effects a *decisive break* with the ordinary world. A space is thus created, a space for breathing, for freedom, for gratuitousness where God may come.[1]

One of the most significant contributions Louis-Marie Chauvet has made to the contemporary renewal of sacramental theology arises from his imaginative use of insights from ritual studies and modern linguistics to clarify how Christian sacraments behave as "language events." I refer, more specifically, to his analysis of the relation between rituality and symbolization. For Chauvet, ritual is not simply "formal behavior prescribed for occasions not given over to technological routine," as Victor and Edith Turner famously proposed in their anthropological study of Christian pilgrimage.[2] On the contrary, one must speak of ritual as a *rupture*—a decisive *break*—that subverts every attempt at causal finality or closure. "The reason the symbolism of the ritual rupture seems to have such significance," writes Chauvet, "is that *we do not master it*; rather, it masters us. In this ritual rupture we do not find a *treatise* on the otherness and graciousness of God, but an *intense experience* of this otherness and graciousness."[3]

---

[1] Chauvet, *Symbol and Sacrament: A Sacramental Interpretation of Christian Existence*, trans. Patrick Madigan and Madeleine Beaumont (Collegeville, MN: Liturgical Press, 1995), 337–38, emphasis added.

[2] Victor Turner and Edith Turner, *Image and Pilgrimage in Christian Culture* (New York: Columbia University Press, 1978), 243.

[3] Chauvet, *Symbol and Sacrament*, 338.

This intense experience resides, above all, in that complex human language we call "the body." For the body is not simply an instrumental organism that registers our response to God's gratuity and otherness; it is the communicative network—the primary relational space—within which that human experience of God reveals itself. In the sacramental situation God meets human participants precisely in the language of the body—a language that begins as air rushing from lungs to throat to mouth and sonic vibrations beating the tympani of our own ears and those of others ("words"). Ritual is bodily inscription, and the ritual rupture that makes symbolic disclosure (sacramental signification) possible is always a matter of blood, breath, and bone. For that reason, too, the body is a primary site of cultural inscription, the place where history—including the history of humanity with God—writes itself.

In this essay, then, I seek to show how the twin notions of ritual rupture and embodied language confirm and expand a central insight of Chauvet's, viz., that

> God is the Different, that God's difference, perceived on the symbolic register as the Other, is Grace . . . [and that] all this is said by being done in a symbolic practice where we do not limit ourselves to speaking about God's grace . . . but where we open up, through an effective break with the useful, a space of gratuitousness where God can come . . . [where] the graciousness of God takes place in practice and takes flesh in us.[4]

IN SEARCH OF A LANGUAGE
FOR CHRISTIAN SACRAMENT

In 1999 David Tracy remarked that modern theology has often "marginalized two traditions: the realism of the cross which acknowledges God's hiddenness, and apophatic theology, which displays God's incomprehensibility."[5] Such marginalizing, Tracy suggests, has resulted at least in part from Western theology's long infatuation with the totalizing pretensions of metaphysics. For centuries, Western theology seemed to forget the crucial difference between infinity and to-

---

[4] Ibid., 339.

[5] David Tracy, "Form & Fragment: The Recovery of the Hidden and Incomprehensible God," *CTI* [= Center of Theological Inquiry] *Reflections* 3 (1999): 62–89; here, 62.

tality. "Unlike the category of infinity," Tracy observes, "any totality demands a *closure*. Therefore eventually in every totality system we find a reduction of everything to more of the same and thereby an exclusion of anything that is genuinely other and different."[6] Here Tracy echoes a point Chauvet makes in *Symbol and Sacrament*: metaphysics is a totalizing system that assaults and restricts infinity, circumscribes God's radical Otherness within a frame of "presence," thereby reducing divine action to the productionist operations of causality.[7]

Not surprisingly, postmodern Christian theology has reacted negatively to this situation, especially because it seriously diminishes our understanding of ritual symbol and sacrament. Chauvet writes of the need to resist "an onto-theological logic of the Same, where the sacraments are controlled by their instrumental and causal system," and to seek instead "a symbolic representation of the Other" that sees sacraments as "language acts making possible the unending transformation of subjects into believing subjects."[8] Other thinkers, such as Jean-Luc Marion, also critique the onto-theological "logic of the Same" but do so from a phenomenological perspective. In "The Present and the Gift," for example, Marion critiques the metaphysical interpretation of transubstantiation, noting that "even if the theology of transubstantiation is not reducible to a particular theme imported from a particular metaphysic," it is still vulnerable to the charge of idolatry, since "substantial presence . . . fixes and freezes the person in an available, permanent, handy, and delimited thing."[9] That "thing," moreover, appears to be at the disposal of the Christian community's consciousness and intentions. "Of this 'God' made thing," writes Marion,

> one would expect precisely nothing but real presence: presence reduced to the dimensions of a thing, a thing that is as much disposed to "honor by its presence" the liturgies where the community celebrates its own power . . . Real presence: "God" made thing, a hostage without significance, powerful because

---

[6] See ibid., 68.

[7] See Chauvet, *Symbol and Sacrament*, 21–45.

[8] Ibid., 45.

[9] See Jean-Luc Marion, "The Present and the Gift," in *God Without Being*, trans. Thomas A. Carlson (Chicago: University of Chicago Press, 1991), 161–82; here, 164. Marion notes that Trent's affirmation of transubstantiation does not require a Thomistic metaphysics.

mute, tutelary because without titularity, a thing *"denuded of all signification except that of presence."*[10]

Still other postmodern thinkers propose that a way out of the totalizing impasse "presence" and "causality" create for sacramental theology should be sought in narrative. Yet here, too, difficulties may arise. In the illuminating essay "Communion and Conversation," Regina M. Schwartz observes that

> like the God of metaphysics, narrative tries to offer up a God of determinate meaning. And like the God of metaphysics, narrative tries to offer up a God of causes. To ask . . . how can the divine God break through narrative is similar to asking how the divine God can survive metaphysics. Both are human stories, preoccupied with Being and beings, cause and effect, motive and meaning. If we were to search for the more divine god, we would need, as Marion puts it, "to think God without pretending to inscribe him or to describe him." *We would turn to a different understanding of language, not one that presumes to convey meaning, but one that performs otherwise.*[11]

DESCRIPTIVE VERSUS DOXOLOGICAL STRATEGIES IN LANGUAGE

In her proposal for a narrative that can "think God without pretending to describe him," Schwartz describes two fundamental strategies of language, one descriptive and the other doxological. The descriptive strategy uses speech as a blunt-force instrument, a "tool to convey meaning" that embodies the author's intention to compress a "universal truth" (note the totalizing claim) within the compact compass of a narrative. For an example of this descriptive strategy and its consequences, Schwartz turns to Genesis 9:18-28, the episode describing a drunk Noah's nakedness, the behavior of his sons, and Noah's sober reaction: "'Cursed be Canaan! The lowest of slaves shall he be to his brothers.' . . . 'Blessed be the Lord, The God of Shem!; Let Canaan be

---

[10] Ibid., 164–65; emphasis in the original. The internal quotation is from Mallarmé.

[11] Regina M. Schwarz, "Communion and Conversation," in *The Blackwell Companion to Postmodern Theology*, ed. Graham Ward (Oxford: Blackwell, 2001), 48–67; here, 49, emphasis added.

his slave.'"[12] Read instrumentally, this brief tale proposes a "cause-and-effect" meaning, a descriptive aetiology that explains—and so justifies—the sociopolitical fate of Canaan and his descendants. Because his father (Ham) sinned, Canaan is cursed, condemned to perpetual slavery. In short, when a reader assumes that the Genesis narrative is "a tool conveying a meaning," this "presumption of instrumentality" becomes "the condition for a legacy of violent uses."[13] As Schwartz points out, this was precisely the consequence. Genesis 9:18-28 became in fact "a weapon to justify slavery in the antebellum American South," where Christian ministers "used a version of the story to preach that a whole race of humankind was cursed by Noah to be subjugated to another race and that this was the will of God."[14] Thus, linguistic forms and strategies that seek closure by "capturing" reality and meaning not only legitimate violence but reduce "everything to more of the same" and thereby exclude "anything that is genuinely other and different."[15]

But language need not always be descriptive; it may also be doxological, speech that "praises or laments, rather than describes."[16] In this doxological strategy, language focuses not on "referential or predicational functions" but on *rhythm*, the "alternation of silence and utterance" that "marks not only the performance of poetry, drama, and ritual, but also conversation."[17] When seen as rhythm and conversation, language becomes an opening for change and transformation, rather than closure around "captured" causes and meanings. Take, for instance, the priestly poem that opens the book of Genesis (Gen 1:1–2:4a). If heard as rhythmic conversation, the poem performs a ritual litany of praise punctuated by a responsive refrain ("And God saw that it was good"). It becomes embodied gratitude, "a hymn of praise, instead of an idolatrous description of divine activity."[18]

Doxological speech is, then, characterized by several qualities that distinguish it from description. First, doxology is open-ended; it seeks to limit (capture, confine) neither the subject nor the object of praise.

---

[12] Gen 9:26-27 (NAB); see Schwartz, "Communion and Conversation," 50.
[13] Schwartz, "Communion and Conversation," 50.
[14] Ibid.
[15] Tracy, "Form & Fragment," 68.
[16] Schwartz, "Communion and Conversation," 51.
[17] Ibid.
[18] Ibid.

Second, doxology is polyglot. Because it speaks several "languages" simultaneously—including metaphor, symbol, rite, culture, and body—its "meanings" cannot be confined to—or exhausted by—a single, closed system of references. Third, doxology "names without naming." The language of prayer and praise is not an act of predication. It does not name God positively as an "essence," nor (in the manner of negative theology) does it annul that essence only in order to reestablish it *per modum eminentiae*. Doxology thus radically *de-nominates*; it addresses God "outside all proper names, without sinking into presence," and hence it is more accurate to say that doxology's naming signals not God's presence but God's absence, anonymity, and withdrawal.[19] Fourth, doxology stammers, oscillating endlessly between joy and sorrow, ecstasy and regret, protestations of faith and confessions of sin. This oscillation is not simply the result of the praying subjects' uncertainty or confusion, but, as Catherine Pickstock has pointed out, belongs to the nature of doxological language as such. "Unlike the view of reality implicit within immanentist language and the power of its textural permanence," Pickstock notes, the twitching "recommencements" of doxology are "supremely but ineffably 'ordered' through genuine mystery and transcendent 'distance' . . . [for] the liturgical stammer bespeaks its admission of distance between itself and the transcendent 'real.' It is this very admission of distance" that avoids the trap of presence and "permits a genuine proximity with God."[20]

A biblical example of language's doxological strategy may be found in the narrative of Isaac's birth (Gen 21:1-8). As Avivah Gottlieb Zornberg remarks, this brief passage combines two themes: laughter and feasting. "To laugh," she writes, "is to counter Spinoza's first great law

---

[19] God's absence and withdrawal are, in effect, what makes "the name" possible, and this withdrawal is nowhere more evident than in the event of Christ's Cross. See Jean-Luc Marion, "In the Name: How to Avoid Speaking of It," from *In Excess*, trans. Robyn Horner and Vincent Berraud, Perspectives in Continental Philosophy (New York: Fordham University Press, 2002), 149, and cf. 142–43. On "de-nomination" as a third way beyond the predicative strategies of affirmation and negation, see ibid., 134–42. See also Chauvet, *Symbol and Sacrament*, 492–502; 513–14.

[20] Catherine Pickstock, *After Writing: On the Liturgical Consummation of Philosophy*, Contemporary Challenges in Theology (Oxford: Blackwell, 1998), 178. Elsewhere, Pickstock calls doxology an "epiphanic naming" of God. See ibid., 204.

of thought: *non ridere, non lugere, neque detestari, sed intellegere*—to laugh, to suffer, to rejoice, to hate, and to weep are to affirm the reality of the self as not simply an undifferentiated part of the world of objects ruled by necessity."[21] Laughter is a language that resists reduction to controlled "meanings;" it "thrives at the expense of normal speech" and rejoices in an "intelligibility" that can be neither described nor scripted.[22] "Abraham and Sarah," writes Zornberg,

> by inviting the laughter to their table, share in it and modulate it. It is a fully human affirmation of affinity, a nonverbal possibility somewhere 'between the wordlessness of animals and the silence of the gods.' . . . The mouth filled with real laughter—like the food of the feast, audible and sensible to others—is an image representing the end of days, the overcoming of separateness and closure. In this world, it remains a mere possibility that constantly destroys itself.[23]

Laughter is, then, the language of the world to come, breaking down boundaries that define the totalizing systems of this world. It is an ebullient, expansive language that limits neither subjects nor objects precisely because reason and will are not its primary referents. Reason, after all, "subjects human beings to a lifetime of evaluation . . . to a world of discontents."[24] But in the biblical account, Isaac's birth initiates the language of the world to come, "the period of feasting and laughter, of the bearable lightness of being."[25] Midrashic commentaries on this story thus imagine Abraham as a "feast-and-festivity maker: I have rejoiced and spread joy everywhere."[26] Laughter and feasting are languages of excess, and hence they belong together as doxological strategies that defy closure. Both are disruptions of the world's temporality—suspensions of a "presence" that seeks to commodify itself in objects totally available to our intelligence and apprehension in *"the* present."[27]

[21] Avivah Gottlieb Zornberg, *The Beginning of Desire: Reflections on Genesis* (New York: Doubleday, 1995), 99–100.

[22] Ibid., 100.

[23] Ibid.

[24] Ibid., 101.

[25] Ibid.

[26] Ibid., 102.

[27] For further discussion of this point see Robyn Horner, "Translator's Introduction" to *In Excess*, ix–xx; here, xii–xiii. Objects are, in fact, never simply

Zornberg's analysis of the story of Sarah and Abraham thus exemplifies Schwartz's understanding of language as doxological rather than descriptive in her model for understanding biblical narrative based on conversation:

> What happens when we hear the creation narrative in Genesis 1 as a conversation, or as an expression of gratitude . . . instead of an idolatrous description of divine activity? Is it possible to read an account of the beginning without satisfying (or frustrating) our craving for an *explanation* of the beginning?[28]

Such questions can be answered, she argues, only if we move from a preoccupation with narrative's performativity to questions about its *reception*. Whether we hear the priestly creation poem in Genesis 1 as a quasi-scientific narrative that explains the world's origins or as liturgical poetry with doxological (praising, thanking) intent depends upon perception and reception rather than upon the nature of narrativity as such.

Reception, then, respects the structure by which realities (whether visual or verbal, human or divine) reveal themselves and give themselves to our experience. For from a phenomenological perspective, objects and events vary through time and are offered only "through successive temporalizations"; hence, "no object ever gives rise to the same lived experience twice."[29] Moreover, events and objects differ from one another in the way they give themselves to us. Historical *events*—such as birth, death, or friendship—differ from *objects* on three grounds: facticity (the event has "always already occurred"); achievement (the event is irrevocable, done "once for all"), and indeterminacy (the event's interpretation can never be fully and finally completed).[30] While an object "will often necessarily first show itself" before giving itself,

> events like death or birth actually only show themselves in the mode of being given. The event is a *fait accompli*, irremediably striking the one who receives it. And this recipient is not the tran-

---

constituted "in the present," but are given only with reference to both past and future; they are basically undefined and hence constituted only over time through a successive series of temporalizations.

[28] Schwartz, "Communion and Conversation," 51; emphasis added.
[29] Robyn Horner, "Translator's Introduction," *In Excess*, xiii.
[30] See ibid., xv.

scendental I—the autonomous human ego—but the *adonné*, the one "given over," gifted, or devoted to the self-giving phenomenon, the one who receives itself from what it receives.[31]

One is reminded here of Chauvet's point that in the sacramental celebration of the Eucharist, the church receives its identity only by "offering itself in what it offers"; it receives Christ's sacramental Body by means of oblation, because the "Christian mode of appropriation is through disappropriation: the mode of 'taking' is by 'giving'—'giving thanks.'"[32]

In short, conversation is a linguistic strategy that resists closure or reduction to a totalizing "system" because it requires multiple perspectives and an endlessly incomplete hermeneutic. All phenomena, to some extent, exceed our capacity to constitute them—above all the human face of the other, which "demands an infinite hermeneutic, proceeding from its priority in appearing to me as a saturated phenomenon."[33] Narratives, too, may exceed our capacity to constitute them. Thus, although biblical stories may be heard or read as objects under the control of a community of interpreters, they may also be experienced as *events* that forever elude the cognitive, hermeneutical grasp of those who hear or read them. "For some readers," Schwartz observes, "Genesis 1 will always *describe* the creation of the world; for others, including those who understand its rehearsal as keeping chaos at bay another year, it creates the world." As poetry, these stories "*can be experienced differently, as praise and lament*" of God inscribed as a Being who forms and promises to protect a people.[34]

FRAGMENTARY LANGUAGES, APOPHATIC AND APOCALYPTIC

This discussion of the differences between descriptive and doxological strategies in language returns us to Tracy's point about the contemporary need to retrieve the theological form of "the fragmentary."[35]

---

[31] Ibid. See Marion, *In Excess*, 32–35. See also the discussion in Shane Mackinlay, "Exceeding Truth: Jean-Luc Marion's Saturated Phenomena," *Pacifica* 20 (February 2007): 40–51; here, especially 42–44.

[32] See Chauvet, *Symbol and Sacrament*, 276–77.

[33] Horner, "Translator's Introduction," *In Excess*, xviii.

[34] Schwartz, "Communion and Conversation," 51.

[35] See Tracy, "Form & Fragment," 63–70.

The fragmentary biblico-theological speech of apocalyptic and apophasis is an antidote to modern theology's amnesia concerning Christ's Cross and the hiddenness of God. From one angle, admittedly, "the fragmentary" may seem to collide with the symbolic. Yet there is good reason to believe that symbol and fragment are not opposite but complementary. Etymologically, it is true, *symbolon* suggests closure, since the word signifies putting together (*syn + ballein*) two separated halves (e.g., of a coin given in pledge) in order to confirm a relationship, ratify a treaty, or seal a contract.[36] Yet the very condition of possibility for the appearance of the symbolic is distance, absence—the suspension or rupture of totality. As even Aquinas recognized, symbols are open-ended actions rather than closed-off objects: *Signa dantur hominibus quorum est per nota ad ignota pervenire* ("[symbolic] signs are directed toward human beings, who use them to proceed from what is known to what is unknown"). Symbolization, in short, is a *process* that oscillates ambiguously between knowledge and ignorance, presence and absence, proximity and distance. What symbols disclose and give, prodigally, is not closure but excess, surplus.

The point is that symbolization is *not* an act of predication. When applied to Christian sacrament, the relation between *signum* (symbol) and *signatum* (symbolized) should be construed as neither a relation between subject and predicate nor a relation between form (signifier) and content (referent). The symbol does not "name" a reality, either cataphatically or apophatically, thereby bringing the process of signification to closure by establishing a graspable "presence" (the *signatum*). On the contrary, symbols are ruled by a "pragmatic theology of absence" and thus opposed to a metaphysics of presence.[37] Sacramental symbols thus "name" without naming, "say" without circumscribing the said, "give" without in any way diminishing the resources of the giver.[38] Marion clarifies this point further by commenting on a passage of *Against Eunomius*, wherein Gregory of Nyssa argues that the Name Christians give God surpasses all signification possible to usual human naming:

---

[36] See, further, the discussion in Chauvet, *Symbol and Sacrament*, 112–13.

[37] Marion, *In Excess*, 157.

[38] Note that "giving" of this kind escapes the ordinary economy of exchange that assigns value and so results in lack, indebtedness, and the implicit or explicit obligation to "return the gift."

The Name does not name God as an essence, it designates what passes beyond every name. The Name designates what one does not name and says that one does not name it. . . . For the Name no longer functions by inscribing God within the theoretical horizon of our predication but rather by inscribing us, according to a radically new praxis, in the very horizon of God.[39]

The language of Christian liturgy and sacrament does not ascribe an identity to God, but opens a space for what Marion calls "denomination"—letting the unnamable God "name and call us."[40] But this requires an understanding of sacramental signification (symbolization) quite different from the Scholastics' totalizing scheme of cause and effect. Chauvet points us in the right direction by noting that the symbolic order requires "an attitude of listening and welcome toward something *ungraspable* by which we are already grasped; a gracious attitude of *'letting be'* and *'allowing oneself to be spoken'* which requires us to renounce all ambition for mastery."[41] As deployed within Christian liturgy, therefore, the primary purpose of symbols (*signa*) is to clear a space that resists and defies every attempt at closure. Thus, for example, it is more accurate to say that the eucharistic bread and wine (sacramental symbols pointing to the reality of Christ's self-gift as our food and drink) are *"signs of a further sign"* rather than causal productions that limit or inscribe Christ's presence within the temporal horizon (the "present") of our celebration.[42] This is a point already recognized centuries ago by, among others, Cardinal Bessarion (d. 1472), who wrote that in the Eucharist the reality of Christ's Body and Blood "is itself the sign of another reality," namely, the ecclesial Body of Christ, the church, gathered in unity by the Holy Spirit.[43] Yet this making of "one body from many" is not a task that permits closure within

[39] Marion, *In Excess*, 156–67. The patristic citation is to *Against Eunomius*, II.14–15.

[40] Ibid., 162.

[41] Chauvet, *Symbol and Sacrament*, 446.

[42] For further discussion of this point, see Marion, "The Present and the Gift," 163–69.

[43] For discussion and text, see Bernard Leeming, *Principles of Sacramental Theology* (Westminster, MD: The Newman Press, 1956), 256. This is the reason, too, why Scholastics such as Thomas Aquinas spoke of the *"res"* of the Eucharist as "the unity of the church" (*"Eucharistia est signum ecclesiasticae unionis"*). See *Summa Theologiae, Supplementum*, Q. 71, art. 9, ad 3um.

the circularity of a ritual-symbolic act, even an action as profound as the Eucharist. Christian liturgy leaves the process of sacramental signification open and ongoing, and hence Mass does not "end" with the last blessing and dismissal of the assembly. As Chauvet insists, the liturgy of the church is joined to "the obligation of an ethical activity": "The ethics of 'living-in-grace,' primarily with regard to those whom humans have reduced to the status of slaves, is the place of veri-fication, the *veritas*, of the filial 'giving thanks' of the Eucharist."[44]

Christian liturgy is thus a site of "de-nomination" whose ritual speech resists reduction to categories of "presence" and "predication" as these have often been understood. If, as Aquinas argued, baptism is *ianua sacramentorum*, it is so not because it enrolls us within a community of *fideles* who "know and name God," but because through it "we enter into God's unpronounceable Name, with the additional result that we receive our own."[45] The language of the Christian assembly at prayer is not a speech of autonomous self-assertion that "names presence" and so guarantees its availability to participants. Moreover, to speak about how symbols work (by *de*-nomination) and to affirm symbolic reality do not require that we think "presence" as that term is often—inaccurately and even idolatrously—used of God's self-giving in sacrament.[46] On the contrary, liturgical language is "never a matter of speaking *of* God, but always of speaking *to* God in the words of the Word."[47]

This is one reason why the postconciliar reforms of the Roman Rite include a proclamation of God's Word within every sacramental celebration. For as Marion remarks, "Christ does not say the word, he says *himself* the Word. He says *himself*—the Word!"[48] Yet that is not all; the Word not only *speaks*; it *is spoken*—spoken in human language, in flesh and bone. Here we may discern the profound reason why, as noted earlier, Chauvet maintains that the Christian symbolic order requires a "gracious attitude of *allowing oneself to be spoken*."[49] The root of this re-

[44] Chauvet, *Symbol and Sacrament*, 279–80.

[45] Marion, *In Excess*, 157. For baptism as *ianua sacramentorum*, see Thomas Aquinas, *Summa Theologiae*, III Pars, Q. 63, art. 6, corpus; cf. Q. 73, art. 3, corpus.

[46] On the danger of an idolatrous presence, see Marion, "The Present and the Gift," 164–65.

[47] Marion, *In Excess*, 157.

[48] Jean-Luc Marion, "Of the Eucharistic Site of Theology," in *God Without Being*, 139–58; here, 140.

[49] Chauvet, *Symbol and Sacrament*, 446.

quirement—essential for understanding the structure of all sacramental signification—lies in the Word's twofold "letting itself be said." "The Word," writes Marion, "says [itself]—Word!—only by letting be said" in human speech, and this in a "double sense."[50] First, the Word lets itself be said in speech that leads *not* to an immediate and accurate *recognition* of who he is, but to progressive *incomprehension* on the part of his hearers. We see this happening in Mark's gospel: Jesus' disciples regularly fail to grasp his message and finally flee at his arrest, while the person who recognizes and "says" the Word at the moment of his death is a Roman centurion (Mark 15:39).[51] Passing beyond the precincts of death, the Word made flesh lets itself be said by an unbeliever! Second, the Word lets itself be said in the vulnerability of a flesh-and-bone incarnation in which he *truly gives himself* to us *yet remains unspeakable*. The Word is unspeakable not because human speech is poor and inadequate (though it often is), but because he exposes us to the unsettling—indeed terrifying—possibility that all our words finally find their *referent* in him. The Word gives itself to us and our history not simply as "thought" or "message," *but as a body*, as One who, letting himself be said in our speech, draws us inexorably into that movement by which he returns to the Father in a "transference [that] designates the Spirit" (see John 19:30).[52] The Word's incarnation thus "occupies and transgresses at once the order of speech and of meaning . . . say[ing] itself, it therefore becomes unspeakable to us."[53] Babbling and stuttering, we say the Word (who lets himself *be* said) in spite of ourselves.

Because it is an ineradicable infection—speech-become-flesh-and-bone-in-history—this Word radically transgresses all human language and so alters the structure of signification itself. For it means that the "referent" we seek in language is no longer "meaning" or "presence" (i.e., predicated objects we speakers can "close in upon" and control), but the uncontrollable, ungraspable advent of a Person.[54] This is

---

[50] Marion, "Of the Eucharistic Site of Theology," 140.

[51] See Paul J. Achtemeier, *Mark*, Proclamation Commentaries (Philadelphia: Fortress Press, 1975), 92–100; and David Rhoads and Donald Michie, *Mark as Story. An Introduction to the Narrative of a Gospel* (Philadelphia: Fortress Press, 1982), 122–29.

[52] Marion, "On the Eucharistic Site of Theology," 142.

[53] Ibid.

[54] See ibid., 147.

perhaps most clearly evident in the Lukan account of post-Easter appearance at Emmaus (Luke 24:13-35). The disappointed disciples are looking for a hermeneutic for Jesus' death. Yet what arrives on the road is not hermeneutics but a person, a Stranger who does indeed interpret the Scriptures, but more important, *lets himself be said* "in the breaking of bread" and *immediately vanishes* (Luke 24:30-35). As a story of "coming to faith," the Emmaus episode reveals that the condition sine qua non for Christian symbolization (sacramental signification) is emptiness, absence, a letting go *"of the desire to see-touch-find" and "to accept in its place the hearing of a word."*[55]

RITUAL STRATEGY: RUPTURE AND FRAGMENTATION

The Christian symbolic order thus fragments all those reductive systems of signification that would seek to limit or circumscribe the unspeakable Word in categories of "presence," whether presence is reified in a delimited object or has been "displaced . . . to the community . . . the present consciousness of the collective self."[56] In short, Christian sacrament's native speech is disruptive and *fragmentary* rather than totalizing. To say sacramental speech is fragmentary is to think "the *impossible*," which for postmodern theorists is not a purely negative category but, rather, one open to multiple interpretations, each fragmentary and incomplete.[57]

John Caputo shows how the fragmenting form of the impossible can be interpreted in relation to either excessive *givenness* (Marion) or endless *deferral* (Jacques Derrida). For Marion, the impossibility of naming God arises "not from a lack of givenness . . . but from an excess in givenness, surplus."[58] The "unnamable, incomprehensible" God's self-giving is an event "of bedazzling brilliance, given without being, visited upon us beyond comprehension, leaving us stunned and lost for words."[59] That is why the fragmented, stuttering language of liturgy, in which every effort to name God collapses in blessed defeat, leads us

[55] Chauvet, *Symbol and Sacrament*, 162; emphasis in the original.

[56] See Marion, "The Present and the Gift," 166.

[57] See Tracy, "Form & Fragment," 69, 71.

[58] John D. Caputo, "Apostles of the Impossible," in *God, the Gift, and Postmodernism*, ed. John D. Caputo and Michael J. Scanlon, The Indiana Series in the Philosophy of Religion (Bloomington: Indiana University Press, 1999), 185–222; here, 194.

[59] Ibid., 185.

to feast on broken fragments of a loaf and to slake our thirst with small gulps of wine poured out. *Impossibility* is a consequence of God's "being given" in an excess so saturating that it exceeds any concepts or limiting horizons that human subjects might attempt to impose on it. But for Derrida, on the other hand, "to affirm the impossible is not to affirm infinite givenness."[60] In Derrida's view, the impossible is always and indefinitely deferred. It is not accessible as an "excess of givenness," and so Derrida's philosophical deconstruction "is a call for the coming of something unforeseeable and unprogrammable, a call that is nourished by the expectation of something to come, structurally to come, for which we pray and weep, sigh and dream."[61]

These two positions about "the impossible" obviously result in differing understandings of messianism and differing views of faith. For Marion, the unspeakable Word has let itself be said—impossibly!—in human flesh and history, without abandoning its gratuity, distance, and otherness. The Word has become a vulnerable "figure of transfiguring glory, the icon of the invisible God, an impossible gift of God" that evokes our faith, which is itself "the gift of having the eyes to see his invisible glory."[62] Derrida, in contrast, confronts us with a much darker figure—a Messiah "who is still to come, unimaginable, unprefigurable," a figure "who is never to be given," whose arrival is endlessly deferred.[63] If this Messiah is "said to be *sans l'être*, this does not mean that he is beyond being or does not have to be," as Christian apophatic theology might hold, but rather, "like a specter, that he neither is nor is not but is yet to come."[64] For Derrida, the "gift of faith" must mean that we will never have "eyes to see," that our tearful groping after God will always occur in the dark, and that our cry "Come!" will always be met with silence.

In the contrast between Marion and Derrida we discern what Tracy calls the "two great fragmentary forms of *both* Judaism and Christianity, the apocalyptic and the apophatic."[65] Note that word "both" in Tracy's comment. Apocalypse and apophasis are *both* embodied in a tradition of theological language common to *both* Christians and Jews.

---

[60] Ibid., 194.
[61] Ibid., 185–86.
[62] Ibid., 186.
[63] Ibid.
[64] Ibid.
[65] Tracy, "Form & Fragment," 77; emphasis added.

Consider once again the original ending of that "strange apocalyptic Gospel" known as Mark.[66] Its original ending (Mark 16:8) is not a cry of triumph, but a whimper, or more accurately, a shudder. The spice-bearing women are left trembling before an empty tomb, afraid to say anything to anyone: *oudeni ouden eipan; ephobounto gar*, the Greek text says ("they said nothing to anyone; for they were afraid"). Mark ends not with closure, but with suspense, incompletion, rupture. Indeed, the Christian testament itself ends with words that lie at the heart of Derrida's darkly elusive messianism: *"Erchou Kyrie Iesou!"* ("Come, Lord Jesus!" Rev 22:20). As exegete Ernst Käsemann famously said, "apocalyptic is the mother of Christian theology," for such language ruptures, fragments, all our pretensions to smooth continuity and final closure within human history.[67]

The Christian sacramental language of giving and givenness is thus not only *apophatic*—a speech that, as Chauvet says, *masters us* and tears open "a space for breathing, for freedom, for gratuitousness where God may come"—but *apocalyptic*.[68] Without the crucial apocalyptic language of a "Second Coming," as Tracy notes, Christianity is liable to "settle down into a religion which no longer has a profound sense of the not-yet, and thereby no longer a profound sense of God's very hidden-ness in history."[69] It is precisely apocalyptic's intent to roil and rupture, to destabilize any and every totalizing claim, to challenge the church's own triumphalism, its mistaken belief in a pure historical "continuity" that "ends in us the victors."[70]

The Roman Catholic understanding of ritual symbolism, of sacramental signification, must be read, therefore, through lenses that are both apophatic and apocalyptic. The apophatic—interpreted, as Marion reads it, not as predication but as "de-nomination"—prevents sacramental signification from collapsing into what both modernity and metaphysics would identify as "the possible." The apophatic *impossible* resists the limiting possible by yielding not causes and objects, being and presence, completion and closure, but rather counter-experiences of bedazzlement, of astonishment at events we cannot comprehend. In short, the celebration of a sacrament does not yield an "object," a

---

[66] Ibid., 79.

[67] Käsemann's comment is quoted in Tracy, "Form & Fragment," 79.

[68] See Chauvet, *Symbol and Sacrament*, 338.

[69] Tracy, "Form & Fragment," 80.

[70] Ibid.

"being," or a "being-present" whose "causes" we can know and name. Instead it opens, as Chauvet would say, an ambiguous, heterotopic "space of gratuitousness where God can come."[71]

At the same time, however, ritual symbols cannot be reduced *exclusively* to experiences of "dazzling excess" flowing from a "saturating givenness beyond Being."[72] The mother tongue of apocalyptic ruptures all expectations and prevents our identifying *any* historical "moment" as so saturated with "givenness" that it becomes immune to "abyss, chasm, chaos, [and] horror."[73] Bedazzlement does not rescue us from what Derrida would call *khora*, the unyielding desert that sinks even below the horizon of biblical history, the "desert in the desert" that resists, absolutely, "the formed structures, the constituted forms of history and culture, of the Western and non-Western, of philosophy and theology, of reason and revelation."[74] This desert (*khora*) "does not happen, does not give, does not desire. It is a spacing, and absolutely indifferent," irreducible to revelation, religion, or any phenomenologically saturating "givenness."[75]

It seems to me that in *Symbol and Sacrament* Chauvet comes closer than Marion to an inclusive understanding of sacrament that embraces both apophasis and apocalyptic. Christian tradition (arguably since the time of Paul's letters to the Romans and Corinthians) has long linked the church's sacramental actions to the Cross and death of Jesus. This linkage was maintained in the medieval era, as well, in axioms such as *"e latere Christi dormientis in cruce fluxerunt ecclesiae sacramenta."* Jesus' experience on the cross can hardly be interpreted as one of "saturating givenness" and bedazzlement; rather, it seems akin to Derrida's *khora*. Jesus' cry of dereliction is surely an experience in which "God manifests God's self by withdrawing."[76] On the cross,

---

[71] Chauvet, *Symbol and Sacrament*, 339.

[72] See Caputo, "Apostles of the Impossible," 215.

[73] See Tracy, "Form & Fragment," 82.

[74] See Caputo, "Apostles of the Impossible," 216, and his *The Prayers and Tears of Jacques Derrida* (Bloomington, IN: Indiana University Press, 1997), 35–36.

[75] See Derrida's comments in "On the Gift: A Discussion between Jacques Derrida and Jean-Luc Marion, moderated by Richard Kearney," in *God, the Gift, and Postmodernism*, 54–78; here, 76.

[76] See Chauvet, *Symbol and Sacrament*, 506; this phrase, as Chauvet notes, comes from the work of Walter Kasper.

Jesus reaches the "desert in the desert" that sinks below the horizon of biblical history—the utterly empty space (neither being nor nonbeing, neither sensible nor intelligible, neither meaningful or meaningless). Thus Chauvet can rightly say that "it is in the experience of [Jesus'] total letting-God-be-God, of this *radical difference* of God, so other that God recedes into God's silence—it is there his *likeness* with the Father is fully revealed."[77]

In sum, Christians celebrate every sacrament in both bedazzlement and *khora*. They celebrate *Eucharist*, to speak more specifically, not in order to inscribe God within an horizon of "being," "presence," and "causality," but to experience God's coming through "unconceptualized symbolisms" that point to God's "otherness and graciousness" taking flesh among us.[78] Sacraments are not celebrations of Christian triumphalism. They speak a language of apocalyptic that challenges the totalizing pretensions

> of every structure, the *khora* that infiltrates or un-forms every historical language and formation, keeps the future open, robs the present of too great an authority or prestige, prevents any current structure or event from declaring itself just, prevents the present order from presenting itself as justice itself. This is said not out of despair or nihilism, but just in order to let justice come, to let the gift come.[79]

For even when God's givenness saturates and bedazzles us who gather to eat the broken holy bread and drink the poured-out saving cup, our cry must still be *"Come, Lord Jesus, come! Come quickly!"*

[77] See ibid., 506.
[78] See ibid., 339.
[79] See Caputo, "Apostles of the Impossible," 218.

Bibliography of Louis-Marie Chauvet

BOOKS:
Du symbolique au symbole. Essai sur les sacrements. Coll. Rites et symbols. Paris:
     Éd. du Cerf, 1979, 306 pp.
Thèmes de réflexion sur l'eucharistie (1. "Eglise et eucharistie"; 2. "Le mystère de la
     présence du Christ"; 3. "L'eucharistie, mémoire de l'Eglise"; 4. "Le sacrifice
     du Christ et de l'Eglise"). Lourdes: International Eucharistic Congress, 1981.
     A booklet of 54 pages for the International Eucharistic Congress of 1981.
Symbole et sacrement. Une relecture sacramentelle de l'existence chrétienne. Coll.
     Cogitatio Fidei. Paris: Éd. du Cerf, 1987, 582 pp.
Les sacrements, Parole de Dieu au risque du corps. Paris: Éd. de l'Atelier, 1993. *De
     la médiation. Quatre études de théologie sacramentaire fondamentale*, appearing
     in an Italian edition (French text and Italian translation) under the title *Della
     Mediazione. Quattro studi di teologia sacramentaria fondamentale.* Rome: Citta-
     della Editrice, Assisi et Pontificio Ateneo Sant'Anselmo, 2006, 236 pp.

DICTIONARY ENTRIES:
"Sacrements" in *Catholicisme* t. XIII, fasc. 60, col. 326–61 (1992).
"Sacrement" in Lacoste, J. Y., ed., *Dictionnaire critique de Théologie.* Paris: Presses
     Universitaires de France, 1998, pp. 1028–33.
"Pénitence" in Lacoste, J. Y., ed., *Dictionnaire critique de Théologie.* Paris: Presses
     Universitaires de France, 1998, pp. 882–88.

EDITED WORKS:
Chauvet, L. M., and P. de Clerck, eds., *Le sacrement du pardon entre hier et de-
     main.* Paris: Desclée, 1993, 225 pp.
Chauvet, L. M., ed., *Le sacrement de mariage entre hier et demain.* Paris: Éd. de
     l'Atelier, 2003, 332 pp.

CHAPTERS IN COLLECTED WORKS:
"L'aveu dans le sacrement de la reconciliation." In L. M. Chauvet, M.
     Balleydier, and F. Deniau : *L'aveu et le pardon.* Chalet, 1979, 11–53.

"Histoire de la liturgie eucharistique." In the collection AGAPE, *L'eucharistie, de Jésus aux chrétiens d'aujourd'hui.* Paris: Droguet-Ardant, 1981, pp. 175–364.

"Sacramentaire et christologie. La liturgie comme lieu de la christologie." In J. Doré, ed., *Sacrements de Jésus-Christ.* Coll. "Jésus et Jésus-Christ." Paris: Desclée, 1983, 213–54.

"Sacrements et institution." In C.E.R.I.T., *La théologie à l'épreuve de la vérité.* Cogitatio Fidei, 126. Paris: Éd. du Cerf, 1984, 201–35.

"Les sacrements de l'initiation chrétienne," and "La confirmation séparée du baptême." In J. Gelineau, ed., *Dans vos assemblées* (new edition). Paris: Desclée 1989, Vol. 1, pp. 226–46 and 281–92.

"Nova et vetera. Quelques leçons tirées de la tradition relative au sacrement de la reconciliation." In *Rituels. Mélanges offerts au P. GY.* Paris: Éd. du Cerf, 1990, 99–124.

"Evolutions et révolutions du sacrement de la reconciliation," and "Propositions pour une pastorale plus diversifiée de la reconciliation." In L. M. Chauvet and P. de Clerck, eds., *Le sacrement du pardon entre hier et demain.* Paris: Desclée, 1993, 33–39 and 203–17.

"Le 'sacrifice' en christianisme: une notion ambiguë." In M. Neusch, ed., *Le sacrifice dans les religions.* Collectif s de l'ISTR. Paris: Beauchesne, 1994, 139–55.

"Le sacrifice comme échange symbolique." In M. Neusch, ed., *Le sacrifice dans les religions.* Collectif s de l'ISTR. Paris: Beauchesne, 1994, 277–304.

"Le rite et l'éthique: une tension féconde." In R. Devisch, C. Perrot, L. Voye, and L. M. Chauvet, *Le rite, source et resources.* Bruxelles: Fac. Universit. St Louis, 1995, 137–55.

"Parler du sacrement de mariage aujourd'hui." In Commission Épiscopale de Liturgie, *Pastorale sacramentelle I, Les sacrements de l'initiation chrétienne et le mariage.* Paris: Éd. du Cerf, 1996, 182–205.

"Quand le théologien se fait anthropologue . . . " In Jean Joncheray, ed., *Approches scientifiques des faits religieux.* Paris: Beauchesne, 1997, 29–46.

"La messa come sacrificio nel Medioevo e nel concilio di Trento: pratiche e teorie." In the collection, *Il sacrificio: evento e rito.* Padova, Italy, 1998, 19–51.

"Baptême des petits enfants et péché original." In G. Medevielle and J. Doré, eds., *Une parole pour la vie. Hommage à Xavier Thévenot.* Paris: Éd. du Cerf, 1998, 225–42.

"La liturgie demain: essai de prospective." In P. de Clerck, ed., *La liturgie, lieu théologique.* Paris: Beauchesne, 1999, 201–29.

"La Bible dans son site liturgique." In J. L. Souletie and H. J. Gagey, eds., *La Bible, Parole adressée.* Paris: Éd. du Cerf, 2001, 49–68.

"Quand la théologie rencontre les sciences humaines." In F. Bousquet, and others, eds., *La responsabilité des théologiens.* Mélanges offerts à Joseph Doré. Paris: Desclée, 2002, 401–15.

"Approche anthropologique de l'eucharistie." InM. Brouard, ed., *Eucharistia. Encyclopédie de l'Eucharistie.* Paris: Éd. du Cerf, 2002, 19–32.

"Le mariage, un défi." In L. M. Chauvet, ed., *Le sacrement de mariage entre hier et demain.* Paris: Éd. de l'Atelier, 2003, 15–26.

"Détendre la sacramentalité." In L. M. Chauvet, ed., *Le sacrement de mariage entre hier et demain.* Paris: Éd. de l'Atelier, 2003, 235–43.

"Sur quelques difficultés actuelles au sujet de l'au-delà." In Commission Épiscopale de Liturgie, *Pastorale des funérailles.* CNPL. Paris: Éd. du Cerf, 2003, 88–104.

"Les sacrements, ou le corps comme chemin de Dieu." In A Gesché and P. Scolas, eds., *Le corps, chemin de Dieu.* Paris: Éd. du Cerf / Univ. Cath. De Louvain, 2005, 103–24.

PRINCIPAL ARTICLES APPEARING IN JOURNALS AND PERIODICALS:

"La dimension sacrificielle de l'eucharistie." *La Maison-Dieu* 123 (1975): 30 pp.

"Une relecture de Symbol et sacrament." *Questions Liturgiques* 88/2 (2007): 111–25.

"Le mariage, un sacrement pas comme les autres." *La Maison-Dieu* 127 (1976): 40 pp.

"L'Eglise fait l'eucharistie, l'eucharistie fait l'Eglise." *Catéchèse* 71 (April 1978): 12 pp.

"La ritualité chrétienne dans le cercle du symbole." *La Maison-Dieu* 133 (1978): 47 pp.

"Réflexions théologiques sur quelques orientations actuelles de la pastorale de la confirmation." *Catéchèse* 75 (1979): 20 pp.

"Le sacramentologue aux prises avec l'eucharistie." *La Maison-Dieu* 137 (1979): 23 pp.

"Pratiques pénitentielles et conceptions du péché." *Le Supplément* (1979): 41–64.

"Le sacrifice de la messe." *Lumière et Vie* 146 (1980): 69–106.

"Nos célébrations sont-elles chrétiennes?" *Masses Ouvrières* 358 (1980): 37–52.

"Le ministère de présidence de l'eucharistie." *Prêtres Diocésains* 1192 (1981): 18 pp.

"La liturgie du prochain: le culte chrétien mis au défi." *Parole et pain* 66 (1984): 378–89.

"Liturgie et agir chrétien. Une tension féconde." *Catéchèse* 98 (1985): 12 pp.

"Rites et symboles. Célébrer Jésus-Christ aujourd'hui." *Masses Ouvrières* 409 (1986): 47–69.

"L'avenir du sacramental." *Recherches de Science Religieuse* 75/2 (1987): 81–106.

"La structuration de la foi dans les célébrations sacramentelles." *La Maison-Dieu* 174 (1988): 75–95.

"La notion de 'Tradition.'" *La Maison-Dieu* 178 (1989): 7–46.

"Le peuple de Dieu et ses ministers." *Prêtres Diocésains*, Numéro special, "Les ministères dans l'Eglise." (March–April 1990): 127–55.

"La vie religieuse comme langage symbolique." *Vida religiosa* (Spanish): 12 pp.

"Ritualité et théologie." *Recherches de Science Religieuse* 78/4 (1990): 197–226.

"Etapes vers le baptême ou étapes du baptême?" *La Maison Dieu* 185 (1991): 35–46.

"La théologie sacramentaire est-elle an-esthésique?" *La Maison Dieu* 188 (1991): 7–39.

"La dimension biblique des textes liturgiques." *La Maison Dieu* 189 (1992): 131–48.

"La singularité du rapport chrétien à la Bible." *La Maison Dieu* 190 (1992): 142–54.

"Appelés à leur dire Jésus-Christ." *Catéchèse* 126/127 (January–April 1992): 167–82.

"Une mémoire inscrite dans le corps: les rites sacramentals." *Cahiers du SCEJI* 7, Montpellier (May 1992): 23–38.

"Nouvelles religiosités et foi chrétienne : un défi pour l'évangélisation." *Revue de l'Institut Catholique de Paris* 43 (July–September 1992): 58–78.

"Les sacrements de l'initiation. Eléments de mise au point théologique." *Croissance de l'Eglise* 108 (November 1993): 35–44.

"Liturgie et prière." *La Maison Dieu* 195 (1993): 49–90.

"Sacramentaire et christologie." *Questions Liturgiques* 75 (1994/1-2): 41–55.

"Los sacramentos en el campo de lo simbolico." *Anamnèsis* (1994/1): 135–48.

"L'espace liturgique comme lieu d'invitation à la prière." *Carmel* 73 (1994/3): 45–60.

"L'organisme sacramentel. Réflexion théologique sur le "système" formé par les sacrements." *Prêtres Diocésains* 1324 (December 1994): 467–81.

"L'acte catéchétique comme initiation à la foi." *Catéchèse* 138 (1995/1): 91–98.

"La liturgie dans son espace symbolique", Concilium 259 (1995): 49–61.

"Communion et dévotion. Réflexions sur les théologies et les pratiques de l'eucharistie." *La Maison-Dieu* 203 (1995/3): 7–38.

"L'initiation chrétienne une fois pour toutes ?" *Catéchèse* 141 (1995/4): 49–56.

"Les lieux du baptême. Eléments de réflexion théologique et pastorale." *Chroniques d'Art Sacré* 44 (Winter 1995): 9–13.

"La fonction du prêtre dans le récit de l'institution à la lumière de la linguistique." *Revue de l'ICP* 56 (October–December 1995): 41–61.

"Pratique sacramentelle et expérience chrétienne." *Christus* 171 (July 1996): 275–87.

"Baptême des petits enfants et foi des parents." *La Maison Dieu* 207 (1996/3): 9–28.

"Le fondement sacramentel de l'autorité dans l'Eglise." *Lumière et Vie* 229 (1996): 67–80.

"Note sur la confirmation des adultes." *La Maison Dieu* 211 (1997/3): 55–64.

"Sur quelques difficultés actuelles au sujet de l'au-delà." *La Maison Dieu* 213 (1998/1): 33–58.

"Théologie et pastorale du sacrement de confirmation." *Prêtres Diocésains* (February 1998): 90–101.

"Les ministères de laïcs: vers un nouveau visage d'Eglise?" *La Maison Dieu* 215 (1998/3): 33–57.

"La symbolique du pain rompu et de la communion." *Souffles* 152 (January 1999): 41–45.

"Sacrements dans l'Esprit." *Prêtres Diocésains* (March–April 1999): 297–317.

"Eschatologie et Sacrement." *La Maison Dieu* 220, (1999 /4): 53–71.

"Les sacrements construisent le Corps du Christ.", *Cahiers de l'Atelier* 489 (September 2000): 31–42.

"Le sacrement de la réconciliation dans les aumôneries: quoi offrir aux jeunes?" *Courrier aux Responsables d'Aumôneries* 6 (June 2000): 2–9.

"La liturgie comme jeu." *Souffles* 159 (September 2000) 36–41.

"Baptisés en Jésus-Christ." *Les Dossiers de la Bible* (...) (2001).

"Le pain rompu comme figure théologique de la présence eucharistique." *Questions Liturgiques* 82 (2001): 9–33.

"L'archi-oralité des textes liturgiques." *La Maison Dieu* 226 (2001/2): 123–38.

"L'institution ecclésiale et sacramentelle dans le champ du symbolique." *Raisons Politiques* 4 (November 2001): 93–103.

"La présidence liturgique en quête d'un nouvel ethos." *La Maison Dieu* 230 (2002): 43–66.

"La présidence liturgique dans la modernité: les chances possibles d'une crise." *Questions Liturgiques* 83 (2002): 140–55.

"Parole et Sacrement." *Recherches de Sciences Religieuses* 91/2 (2003): 203–22.

"Humanité de la prière." *Unité Chrétienne* (November 2004): 22–26.

"Les nouveaux lieux de vérification du discours théologique." *Transversalités* 94 (April–June 2005): 113–29.

"La dimension vocationnelle de l'initiation chrétienne." *Jeunes et vocation* 123 (November 2006): 915.

"Le vocabulaire liturgique: des mots usés?" *Chemins d'Evangile*, Vicariat de Bruxelles (December 2006): 4–9.

AMERICAN DISSERTATIONS ON LOUIS-MARIE CHAUVET

Ambrose, Glenn. "Eucharist as a Means for Overcoming Onto-theology?: The Sacramental Theology of Louis-Marie Chauvet." PhD diss., Graduate Theological Union, Berkeley, 2001.

Brereton, Andrew. "The Sensus Fidelium and the Sacramentality of the Teaching Church: A Model Based on the Theology of Louis-Marie Chauvet." PhD diss., Fordham University, 2006.

Brunk, Timothy. "A Critical Assessment of Sacrament and Ethics in the Thought of Louis-Marie Chauvet." PhD diss., Marquette University, 2006.

Burke, Thomas. "Kenosis as Symbolic Framework for the Sacraments: An Exploration of the Work of Louis-Marie Chauvet and Others." PhD diss., Boston College (in progress).

Fortuna, Joseph John. "Two Approaches to Language in Sacramental Efficacy Compared: Thomas Aquinas in the *Summa Theologiae* and Louis-Marie Chauvet." PhD diss., The Catholic University of America, 1989.

Mudd, Joseph. "Eucharist and Metaphysics: Louis-Marie Chauvet and Bernard Lonergan on Disputed Questions in Thomas Aquinas's Eucharistic Theology." PhD diss., Boston College (in progress).

Sauer, Stephen J. "Naming Grace: A Comparative Study of Sacramental Grace in Edward Kilmartin and Louis-Marie Chauvet." PhD diss., The Catholic University of America, 2007.

Contributors

Philippe Barras, director of Centre Interdiocésain de Formation Pastorale et Catéchétique (Lille) and assistant professor, Institut Supérieur de Liturgie, Institut Catholique de Paris, is author of "Adap en France" (*La Maison-Dieu* 206, 1996).

André Birmelé, professor of systematic theology, Faculty of Protestant Theology, Université Marc-Bloch, Strasbourg, is author of *Kirchengemeinschaft: Ökumenische Fortschritte und methodologische Konsequenzen* (LIT, 2003).

Lieven Boeve, professor of fundamental theology and coordinator of the Systematic Theology Research Unit, Faculty of Theology, K.U. Leuven, Belgium, is author of *God Interrupts History: Theology in a Time of Upheaval* (Continuum, 2007).

Philippe Bordeyne, professor of theological ethics and dean of the Faculty of Theology, Institut Catholique de Paris, is author of *L'homme et son angoisse: La théologie morale de Gaudium et spes* (Éditions du Cerf, 2004).

Elbatrina Clauteaux, assistant professor of fundamental and systematic theology, Institut Catholique de Paris, is author of *Panton Pata Pemonton, Histoires de la Terre des Hommes. Contes, Mythes et Légendes des Indiens Pémon du Venezuela* (L'Harmattan, 1997).

Judith M. Kubicki, CSSF, associate professor, Theology Department, Fordham University, is author of *The Presence of Christ in the Gathered Assembly* (Continuum, 2006).

Gordon W. Lathrop, professor emeritus, The Lutheran Theological Seminary at Philadelphia, is author of *The Pastor: A Spirituality* (Fortress, 2006).

Nathan D. Mitchell, professional specialist, Department of Theology, and concurrent associate director, Notre Dame Center for Liturgy, University of Notre Dame, is author of *Meeting Mystery: Liturgy, Worship, Sacraments* (Orbis, 2006).

Bruce T. Morrill, SJ, associate professor and graduate program director, Theology Department, Boston College, is contributing coeditor of *Practicing Catholic: Ritual, Body, and Contestation in Catholic Faith* (Palgrave Macmillan, 2006).

Patrick Prétot, OSB, professor of liturgy and sacramental theology, director of Institut Supérieur de Liturgie, Institut Catholique de Paris, is author of "Pierre-Marie Gy, O.P.: Historian and Theologian in Service to the Church and the Liturgy" (*Studia Liturgica*, 37, 2007).

David N. Power, OMI, professor emeritus, School of Theology and Religious Studies, The Catholic University of America, is author of *Love Without Calculation: A Reflection on Divine Kenosis* (Crossroad/Herder & Herder, 2005).

Jean-Louis Souletie, FMT, professor of fundamental and systematic theology, Institut Catholique de Paris, is author of *Les grands chantiers de la christologie* (Desclée, 2007).

Index of Names

Index of Subjects

narrative, narrativity, xvi, 8, 11, 20–22, 47–49, 53, 56, 122–23, 141, 143, 145, 149, 152, 210, 215
nature, natural (*see also* body, creation), xvi, 34, 73, 142, 189
North American Academy of Liturgy (NAAL), 103, 105

obedience, 58, 138, 197–98
ordination, 64, 75
otherness (*see* difference)

participation, xvi, xix, 48, 72, 103–04, 110, 114, 124, 135, 139, 167, 176–77, 184
paschal mystery
  Christ's death and resurrection, xv, xv, xix–xxi, 1, 30, 31, 40, 51, 55, 65–66, 69, 71, 79, 143, 172, 175–76, 179–84, 202
  in liturgy, sacraments, xiv, 28, 31–33, 40, 43–44, 56, 61, 77, 88, 95, 100, 116, 133, 139, 152, 154, 177, 206, 223
  in Scripture, xv, 32, 48, 61, 70
pastoral care, service (*see under* practice)
patristics, patristic era (*see under* theology)
peace, 182, 185
penance, reconciliation (*see under* forgiveness)
philosophical, philosophy, 16
  anthropology, xxi, 8, 9, 14, 17
  cosmology, 144, 147
  deconstruction, 221
  epistemology, 9, 21, 28, 120, 124, 127, 143, 156
  ethics (*see under* ethics, theory of)
  hermeneutics, 6, 11, 17, 19–23, 48–49, 54, 58, 153, 158, 164, 190–91, 215, 220
  humanism, 203
  of language, viii n4, 48

metaphysics, ix, xvi, 2, 10, 11, 141, 162, 164, 188, 190, 208–09
  ontology, xiv, xvii, 7, 11, 14, 17, 23, 153–54, 164, 166, 193
  scholastic, 204
  semiotics, 154
  structuralism, 145
  phenomenology, xvi, 11, 17, 20, 21, 145, 147, 153, 158, 161, 164, 167, 210, 223
  pragmatism, 190
piety, 44
pluralism, plurality, 9, 23, 48, 61
politics, poltical-economic order, 53, 55, 141–42, 146, 148, 195
Pontifical Biblical Commission, 47, 52, 54
post-colonialism, 50
postmodern, postmodernity, 6, 14, 17–19, 22, 27, 50, 108–09, 120, 141, 151, 210
poverty, the poor, 49, 51, 79, 106, 110, 132, 139, 178, 185
power, 80, 108, 131, 136, 154, 166, 172, 197, 209, 212
practice
  ecclesial, xix, 38, 64–65, 69, 76, 90, 187–88, 193, 204, 206
  ethical, moral, xv, xvii, xviii–xx, 1, 12, 55, 57, 58, 60, 80, 110, 113, 119, 121, 127, 133, 149
  liturgical-sacramental, x–xvi, 2–3, 27–29, 34–39, 48, 58, 65, 67, 70, 75–77, 83, 89, 93, 98, 105–06, 108–09, 113, 116, 174, 176, 179, 183–85, 188, 190, 193, 195, 204, 222–23
  mission (of church), missionary, 91, 97, 105, 107, 139
  musical (*see also* music), xi, 167
  pastoral, x, 79–80, 83–100, 125, 188
  practical reason, 130, 140–41
  praxis, 6, 12, 89, 125–26, 191, 217

lectionary, 50, 113
and liturgy-sacrament, 47, 50–52,
61, 64, 66, 70–77, 79–80, 102, 105,
108, 149, 179
proclamation, xviii, 32, 51, 53, 70,
74–75, 102–03, 107, 110, 113, 124,
135–36, 152, 182, 193, 218
sacramentality of, 43, 64–65
theology of the Word, 43, 44, 104,
115, 206, 218–19
and tradition, xiii, 50, 86, 116, 122,
137–39
Second Synod of the Churches of
Africa and Madagascar, 48
Second Vatican Council (Vatican II),
88, 91, 100, 101–04, 110, 173
secular, secularism, secularization,
18, 88
sharing (see communion)
sin, 75, 151, 179, 181, 212
slavery, 50
social sciences, 2, 16, 137, 156, 187–88,
189–206
anthropology (ethnology), 35,
158–61, 165, 170, 194, 196
linguistics, 194
psychoanalysis, psychology, 10,
14, 33, 93, 95, 164–65, 190–92,
194, 196–202
ritual studies, ritual theory, 14,
127–28, 137
sociology, 33, 165, 191–92, 194
society (see under body, culture)
solidarity, 146
soul, xvi, 142
spiritual, spirituality, 12, 73
subject, subjectivity, xvi, xvii, 1, 13,
20, 26, 120, 126, 130–36, 164, 173,
176, 190–92, 195–98, 202, 215
suffering, 49, 79, 112, 135, 140–43,
146, 149, 151, 172, 213
Sunday, Lord's Day, xx, 106, 113, 131,
139–40, 152

symbol, symbolic, symbolism
exchange, 10, 35, 127, 129–30,
174–75, 193, 209, 215
fragmentation, rupture, 207–08,
215–16
gestures, xviii, 174, 182
language, xvi, xvii, 153–54, 158,
161–63
mediation, 7–8, 13, 25, 94, 126, 150,
154, 159, 166–68, 175, 183, 188,
194–95, 216
and reality, 74, 77, 144–47, 149, 153,
157, 161–69, 184, 201
symbolic order, xviii, xxi, 1, 8, 9,
13, 22, 26–27, 34, 109, 153–54,
157–60, 170, 177, 213, 218

technology, 141–42, 144–46, 171–72
theological, theology, 15–16, 70,
190–206
anthropology, xiii, 8, 25, 120, 134,
154, 173–76
biblical, 71
christology (see christology)
doctrinal, dogmatic, 64, 154, 204
ecclesiology (see also church), 6,
25, 31–35, 79–81, 101, 154
fundamental (see also grace,
revelation), xiii, xx, 1–3, 6, 44, 69,
116, 162, 188
liberation, 12
linguistic, hermeneutical, 7–19, 65,
68, 83, 94
liturgical, xiii, 27, 101, 105
medieval, xi, 34, 36, 121, 124
moral (see ethics)
onto-theology, 7–8, 11, 14, 23
pastoral, x, xiii, 79–80, 83–100, 109,
125
patristic, 38, 40, 51, 52, 55, 56, 60,
66, 92, 143
pneumatology (see Holy Spirit)
political, 12, 140–43, 148